"Rabbi Marla Feldman has created a dynamic and compelling conversation among the generations. Both individuals and groups will admire her captivating modern midrashic interpretations and her expert navigation of traditional texts. Feldman shows us how fresh and relevant our sacred tradition can be!"
—RABBI MARY L. ZAMORE, executive director, Women's Rabbinic Network

"Rabbi Marla Feldman has added an imaginative, insightful contribution to our collective Jewish library. As she creatively gives voice to both familiar and lesser-known female biblical characters, she shows why their stories matter for us as contemporary readers."
—RABBI ANDREA L. WEISS, Jack, Joseph and Morton Mandel Provost, Hebrew Union College—Jewish Institute of Religion

BIBLICAL WOMEN SPEAK

The Jewish Publication Society expresses its gratitude for the generosity of the sponsors of this book:

Wendy and Leonard Cooper, for all of the girls and women in the Cooper family: Ziva, Liora, Ariella, Rafaella, Regan, Cherylle, Michelle and Adriana.

With love from Bubbe/Mom/Wendy and Poppi/Daddy/Leonard

University of Nebraska Press

LINCOLN

Biblical Women Speak

HEARING THEIR VOICES THROUGH
NEW AND ANCIENT MIDRASH

Rabbi Marla J. Feldman

The Jewish Publication Society

PHILADELPHIA

"Keturah, the Great Mother of Many Generations" was originally published in a different form in CCAR *Journal* (Summer 1999). "Testament of Shelomith" was originally published in a different form in CCAR *Journal* (Spring 1991). "Miriam's Fringes" was originally published in a different form in CCAR *Journal* (Summer 1993). All are reprinted by permission of the CCAR.

Library of Congress Cataloging-in-Publication Data
Names: Feldman, Marla J., author.
Title: Biblical women speak: hearing their voices through new and ancient midrash / Rabbi Marla J. Feldman.
Description: Philadelphia: Jewish Publication Society; Lincoln: University of Nebraska Press, [2023] | "Published by the University of Nebraska Press as a Jewish Publication Society book." | Includes bibliographical references.
Identifiers: LCCN 2022043569
ISBN 9780827615144 (paperback)
ISBN 9780827619081 (epub)
ISBN 9780827619098 (pdf)
Subjects: LCSH: Women in rabbinical literature. | Women in the Bible. | Midrash—History and criticism. | Aggada—Commentaries. | Feminism—Religious aspects—Judaism. | Bible—Feminist criticism. | BISAC: RELIGION / Biblical Studies / Exegesis & Hermeneutics | SOCIAL SCIENCE / Women's Studies.
Classification: LCC BM509.W7 F45 2023 | DDC 221.9/22082—dc23/eng/20220930
LC record available at https://lccn.loc.gov/2022043569

Set and designed in Adobe Text by N. Putens.

TO MY SISTER, PAMELA

"And my sister I shall love above all flesh;
For I have not a sister in all the earth but her alone;
This is no great merit for me if I love her, for she is my sister,
And we were sown together in our mother's body,
And together we came forth from her womb,
If I do not love my twin, whom shall I love?"

—Adapted from Jubilees 35:22, Esau's expression
of devotion to his twin brother Jacob

AND TO MY MANY SISTERS BY CHOICE—
the women who have inspired, encouraged, and
uplifted me throughout my life and my career.

.

CONTENTS

ACKNOWLEDGMENTS

My interest in midrash was first ignited by incredible scholars who shared with me their knowledge and passion for this unique form of Jewish literature. Dr. Judah Goldin z"l first introduced me to midrash when I was an undergraduate student at the University of Pennsylvania. Later, my appreciation of midrash as both a scholarly and a creative endeavor blossomed during my rabbinical studies with Dr. Norman Cohen at Hebrew Union College—Jewish Institute of Religion. I am particularly grateful for his expert insights in reviewing parts of this book related to the history of midrash and specific classical compilations. I would never have embarked on this journey had it not been for their support, wisdom, and gentle guidance in those early years, for which I am eternally grateful.

I would be remiss if I failed to acknowledge the role of women rabbis and scholars who came before me. Not only did they open the professional doors through which I entered, but they also exposed the dearth of women's perspectives in Jewish scholarship, paving the way for future generations to discover those missing voices. I owe a debt of gratitude to all those who blew open the doors, shattered the glass ceilings, and leveled the playing field for those of us who followed.

Over the course of my rabbinical career, I have taught many adult education courses in midrash, often focusing on particular biblical personages, and encouraged students to engage creatively with the text. My students have challenged me, expanded my vision, and enhanced my own understanding of our sacred texts. Heartened by my students and friends, I have been inspired to write modern midrash periodically over the years. I am grateful to the editors of the *CCAR Journal: The Reform Jewish Quarterly*, in which several of my creative renderings first appeared.

It has long been a dream to publish a collection of my modern midrash and share my passion for this literary form with a wider audience. I am incredibly grateful to the folks at The Jewish Publication Society and University of Nebraska Press for making this possible. In particular, I am indebted to Joy Weinberg, the JPS managing editor, for her keen eye, diligent editing, and patience with my many questions. And I am grateful to my friend and colleague Rabbi Barry Schwartz, director of The Jewish Publication Society, who believed in this project and helped shape it from the beginning.

My sister and womb-mate, Pamela, is my "reader in chief" and dependable sounding board. In addition to having a great eye for grammar and nuance, I know I can count on her honest feedback and the end result will be better for it. She read nearly every word of this book, often more than once, before it went to the editors. Not only is she a master of the written word; she is also a creative partner in exploring midrash through her own artistic endeavors.

I have many "sisters by choice" who have supported my efforts and cheered me on during this journey. I am immensely grateful to my Women of Reform Judaism (WRJ) sisters, who provided the sabbatical time I needed to undertake this project and have patiently awaited the final product. Many friends and colleagues have provided enthusiastic encouragement throughout my career and in my personal life, giving me the confidence to turn aspiration into reality. There are far too many to name them all, but I trust they will read this and know who they are.

I am fortunate to be one of the many beneficiaries of the remarkable vision of the creators of Sefaria: A Living Library of Torah Texts Online (sefaria.org), perhaps the most impactful tool available for the study of Jewish texts today. Sefaria provides the Bible, Mishnah, Talmud, major commentaries, and many midrashic compilations in both Hebrew and

English in an easily searchable format. One can explore the commentaries related to a particular verse or use the word search feature to see all the references to a particular biblical character. Sefaria was used extensively in the research for this book.

Of course, none of this work would have been possible without the love and encouragement of my family. My parents supported my educational pursuits long before any of us imagined that rabbinical careers eventually would become possible for women. My siblings and extended family continue to be my greatest cheerleaders, allowing me to soar, even while helping me remain firmly grounded. Any success I achieve is a credit to their faith and confidence in me.

INTRODUCTION

Finding Ourselves within the Biblical Text

For generations upon generations, week after week, Jews around the world have read and reread the stories of the Torah, drawing wisdom from the many rabbis and scholars who engaged in dialogue with prior generations to reveal the hidden nuances of the text and discover meaningful lessons for their own communities. Through this process of interpreting and expounding upon the biblical text, an ancient art that developed over millennia, midrash and biblical commentaries emerged, enriching our understanding and bringing creative energy to the study of our sacred texts.

Midrash (from the Hebrew verb root *d-r-sh*, meaning "to seek") is a type of Hebrew literature that seeks to understand sacred texts through traditional interpretive methods. To truly understand the biblical text, we are encouraged to delve into it deeply, searching out not only the most obvious explanations, but the hidden meanings as well. Most importantly, as we encounter the text, we need to ask questions, lots of questions. Some questions may be as simple as what a word means or as deep as what a biblical character may have been thinking or feeling in a given moment.

Using various linguistic techniques and rules of construction to answer their own questions, the rabbis continually teased out new meanings and discovered ancient truths within the text. Over time, rules developed to provide structure and logic to those engaged in deciphering the text. For example, if the words and even the letters of the Torah come directly from

God, then every jot and tittle must be meaningful and contain important lessons. Any repetition in the text, any missing letter, or any unusual word choice is significant and might be the clue to unlocking that text's meaning. To understand the proper nuance of a word, commentators would compare it to how it is used elsewhere in the Bible or examine nearby verses for context. These principles, known as hermeneutical rules, eventually became codified (to learn more, see the appendix, "Overview of Midrash").

As midrashic literature developed over hundreds of years, scholars identified and classified various types of midrash and organized compilations of midrashic material. There are two primary types of midrash, based on the purpose behind the interpretive endeavor. Halakhic midrash (*midrash halakhah*) expounds upon the biblical text to clarify the rules and regulations governing Jewish communities and individual behavior. Aggadic midrash (*midrash aggadah*) explores the narrative elements of the biblical text, seeking to gain insights into the lives of our ancestors through stories, parables, and legends. The new midrashim and classical midrash discussed in this book would be characterized as *midrash aggadah*, focusing on the narrative, rather than the legal, aspects of the biblical stories.

Midrash can be found embedded within many Jewish sources. Translation is a form of interpretation, and as such, early Aramaic translations of the Bible provide a rich source for early midrash by virtue of the nuances of words chosen and embellishments added within the texts. Although not typically categorized as midrash, source material from the Hellenistic period, including books from the noncanonical Apocrypha and Pseudepigrapha from the second to first century BCE and Josephus's *Antiquities of the Jews* from the first century CE, provide insights into how early Jewish communities understood and amplified the biblical stories. Although organized as a legal code, Talmud also contains a great deal of midrashic material, which provided the foundation for later compendia and commentaries. Midrash Rabbah (the "Great" Midrash), an extensive compendium of midrash developed from the fifth through the eleventh centuries and organized according to the books of the Bible, is cited throughout this book.

Biblical commentary emerged in the Middle Ages as scholars synthesized hundreds of years of Jewish texts, including midrash, and applied hermeneutical principles to uncover deeper truths in the texts. Many scholars sought to clarify the *peshat* (simple meaning) of the biblical text, while others embraced a more homiletical approach, adding their own *derash* (interpretation) to teach lessons from the text. According to Barry Holtz in *Back to the Sources: Reading the Classic Jewish Texts*, "Their commentaries function on the one hand as lenses through which we can see the facets of the text more sharply, and on the other as windows on some of the most interesting minds of medieval Jewry."[1]

Rashi (Rabbi Shlomo ben Yitzhak, 1040–1105, France) was the most prominent of these commentators. His work, which laid the foundation for many who followed, appears throughout this book. Readers also will discover numerous other well-regarded medieval commentators, including Rabbi Abraham ben Meir Ibn Ezra (1089–1164, Spain), Rabbi David Kimhi (Radak, 1160–1235, Provence), and Rabbi Moshe ben Nahman (Ramban or Nahmanides, 1194–1270, Spain).[2] For more information about their major collections of midrash and commentaries, see the appendix and the glossary of classical sources.

It is important to note that midrash is an interpretive literary process, not a finite or time-bound relic of the past. Some midrashim are as old as the biblical text itself, while others are "revealed" much later in the Talmud and medieval commentaries. The midrashic process continues even today, as we continue to peel back the layers of our sacred texts to unveil new lessons by posing fresh questions and reading with modern eyes and contemporary sensibilities. Thus, new midrash continues to unfold through human engagement with our ancient texts as we seek to elicit their meaning and keep them relevant throughout the generations. Holtz explains:

> Primarily we can see the central presence of cultural or religious tension and discontinuity. Where there are questions that demand answers, and where there are new cultural and intellectual pressures that must be addressed, Midrash comes into play as a way of resolving crisis and reaffirming continuity with the traditions of the past. . . .

In the laconic style of the Bible, we find one significant cause of the necessity for Midrash. Midrash comes to fill in the gaps, to tell us the details that the Bible teasingly leaves out.... The human mind desires answers, motivations, explanations. Where the Bible is mysterious and silent, Midrash comes to unravel the mystery.[3]

JOURNEY TO THIS BOOK

When I was first introduced to midrash as a college student, I was enthralled by how rich and deep Torah study can be when embellished through interpretation, commentaries, and the insights of prior generations. In rabbinical school I continued to explore how classical midrash treats various biblical characters, particularly the underrepresented women of the Bible, and I eventually sought to give voice to biblical women's experiences and perspectives through my own creative renderings.

Unfortunately, until the modern era, midrash was the exclusive domain of male rabbis and scholars, who too often excluded the voices and insights of women. The biblical text itself gives short shrift to women's experiences. Even when female personages like the matriarchs are prominent in the text, their perspectives, feelings, and personal experiences are rarely explored with the same depth as those of the male characters. This significant gap makes the role of modern midrash about biblical women particularly important: to discover the women whose names are missing from our texts, to amplify the voices of unnamed and named women, and to reconsider and reimagine what additional and/or alternative meanings these texts might hold for us today when filtered through the lens of women's experiences. While there is much to be learned from the wisdom of the sages who wrestled with these texts in the past, their perspective was diminished and defective because of their failure to consider these aspects of the text.

Fortunately, feminist thought and scholarship has had a growing influence on biblical studies in recent decades. Opening our eyes to the biases and deficiencies of Jewish text study devoid of women's voices has led to the growth of more multidimensional and inclusive perspectives that have enriched biblical studies. In the 1980s and 1990s, Peter Pitzele's Bibliodrama used improvisational techniques to help people put themselves into the text as a form of midrash, much as Amichai Lau Lavie's Storahtelling uses theatrical techniques today. In the 1990s and 2000s, the Institute for Contemporary Midrash held several conferences and briefly published *Living Text: The Journal of Contemporary Midrash* to encourage and support further development of modern midrash. Novels like Anita Diamant's *The Red Tent* exposed millions to the concept of retelling ancient tales for modern readers. Courses have been offered not only for the study of traditional midrash, but also to empower individuals to create their own midrash to bring our biblical tradition to life. New, modern Torah commentaries, such as *The Torah: A Women's Commentary*, published by Women of Reform Judaism and the Central Conference of American Rabbis, have added new approaches to the text and the insights and wisdom of new scholars to the conversation.

In this work, I have tried to fill in the gaps of select biblical stories from the first-person vantage point of certain female biblical characters, some who are named and central to the biblical storyline and others who are unnamed and considered minor figures. In the biblical era, women were defined by their relationships; they were daughters, sisters, wives, and mothers. As such, the locus of their (limited) power, authority, and influence would have been in their family lives. Women like Leah, Bilhah, and Miriam are significant characters in the Bible, yet the rabbis failed to explore critical moments in their familial lives.

For instance, we know that Leah and Rachel were jealous rivals for Jacob's affection and progeny, yet they also were sisters with a common cause: seeking the welfare of their clan. After Rachel dies, midrash tells us how Jacob felt at the loss of his beloved wife and how he doted on his sons with her, Joseph and Benjamin, yet rabbinic literature does not consider how Leah would have mourned for Rachel too. We are left to wonder how she felt about the loss of her sister (chapter 2), and this in turn might shed light on our own lived experiences of sibling relationships and loss.

We know that Bilhah, Rachel's handmaid, gave birth to two of the Israelite tribes, and there is a curious interlude with Jacob's son, Reuben, but other details of her story are missing; we can only speculate about the life of a handmaid and what really happened between her and Reuben (chapter 4). While the rabbis imagined her "affair" with Reuben as either a lover's tryst or a violent attack, if we consider the full range of family dynamics and possibilities, there are more nuanced ways to imagine that moment.

As for Miriam, perhaps the most notable woman in the Bible (chapter 9), her affliction and subsequent exile from the Israelite camp in the wilderness is generally understood to be the result of gossip against Moses. This midrashic notion is so ubiquitous that the story has become a cautionary tale to all women who might be guilty of that sin. This assumption, however, squelches other questions that might otherwise have arisen from the text, such as consideration of Moses' and Aaron's own complicity, curiosity about what might have taken place during the seven days of her exile, and the broader perspective Miriam might have gained as she struggled to face a significant challenge in her life. Such lacunae in the biblical text provide a wide opening for creative interpretation and exploration. Many of the questions that have intrigued me most are not considered by the rabbis of ages past.

In most cases, the rabbis recognize even the most minor female characters in their commentaries, although generally their interest is limited to how these characters further the narrative of the (male) protagonists. There is a lack of interest in these women as individuals, separate and apart from how they are connected to their male counterparts. Women who are not part of the Israelite family tree leading to King David are minimized in rabbinic literature. For example, Abraham's third and final wife, Keturah (chapter 1), is largely ignored, despite her being the mother of numerous neighboring clans descended from the patriarch. The rabbis exhibit little interest in who she was or how she came to be married to Abraham. Judah has a wife who bears him three sons, buries two sons, and then dies, setting the stage for Judah's later union with Tamar, through whom the messianic line will flow. Judah's wife (chapter 3) has no name and no story of her own, and the rabbis make no attempt to explore that gaping hole in the narrative. She is usurped by her daughter-in-law Tamar, who will claim the Davidic line as her legacy.

The rabbis take note of some female characters in order to convey a specific lesson about values or law, but there is little depth to their portrayal in rabbinic literature. As a generalization, rabbinic commentaries posed transactional questions. They wanted to know how to understand a particular word or text, what actually took place in a particular narrative from the perspective of the primary characters of the Israelite saga, and what lessons were to be learned for their own day and age. In contrast, when this volume asks about what transpired from individual women's point of view, that perspective is a relational one. By way of illustration, the book of Leviticus uniquely mentions Shelomith Bat Dibri (chapter 8), the infamous blasphemer's mother, yet other than naming and shaming her to teach a lesson about the crime of blasphemy, the rabbis do not explore the intensity of emotions that would have been experienced by the mother of a young man who was stoned to death. By contrast, the modern midrash "Testament of Shelomith" envisions her relationship with her son's father, asks what it might have been like for this mother and her half-Egyptian child to be on their own in the wilderness, and imagines her distraught, impassioned, and accusatory words after her son dies by divine decree communicated by Moses.

Like Shelomith, the rabbis consider the story of Zelophehad's daughters significant because of the underlying property laws at issue, and even today we celebrate the progressive ruling allowing them to inherit land in the absence of male siblings. Yet, though their names are memorialized in the biblical text, the rabbis—and many of us today—fail to consider the potentially devastating impact of the additional requirement of intratribal marriage imposed upon women. These sisters' personal and nuanced stories of love and loss beg to be told (chapter 10).

I was particularly interested in some of the non-Israelite biblical women who play key roles in the biblical saga and yet are of even less interest to the rabbis, given their non-Israelite status. These include Keturah and Judah's unnamed wife, as noted above, along with Potiphar's unnamed wife (known as Zuleikha in numerous sources; chapter 5), the Egyptian midwives Shiphrah and Puah (chapter 6), and Pharaoh's unnamed daughter (chapter 7). In the traditional commentaries, Potiphar is depicted as cruel, licentious, and wicked, and Zuleikha, who falsely accuses Joseph of attempted rape, is cast as the villain. If we want to know more about her character, however, we need to ask different questions than the rabbis asked. Why, for example, would the wife of an Egyptian minister demean herself with a servant? What in her background would lead her to such deviant behavior, and why would she risk her station by dallying with a slave? The rabbis never investigate what it must have been like to be married to an abusive man like Potiphar. In asking that question, the modern retelling of her story changes the story itself and, perhaps, may lead us to compassion rather than judgment for victims of abuse today.

The rescue of the Israelite children, including Moses, is the work of a network of Egyptian women, from the midwives Shiphrah and Puah to Pharaoh's daughter and her servant. While these women are celebrated for their heroism, these stories only scratch the surface. What moral code compelled the midwives to defy their king, the most powerful ruler on earth, whom they themselves considered a god? Why did Pharaoh's daughter disobey her own father's edict? And what gave her servant the courage to jump into the Nile to pluck Moses from the waters? I want to know much more about these brave women than the Bible or classical midrash tells us. In a modern world that knows the horrors of genocide and terror, finding role models within our ancient texts for defiance in the face of evil makes our tradition relevant and meaningful for today's realities.

In all of these modern midrashim, bringing a woman's perspective to the text inevitably leads to a story about relationships and emotions. While some of the portrayed relationships are loving and joyous, they also are nuanced and fraught with challenging life circumstances that lead our protagonists to sorrow, loneliness, and loss. Yet in exploring the hidden mysteries of their stories, we can discover their uplifting capacity for love, hope, resourcefulness, fortitude, and courage in their tenacious determination to fulfill their dreams and live their best lives. By asking new questions with modern eyes, we can shed new light on our ancient tradition and find meaning for our own life journeys.

Each of the book's ten chapters brings to life a different biblical woman's story. Every chapter contains four sections. The "Biblical Text" sets the stage for both the modern and classical midrash. The "Modern Midrash" tells the biblical woman's story in her own voice, imagining the narrative from her perspective and considering her thoughts, motivations, struggles, and choices. "Classical Midrash and Commentary" explores historical interpretations found in the traditional midrash and the commentaries of the most prominent medieval scholars related to that character and storyline. It also integrates insights from Hellenistic literature such as the Apocrypha, the Pseudepigrapha (especially the book of *Jubilees* and the *Testaments of the Twelve Patriarchs*), and *Antiquities of the Jews* by Josephus Flavius (for more information, see the appendix and the glossary). While technically these works are not considered midrash, I have included them because the material supplements the biblical text and sheds light on how early sages expounded upon the biblical stories, just as midrash does. Finally, the "Author's Commentary" compares the traditional interpretations to the modern retelling of the story, reflecting upon the conventional understandings of the text and why I then chose to maintain, adapt, or in some cases reject these historical perceptions. An appendix, "Overview of Midrash," does just that, providing a more detailed overview of the major sources of midrash and some of the traditional hermeneutical rules of its construction used by the rabbis. The glossary lists the sources referenced throughout the book, providing their chronological, historical, and geographic framework.

In sum, this book offers a taste of the diversity and possibility of rabbinic interpretation through the generations through examination of both the classical midrash and my own modern midrash on biblical stories. It delves into ten female characters mentioned in the Bible, considering missing details of their background, reflecting on their experiences, and imagining their thoughts and emotions at seminal moments in their lives. In some cases these are well-known figures, and in other cases they are unnamed and underappreciated, but in all cases there are gaps in the traditional text that, when filled, may enhance our understanding of our history and tradition and, perhaps, offer insights into our own lives.

To be clear, this volume is not a comprehensive exploration of all the sources commenting on these biblical texts, but rather intended to introduce major concepts and common themes found in the traditional midrash and commentaries that shed light on these women and their experiences. Also, I have not explored the rich and growing body of modern feminist scholarship, midrash, and theology that are enhancing our understanding of these and other biblical women. Many individuals are continuing the development of midrash as I have in this book, expanding upon the teachings of the past and contributing modern interpretations of biblical characters. As we put ourselves and our own life experiences into the text, there are many "truths" to be uncovered. Others may offer similar or vastly different depictions of these biblical women and their stories, all of which will augment our understanding of and connection to our sacred tradition.

HOW TO USE THIS BOOK

The structure of this book allows for multiple uses. The modern midrashim may be read as short stories for discussion groups or book clubs. Readers are encouraged to consider what questions they would ask of the texts and how they would answer those questions. Those interested in learning about midrash and the midrashic process may delve into the sections on classical midrash and commentary in order to study how earlier scholars interpreted these texts. Discovering what questions the classical commentaries considered may spark conversation about what was deemed important to these scholars and how they applied both logic and the influences of their worldview to bring greater understanding to the texts. Adult learners who engage in weekly Torah study may find these chapters to be a useful supplement to other resources.

For rabbis and educators teaching courses about midrash or about these particular biblical characters and stories, these chapters provide insights that students can share, explore, and expand upon. The endnotes lead to primary sources that can be used to create source sheets and other course materials.

The author's commentary provides insights for those seeking a deeper, more personal connection to the text and hopefully will empower readers to explore their own modern interpretations of the text. This book is an invitation to put ourselves into the text, to challenge the conventional wisdom, and to see the biblical narrative through the lens of our own lives. Generations of scholars before us engaged with the text in this way, and it is no less our prerogative to do so today. Modern technology makes the ancient conversations among scholars readily accessible to anyone. With the click of a computer button, any student of the Bible can explore the vast array of commentaries and midrash. Thanks to Sefaria: A Living Library of Torah Texts Online and other online open-source websites, the vast world of midrash is available to all who seek it.

NOTES ON STYLE

Various English translations have been utilized. The style and tone of translations vary over time and location, so, for example, an English translation from nineteenth-century Great Britain will differ from an American one in our twenty-first century. When a particular translation is quoted, the original gendered language and spellings have been retained, including abbreviations for God, such as G'd. Hebrew words and biblical quotations are shown in italics, and translators' clarifying language appears in brackets.

In citations, Babylonian Talmud is abbreviated as BT and Charlesworth's *Old Testament Pseudepigrapha* is abbreviated as OTP. For Midrash Rabbah, the name of the biblical book is abbreviated, with "Rabbah" as "R." (e.g., Gen. R., Exod. R.). Some translations also use "R." as an abbreviation for "Rabbi." Endnotes that contain multiple citations are organized chronologically where possible. In some cases, the dating of texts is the subject of scholarly debate, as collections of midrash may have been compiled over a long period of time and scholars may have been active contemporaneously. In these instances, the author has made judgment calls as to the order of placement.

Gazing back, Rashi and others of his era looked to the sages who preceded them for inspiration and wisdom as they engaged in the task of decoding the mysteries of our ancient texts to make them understandable for their medieval communities. Looking forward, they inspired generations of later scholars, who built upon their work and continued the process of interpretation and exegesis, setting the stage for the modern era of biblical scholarship. So, too, contemporary students of Torah look to those who came before to gain insight into our texts and traditions. And like the rabbis of the Talmud and the commentators of the Middle Ages, we, too, bring our own questions, sensibilities, and cultural experiences with us as we continue the process of searching for the deeper meanings of the biblical text. For this place and time, in our own moment in history, we follow in their footsteps by learning from the wisdom of past generations, engaging with the text to ensure its relevance for today, and laying the groundwork for future generations to continue the process.

Through this volume, I hope to share my appreciation for midrash as a literary art form and empower others to bring their own questions and imagination to the text, to explore the empty spaces between the words, and to discover the missing voices of our ancestors. As we delve into the text, challenge it, and strive to garner new understandings and seek relevance for our modern world, we keep our ancient tradition alive and vibrant. And if we look deeply enough, we may even find ourselves within our ancient texts.

BIBLICAL WOMEN SPEAK

1

Keturah

Abraham's Last Wife

BIBLICAL TEXT: *Genesis 25:1–6*

Abraham took another wife, whose name was Keturah. She bore him Zimran, Jokshan, Medan, Midian, Ishbak, and Shuah. Jokshan begot Sheba and Dedan. The descendants of Dedan were the Asshurim, the Letushim, and the Leummim. The descendants of Midian were Ephah, Epher, Enoch, Abida, and Eldaah. All these were descendants of Keturah. Abraham willed all that he owned to Isaac; but to Abraham's sons by concubines Abraham gave gifts while he was still living, and he sent them away from his son Isaac eastward, to the land of the East.

MODERN MIDRASH:

Keturah, the Great Mother of Many Generations

They used to call me the Great Mother of Many Generations, for it was through me that the human species was restored after the Great Tower collapsed. Though my own name is barely remembered by my descendants, the names of my offspring are proclaimed as my legacy. Their deeds, and their misdeeds, are my sole bequest to the future. *Zimran, Jokshan, Medan, Midian, Ishbak, Shuah.* The litany of their names reads like a curse, and the recitation brings no pride. What has become of Keturah—the daughter, the wife, the mother, the woman? Who will restore my name among the mothers of our people?

My mother named me Keturah. Proclaiming my life a blessing, she said I embodied the qualities of both piety and grace. My father called me his Sweet Bouquet, as he remembered the fragrances of my childhood, when I would gather wildflowers to beautify our home and hearth.

When Abraham came upon me, I was a slight, modest girl, awed by the elder who had journeyed so far and survived so many trials. He had traveled to Beer-sheba to find Hagar, the Egyptian handmaid of his deceased wife. She would not receive her son's father, having been rejected and turned out by her mistress and left to raise her son and face the world of men alone. When Abraham saw me gathering flowers in the field, he thought I was the handmaid. Indeed, I appeared as Hagar had in her youth: pure and innocent, before life pressed down hard upon her and twisted her features.

Since he could not have Hagar as his wife, he chose me instead to tend to his hearth. Our union was blessed by all who knew our families. Though I was just a young girl, I was a skilled healer, with ample herbs and tinctures to comfort him as the years claimed their due. Abraham provided me with a name and the protection of his camp. He brought honor to my family and our kin. What I lacked in love, I gained in security and prosperity.

Though distant and distracted, Abraham was nonetheless kind, treating me like a favored daughter among the women of the clan. I spent my days collecting the local herbs and flowers to refresh his meals and perfume his tent. I hoped the sweet smells would ease his troubled, aged spirit, though he never seemed to notice. The only time he acknowledged my gifts was when the aromatic incense enhanced his worship at the altar of his God.

When Zimran, my first-born, was given to us, a flicker of joy shone in Abraham's eyes, and he swelled with pride, as any father might. I felt fulfilled in body and soul, sensing that my calling to be a mother was just beginning. But as he gazed upon our son, his joy slowly turned to sadness, and his face turned ashen. I could tell that some memory of the past troubled him as his shook his head and handed Zimran back to me as if his hands were on fire. As Abraham turned to leave, I heard him whisper, "I will not love this child, lest he, too, be taken." A week later, as the camp readied for the covenant ceremony, he abruptly told the servants to cease their preparations. "No more sacrifices," he said. I rose from my birthing bed, weak and sore, to plead for my child, but Abraham would not be moved. He just kept muttering, "No more sacrifices." Over and over, like a mantra: "No more sacrifices." And so my children would remain whole, uncircumcised, never to be part of the covenant of Abraham.

I bore many children to strengthen Abraham's camp. Each birth was different, each child a blessing. The other women grew jealous of my fertile womb but sought my wisdom in birthing nonetheless. I gave them remedies and teas to help them conceive. Soon I became known as the Great Mother to their young ones as well as my own. Only Rebekah—an outsider among the women of our camp, holding steadfast to the ways of her far-off people—refused my help, even as she grew desperate for a child for Isaac.

I thrived in those days and was treated with the respect due the wise matriarch of the clan. Other women sought to honor me by suckling my young, but I gently brushed them away, preferring to keep my children at my own breast. Nurturing my children was the crowning achievement of my life. Being a mother brought me as much honor as any woman could expect.

With each birth I begged Abraham to teach our children the ways of his God, to cut their flesh and bring them into the covenant with the God of heaven and earth. But he had no heart for it. Instead of finding joy in the youth of his camp, his progeny brought him sorrow. How could it be that he, who never knew the agony of childbirth, felt such pain in fatherhood? Even his beloved son Isaac brought him anguish. Something must have happened between them, but no one told me what it was. Abraham cowered in Isaac's presence and turned away from his clouded, reproachful eyes.

My sons grew strong and healthy but never knew the love of their father or his God. If they felt rejected, they never showed it. Instead, they avoided Abraham and turned to Ishmael to learn of the hunt and the ways of men. He became more like their beloved uncle than their older brother. Eventually, they also learned to worship Ishmael's gods. As they cavorted with the neighboring clans, they brought shame to their father. "This is my penance," he would say as he pushed us all away.

As my sons grew to manhood, they sought wives from among our neighbors, as Ishmael had done. Abraham dutifully paid the bride-price for each, though he despised our sons' foreign wives and refused their families a place in the camp. As each son emerged from his wedding tent, Abraham gave him a token as a remembrance—an amulet inscribed with mysterious words—and then sent him toward the sun to make his own way in the wilderness.

As my womb shriveled, Abraham had no more use for me. The farther apart we grew, the closer Abraham became to Isaac and Rebekah. In his final years, he finally made peace with the son of Sarah. He joined Isaac and Rebekah in Sarah's tent, bequeathing to them the secrets of his faith and his visions, leaving behind all that had separated him from her memory, including me.

I once tried to bring Abraham back to me. With humility I confessed my failures. I admitted that I had never been the wife Abraham wanted, never filled his heart with laughter, never been a companion or confidant. I pledged to do all I could to make him proud and bring honor to his camp. I stood outside their tent and pleaded for Abraham to return, but Rebekah turned me away, gently, yet firmly. "When you entered his tent," the prophetess said, "Father Abraham ceased speaking with his God. After you leave, the Almighty will speak through me."[1]

"But I have done all that has been asked of me!" I cried. "I have served Abraham with devotion. I have nurtured many sons to carry on his name. I am the Great Mother of Many Generations!"

"No matter," Rebekah replied. "It is through Isaac that Abraham's seed will be counted."

Resigned, I left Abraham's camp and returned to the tent of my father. Like Hagar before me, I had become a mere shadow, a servant cast aside, with no husband or sons to give me status. I had tried to mold my sons into the men Abraham hoped they might be, but I myself did not understand his clan's ways. Despite my pleading, Abraham had refused to embrace our sons and teach them his ways. Under Ishmael's tutelage, they became cruel, vulgar brutes who showed no concern for me or their father. As they were sent away, I, too, was destined to spend the rest of my years as an unwanted burden to the family of my youth.

Not long after we separated, I heard that my husband had died. He was 175 years old. Thirty-five of those years had been spent with me, but no one thought to tell me! I only learned of it from a passing caravan.

Isaac buried his father alongside his mother, Sarah, Abraham's first wife. Even Hagar's son, Ishmael, joined in honoring their father. But neither I, nor our sons, nor our many grandchildren living in the east were acknowledged. We were denied the opportunity to mourn for our beloved Abraham—even to place dirt on his grave. I deserved better than that.

Once severed from my union with Abraham, the sweet, wise Keturah was lost forever. And so I, the Great Mother of Many Generations, became but a footnote of history.

CLASSICAL COMMENTARY AND MIDRASH: Devoted Wife or Concubine?

The life of the first patriarch, Abraham, is a major focus of the biblical text, though his final years are sparsely described. We know significant details about Abraham's first marriage to Sarah and their many adventures. At her insistence, he consorts with her handmaid, Hagar, who bears him a son, Ishmael. After her own miraculous pregnancy and birth of Isaac, Sarah has Hagar and Ishmael sent away. The *Akedah* (story of the Binding of Isaac), the subsequent death and burial of Sarah, and the search for a wife for Isaac occupy several chapters.

Yet this third union for the patriarch, Abraham's marriage to Keturah, which produces six sons, is covered by a scant six verses. Because this interlude is bracketed by the story of Isaac and Rebekah's marriage immediately prior, and Abraham's death at age 175 immediately following, most commentaries calculate that Abraham and Keturah would have been married thirty-five to forty years, yet the text never tell us what transpired during these years other than the birth of their children. And unlike Ishmael and Isaac, we know nothing about their sons other than their names, the fact that they were sent away, and an indication that they would themselves become the heads of neighboring tribes. Most of all, we know nothing of Keturah herself. And so we are left to wonder who she was and the nature of her relationship with Abraham and their children.

The silence around Keturah and this time in Abraham's life left space for the rabbis to fill in the gaps through midrash, and yet, outside of addressing some of the most obvious questions, the rabbis seem largely disinterested in Keturah or her descendants. Their interest is reserved for the progenitors of Israelite lineage that will come from Isaac and Jacob. As such, much remains to be discovered about Keturah and her legacy.

Keturah and Hagar

A strong midrashic thread connects Keturah with Hagar. This stems from the unusual framing of Gen. 25:1, which introduces Keturah. The verse literally reads, "*And he* [Abraham] *continued* [va-yosef] *and he took a wife.*" Most commentaries understand this unusual phraseology as meaning simply that he "married again" or that he "took another wife." However, some read "married again" as suggesting that Abraham actually remarried someone—and since Sarah had already died, that could only refer to the handmaid Hagar, even though she and Abraham had not formally wed. Rashi and other scholars, citing Genesis Rabbah, suggest that a defective spelling of the Hebrew word for "*concubines*" in Gen. 25:6—"*To Abraham's sons by concubines* [p-l-g-sh-y-m] *Abraham gave gifts*"—proves that Keturah was actually Hagar. Apparently, in earlier texts that were extant in Rashi's time, the biblical word for concubine had been written without a letter that would make the word plural (*p-l-g-sh-m* instead of *p-l-g-sh-y-m*, as written in current texts). According to this interpretation, the spelling suggests that there was only one concubine, not two.[2] Thus Rashi's commentary on this verse simply states, "This is Hagar," as if Keturah being Hagar is a generally accepted fact,[3] and Aramaic translations of the Bible make this connection explicit.[4] Meanwhile, current Hebrew texts use the complete spelling of the word, rendering this midrash somewhat confusing.

Other commentators, most notably Ibn Ezra and Rashbam, dispute the association between Hagar and Keturah. Ibn Ezra suggests that the use of the plural in Gen. 25:6—Abraham's "*concubines*"—implies two separate women, while Rashbam cryptically notes that according to the simple meaning of the text, she could not be Hagar.[5]

Despite this dispute, throughout most midrash there is an assumed connection between Hagar and Keturah. That assumption requires additional interpretation to explain how and why Abraham would reunite with Hagar. In a play on the Hebrew root *k-t-r*, meaning "to connect" or "to bind together," the rabbis said Keturah combined the qualities of piety and good deeds.[6] Rashi cites Genesis Rabbah's play on the etymology of the name "*Keturah*," which stems from the same Hebrew word as *ketoret*, meaning "incense," explaining, "She was named Keturah because her deeds were as beautiful [sweet] as incense [*Ketoreth*]."[7] Later commentaries clarify that her good deeds referred to Keturah/Hagar's piety; during the forty years between Abraham's initial involvement with Keturah/Hagar and his reunion with her at the end of his life, she had been righteous, remained virtuous, and renounced her idolatrous ways, thereby being worthy of Abraham once again. Those good deeds merited a new name, as summed up in the thirteenth- to fourteenth-century compendium *Tur ha-Arokh*:

"*Whose name was Keturah.*" Rashi claims that Keturah was identical with Hagar, who appears in a new guise. Her new name reflected her new and improved attitudes, comparable to the incense offered on the altar, the most beloved of Israel's sacrificial offerings. In order to reconcile this comment with what Rashi had written on Genesis 21:14 where Hagar is described as . . . returning to the idolatrous practices she had absorbed in her home as a child, we would have to postulate that in the interval she had become a penitent. Although she was of Egyptian origin she was not only of perfectly good character, but seeing that the first time Avraham had married he had done so with Divine approval, she was now also permissible to him as a wife. I have seen a comment in *Bereshit Rabbah* 61:4 that even at this stage Avraham married her at G'd's instructions. This is why the Torah wrote "he again married, etc." The word *vayosef* is to tell us that just as it had been with G'd's approval that he had married Hagar the first time, he still enjoyed G'd's approval when he took her back.[8]

The sixteenth-century commentary *Kli Yakar* adds that the incense associated with Keturah signified this transition:

> Avraham named her in honor of the holy incense to make it known that she had repented fully after having lapsed into idolatry, so that now even her former deeds ascended to Heaven like the incense.[9]

The placement of Keturah's story immediately after Isaac and Rebekah wed suggests a chronological connection between these two events. The Talmud presumes that seeing Isaac and Rebekah so happily wed made Abraham long for marriage himself.[10] There is a rather sweet midrash that Isaac himself had sought out Hagar after his mother, Sarah, passed away in order to reunite Hagar with his father. Immediately prior to this section, the biblical text notes that Isaac had traveled from the Negev region to greet his bride-to-be Rebekah at Beer-lahai-roi (Gen. 24:62)—the same location to which Hagar had fled after being cast out of Abraham's household (16:14). The juxtaposition of these two passages implies that Isaac and Rebekah's meeting took place just prior to Abraham's marriage. The confluence of Isaac and Rebekah's meeting place, Hagar's retreat locale, and Abraham's marriage makes for a nice storyline:

> What is written before this passage (Gen. 25:1)? (Gen. 24:62:) *Now Isaac had come by way of Beer-Lahai-Roi.* And afterwards [it is written] (in Gen. 25:1): *Then Abraham took a wife again.* It is simply that when Isaac took Rebekah, Isaac said: Let us go and bring a wife to my father. Hagar and Keturah are the same person [according to] the words of Rabbi, but our masters say he took another wife. What is the logic of Rabbi? Hagar and Keturah are the same person because it is written (in Gen. 24:62): *Now Isaac had come by way of Beer-Lahai-Roi.* [Here is a reference to] the same woman about whom it is written (in Gen. 16:14): *Therefore the well was called Beer-Lahai-Roi.*[11]

For those commentators who do not associate Keturah with Hagar, who was Egyptian, the question of her ancestry remains unanswered. The first-century book of *Jubilees* (see glossary) refers to Keturah as the child of household servants and specifically notes that Hagar had already passed away.[12] Linking this narrative with the preceding biblical text, some commentators hold that Abraham's marriage was a likely consequence of having just married off his son Isaac to Rebekah and his natural longing likewise to enjoy marriage.[13] Since the divine decree that Isaac was to inherit Abraham's wealth and his legacy had already been secured, Abraham was free to marry as he chose and enjoy comfort in his old age.

A common midrashic thread suggests that Keturah was a Canaanite woman. Although the Torah doesn't stipulate the prohibition against marriage with Canaanite tribes until much later,[14] the rabbis nonetheless question how Abraham could have deigned to marry into a forbidden union. Since Abraham himself had insisted that his servant find a wife for Isaac from among his kin and not the local tribes (Gen. 24:3), commentators explain that marriage to a Canaanite woman would thereby have been forbidden to Isaac and his descendants, but not to Abraham. Even if Abraham had not been forbidden to marry a Canaanite woman, the shame of such a marriage helps explain why the rabbis avoided the subject—they did not wish to impugn the memory of the patriarch. According to Rabbeinu Bahya (Rabbi Bahya ben Asher, thirteenth-century Spain):

The reason why the Torah did not tell us whose daughter Keturah was may have been that she was a Canaanite and therefore the Torah did not want to bother with her genealogy, (Nachmanides). Had she been Egyptian, or from any nation other than the Canaanites, the Torah would have given us more details about her background. We have proof of this when the Torah detailed the genealogy of the women whom Esau and Ishmael married (compare 28,9). Seeing that Keturah was a member of an accursed nation, the Torah preferred not to go into details (for the sake of Avraham?).[15]

While some commentators agree that Abraham might have married a Canaanite woman, others could not imagine such an act. Believing that Abraham's marriage here would have been a pious act in fulfillment of the commandment to procreate, these commentators presume that his selected bride had to have been of more respectable ancestry. According to Radak (Rabbi David Kimhi):

> He took another wife although he already had had two wives. He meant to continue siring children in his old age in order to comply with the blessing/command to increase the world's population. Seeing that the continuity of his own seed had been assured, he was not concerned with the antecedents of Keturah. We can be certain, however, that he selected a woman who personally possessed all the good qualities he would have desired also for a wife for his son. The only thing he did not insist on was such a woman's national background. He was certainly not looking for experiencing disappointments with any children from Keturah, having experienced enough disappointment with Ishmael. We may safely assume that Keturah was not of Canaanitic descent, seeing that even Hagar the Egyptian had not been of such descent.[16]

Commentators also attempt to resolve a major textual ambiguity regarding Keturah's status. Whereas Gen. 25:1 refers to Keturah as Abraham's wife, verse 6 calls Abraham's male progeny the "*sons by concubines.*" Later in the biblical text, the genealogy in 1 Chron. 1:32 uses the term "*concubine*" for Keturah. The *Tur ha-Arokh* offers a simple explanation for the apparent discrepancy: the "*sons by concubines*" do *not* refer to Keturah's progeny, but rather to Abraham's children from other women who were, in fact, concubines like Hagar. This source also reinforces the notion that Keturah could have been a Canaanite woman like these other women:

> No doubt Hagar's status in the household of Avraham had been that of a concubine, whereas Keturah was his wife in the full sense of that term. If she had been a servant maid in his household and

he had raised her to the status of concubine the Torah would not have described this as "*He married a woman named Keturah*." If the Torah here describes Keturah as a concubine, this was only since G'd had decreed that Yitzchok would be Avraham's sole heir, so that sons from any other woman would have to content themselves with gifts handed to them during their father's lifetime. Avraham had taken these women from the Canaanite women, for if Keturah had been an Egyptian or Philistine by birth the Torah could not have said that Avraham dispatched these sons somewhere to the Far East, but he would have sent them back to Egypt or the land of the Philistines when [*sic*] their mother had come. The prohibition of marrying Canaanite women applied only to Avraham's heirs, not to children who would not inherit his estate, and thus represent his outlook on life.[17]

In characterizing Abraham and Keturah's relationship as a fully legitimate marriage, later rabbis describe their marriage ceremony in clearly anachronistic terms, suggesting that Abraham gave Keturah a *ketubah*, proving that she was a wife and not a concubine. Ignoring historical chronology is a classic biblical interpretive device known as *ein mukdam ume'uḥar ba-Torah*, meaning "nothing is earlier or later in the Torah." According to Radak:

> Keturah was not a concubine. This is why the Torah writes "*he took a wife*," as opposed to the mention of concubines (verse 5). The sons of the concubines are not mentioned by name whereas the sons of Keturah are all mentioned by their names. This fact alone clearly shows that their status was superior to the sons of Avraham's concubines. The essential difference between a wife and a concubine is that though both are exclusive partners of the men with whom they live, the former, when becoming wives, underwent the ceremony known as chuppah, and the union was celebrated with a wedding party, whereas a concubine was not accorded all this pomp and ceremony.[18]

Other commentaries explain the ambiguity by suggesting that despite having a *ketubah*, Keturah was not a "full" wife, but rather a "half" wife, and thus more like a concubine:

> [Quoting Rashi:] *Wives are with a kesubah, concubines are without a kesubah.* Rashi is answering the question: If the concubine mentioned here is Hagar, why before (v. 1) is she called a wife? The answer is: Scripture called her a wife because she had a kesubah like a wife. And it calls her a concubine because Avraham took her only for conjugal relations and not for child-bearing. The word *pilegesh* connotes *peleg 'shah* (a half wife): one who is for conjugal relations and not for child-bearing.[19]

Status of Keturah's Children

The rabbis were more interested in Keturah's children than in Keturah herself. According to midrash, when the Tower of Babel was destroyed, thirty families were swept away and then were replaced by thirty others: Keturah's sixteen, Ishmael's twelve, and Rebekah's two.[20] Commentaries referring to Keturah's children vacillate between acknowledging their companion status to the Israelites and perceiving them as evil, unworthy descendants of Abraham. For example, her son Zimran's name is interpreted as "they who wrought destruction [*mezammerin*] in the world," and Jokshan's name is interpreted as "they were cruel [*mith-kashin*] in the world."[21] The simple reading of the text reveals that her children were dispatched to populate adjacent lands to the east; they were not to dwell with their brother Isaac and his clan. Some commentators suggest that this was to protect Isaac's inheritance from any claims by his half brothers, which would also explain why Abraham gave Keturah's children their share of his estate prior to his death.[22] Other commentators focus on the geography, associating the "lands to the east" with Abraham's ancestral property, the lands of his father Terah, without judgment or critique.[23] Rashi adds that the gifts Abraham bestowed upon Keturah's children were properties he had acquired through Sarah that he no longer wanted. Thus Isaac would inherit the land, while the children of Keturah would inherit the transferable gifts of herds and other wealth that could be taken with them to the east.[24]

The Talmud describes the children of Keturah as joining the children of Ishmael and the children of Esau in participating in the burial of their kinsman Jacob, suggesting that Keturah's children were counted as part of Abraham's extended clan.[25] Yet, commentators debate as to whether Keturah's children were obligated to partake in the rite of circumcision, which would define their status as either within or outside of the covenant.[26]

One midrashic strand characterizes the children of Keturah, along with Ishmael and his descendants, as a blemish on Abraham's name.[27] The gifts Abraham bequeathed to them are also the subject of speculation. According to the Talmud and later commentaries, Abraham granted them magical knowledge through the names of demons, which allowed them to perform sorcery.[28] Other texts associate them with idol worship and other unacceptable behavior.[29]

AUTHOR'S COMMENTARY:
The Missing Story—Filling in the Blanks

The rabbis seem to disagree as to whether Abraham's marriage to Keturah and their resulting progeny was a positive or negative occurrence in the life of our first patriarch. As a result, no clear picture emerges as to their characters or their role in the family history. Equally confounding is the lack of information about Keturah herself. Even though the biblical narrative and commentaries center around Abraham's descendants through Isaac and Jacob, they nonetheless provide significant insights into the lives of Ishmael and Esau, who are similarly adjacent to but not directly part of this lineage. Why, then, is so little thought given to Keturah, who is at the same genealogical level as Sarah and Hagar, and Keturah's children, who are half-siblings to Isaac and Ishmael? Furthermore, the timeline of the biblical narrative suggests that Abraham was at least 140 when he wed Keturah; thus, the two would have been married for more than thirty years at the time of his death at age 175—a significant period of time shrouded in mystery.[30] While rabbinic discussions help to characterize the relationship between the descendants of Keturah, Sarah, and Hagar, they do not shed light on Abraham and Keturah's marriage or relationship. Thus her story becomes ripe for modern midrash.

The rabbinic association between Keturah and Hagar flows very naturally from the text. Both were the matriarchs of significant, but not primary, generational lines of Abraham. Both have an ambiguous familial status as wife, handmaid, or concubine. Accepting the geographic juxtaposition of the prior passage about Isaac and Rebekah in Beer-lahai-roi, both women could be found in the same location. And the idea that Abraham might search out Hagar after the death of Sarah is not too far-fetched.

The modern midrash "Keturah, the Great Mother of Many Generations" picks up these threads to imagine Abraham traveling to Beer-lahai-roi to find Hagar but instead discovering a younger version of her in the personage of Keturah. In the end, Keturah's fate is the same as Hagar's. Both women are destined to be matriarchs of substantial nations, and both women fulfill their duty to provide heirs for Abraham. Yet, both women are usurped by others with a preferred bloodline, and both are discarded and abandoned when their wombs are no longer needed.

Playing on the meaning of her name, the classical commentaries characterize Keturah as righteous and associate her with sweet-smelling incense—elements also found in the modern midrashic depiction of Keturah as young, pure, and empowered with the wisdom to use fragrant herbs and flowers for healing. The similarity between this portrayal of Keturah as a young caregiver to her elder spouse and Abishag, the maiden who cared for King David in his old age (1 Kings 1:1–4), is intentional and may even have resonance in more modern May-December romance stories. Theirs may not have been a passionate love affair, but Keturah feels admiration and loyalty towards her husband.

It is difficult to imagine what it might have meant to Abraham to have additional children after what transpired between him and his other sons. He had doted on Ishmael until Sarah insisted that he and Hagar be banished. He then loved Isaac, only to have been commanded by God to sacrifice him: "*Take your son, your favored one, Isaac, whom you love, and go to the land of Moriah, and offer him there as a burnt offering on one of the heights that I will point out to you"* (Gen. 22:2). As Abraham raised the knife to sacrifice his beloved son, God interceded at the last moment. Surely the trauma of that experience would have influenced his emotional connections with Isaac, Ishmael, and future progeny. While the biblical text does not offer any insight into these relationships, this modern midrash considers the possibility that Abraham might have been reluctant to bond with the sons of Keturah or to bring them into the covenant for fear of a repeat of that horrific test of faith. The psychological baggage Abraham carried would have also intruded upon his marriage with Keturah.

In filling in the gaps of Keturah's story, the modern midrash focuses on her motherhood because that is all that is shared about her within these six verses of biblical text. Being a mother to their many children is her "power," her gift, and the source of her strength, and she wields her "great motherhood" status firmly. Yet that same power is also the cause of her shame and downfall in the years to come as, one by one, her children depart, leaving her bereft, loveless, and, like Hagar before her, alone in the world.

2

Leah and Rachel

Devoted Sisters and Bitter Rivals

BIBLICAL TEXT: *Genesis 35:16–21*

They set out from Bethel; but when they were still some distance short of Ephrath, Rachel was in childbirth, and she had hard labor. When her labor was at its hardest, the midwife said to her, "Have no fear, for it is another boy for you." But as she breathed her last—for she was dying— she named him Ben-oni; but his father called him Benjamin. Thus Rachel died. She was buried on the road to Ephrath—now Bethlehem. Over her grave Jacob set up a pillar; it is the pillar at Rachel's grave to this day. Israel journeyed on, and pitched his tent beyond Migdal-eder.

MODERN MIDRASH: *Leah's Eulogy*

I've torn my clothes, sat among the ashes, sprinkled the dust of the earth on your grave, but nothing lessens the ache in my heart. How can I live with my grief?! Despite our childish rivalry, there is no one in this world who knows me—knew me—like you, my little sister. Oh Rachel! It's so unfair. Finally, we had reached peace between us, and now, just when we should be enjoying the wealth of our years, you come to this bitter end. I don't know how I will go on without you.

I remember our childhood like it was yesterday. We were so different on the outside, yet so similar within. Though born only a few moments apart, I somehow became the "big" sister, and you, the baby of the family.

As Father always said, I was born larger, stronger, and sturdier for bearing children. You were the pretty one, graceful and enchanting.

After Mother died, I tended the hearth and looked after the family, while you threw decorum to the wind and tended the herds along with the shepherd boys. You knew how to get what you wanted from Father, who loved you best. Of course, I was jealous of your beauty and popularity, but I also admired your bravery and adventurous spirit.

When Jacob arrived, you saw your chance to escape our predestined lives. You found him alluring and exotic, since he came from afar, and even Father approved, since he was our cousin. So you worked your womanly magic, and he was smitten. His passion was so consuming, he could see beauty in no one else—he barely noticed me during the seven years he worked for Father to earn your hand, suffering every moment in his longing for you.

When your wedding day finally arrived and Father proposed our prenuptial switch, I thought I would faint. I had secretly loved Jacob all those years but of course never divulged my feelings for him lest I betray you. To this day, I do not know why Father insisted I marry him first. Was it really because propriety and custom demanded it? Was it just a ruse to keep Jacob indentured to him for seven more years? Did Father somehow know I loved Jacob despite my best efforts to hide it? Or, I sometimes wonder, did Father come to believe that he would never find a match for me, his homely, spinster daughter, and I would forever remain a burden to him?

Whatever the reason, I was immensely grateful. If not for my marriage to Jacob, Father might have insisted that I wed Jacob's twin brother, Esau, who I had heard was a vulgar brute. It all seemed too good to be true; I would have the man I loved, my sister and I would stay together, and I would be spared from marrying Esau or some unknown stranger.

When you agreed to help me deceive Jacob, I knew you did not love him as much as I did. You gave him up too easily. I actually felt sorry for you, Rachel. I understood how trapped you felt, like one of your sheep caught in a thicket, reliant on the protection of a man, yet needing your freedom as much as air. You weren't prepared to give up your independence just yet. I loved you for your generosity that night, but I also pitied you. For all your gifts, you would never be satisfied.

As much as I loved Jacob, the way we were wed forever tarnished our marriage. Our deception wounded him deeply and undermined the trust between us. The next morning, he expected to see you by his side, only to discover the cruel truth—you did not love him as much as he loved you; you could live without him. I finally had my beloved, but his beloved was not his.[1]

I knew Jacob would never love me with the same youthful passion he once had for you, but I hoped we could create our own love story by building our beautiful family together. Well, at least the last part of my dreams came true. The blessings of my womb made his clan large and strong and gave me the matriarchal status I thought I deserved.

Once you saw the joy my sons gave me, it was your turn to be jealous. You couldn't stand that I finally had something you did not. So you used your wiles and charm, now to try to gain a child. By this point, though, Jacob had little sympathy for you. In desperation you gave him your hand-maid Bilhah to bear your children. And then I gave him Zilpah to bear more children for me. Thus, our ridiculous womb-contest began. My children, Bilhah's children, Zilpah's children, but never yours. Exhausted, Jacob had to be coaxed, so I sent my children to find seductive potions like the mandrakes you demanded from my first-born. But even then, your manipulations backfired. I had more children, and you remained barren, unfulfilled.

After Joseph's birth, so much changed. We found common cause in our desire to leave Father's home and establish our own clan in Jacob's homeland. Together we convinced our husband to return home, confront his brother, and take what was rightfully his. Jacob, finally at peace with himself and his past, seemed ready to forgive and possibly love again.

So we headed to a new home in a new land, away from Father and all the rivalries and envies that had divided us.[2] Each of us had enough in our respective lives. Wisdom had finally caught up with us, and we were just beginning to enjoy each other as siblings should—with love, compassion, and friendship.

With this final birth, there was no jealousy in my heart. I cried with you as you screamed in agony and prayed that out of your pain there would be born a child who would awaken our beloved's heart. I tried to comfort you in your last moments. *"It is another boy for you,"* I whispered, holding you as you delivered your son with your dying breath. For you and not for me.

I knew that Ben-Oni, the offspring of your pain, was destined to become Ben-Yamin, our husband's heartsong. Jacob would love and cherish this child over all the others.[3] I knew that, and I was no longer jealous.

Oh, Rachel, it's just not fair. How could you leave me now when we have so much left to share? I will miss you more than you could know, more than even I ever realized. You were part of me, the best part . . . the part that was unafraid, bold, willful, daring. And strong. The part that could show love. I will never again be whole without you in my life.

Finally having Jacob to myself, I feel nothing but guilt and sadness, like that first morning in his bed, when he discovered our betrayal. I feel guilty to have our husband all to myself after all these years of sharing him with you. And I am saddened by all the time we lost together with our rivalries. We should never have let Jacob come between us. Now, henceforth, I never will.

Dear Sister. I pledge to remain here with you the rest of my days. I will tend to your grave, even as Jacob moves on—too easily it seems. My tears will leave a pillar of salt to mark your final repose. Here you are buried, and here I, too, will die. Together we will cry for our children.[4]

CLASSICAL COMMENTARY AND MIDRASH:
Sisters, Wives, Rivals, and Matriarchs

The book of Genesis provides significant insight into the lives of the matriarchs and patriarchs, and the scope of commentaries and midrash about them are plentiful. We know, for example, that Leah and Rachel were jealous rivals, competing for Jacob's affection and children, and the midrash fills in information about their youth and what really transpired on Jacob's wedding night. From these and other teachings, we might begin to envision their story from their own perspective and imagine how their relationship might have developed and matured over time.

Rachel and Leah's Youth

There are snippets in rabbinic literature about Leah and Rachel's youth before Jacob enters their lives. Some commentators presume the two sisters were twins, born in parallel with Esau and Jacob,[5] though all we know from the biblical text is that Leah was older and had "weak eyes" and that Rachel was a beautiful shepherdess.

Loath to perceive criticism of one of the matriarchs in this characterization, the rabbis explain these differences to Leah's credit.[6] Some suggest that Leah was just as beautiful as Rachel, and her eyes were soft and tender, yet weakened by tears due to her distress at the prospect of being wed to Esau. This understanding is based on a commonly referenced midrash that the daughters of Laban were destined to marry the sons of Isaac. The two elder, Leah and Esau, and the two younger, Rachel and Jacob, would naturally wed. When Leah discovered the kind of man Esau was, she grew distraught and cried until her eyelashes fell out. God compensated her for her righteousness by blessing her with children.[7]

Noting how unusual it was for a father to allow his younger daughter to be on her own among the shepherds, the rabbis offered several possible explanations for Rachel's occupation. Some commentaries suggest that Laban's herds had been diminished by a plague, and the family was so poor and the flock so meager that his young daughter alone could perform the task sufficiently.[8] Others presume the reverse, suggesting that Laban was so well regarded in the community that his daughter would be safe from any public harm.[9] In asking why Rachel, and not Leah, fulfilled this duty, some explain that Leah's weak eyes made it difficult for her to tend the sheep. Others conjecture that Leah was older and of marriageable age and therefore stayed home to protect her virtue, while Rachel was too young to be considered at risk.[10]

This characterization of Rachel's youth also serves as an explanation for Jacob's waiting seven years until Rachel becomes old enough to marry. Lest there be concern for Rachel's virtue, the rabbis provide assurance that Jacob's impromptu kiss when they meet at the well was not one of passion but of affinity.[11] Although the biblical text itself states first that Jacob kissed Rachel (Gen. 29:11) and then that he informed her that he was a relative (29:12), the commentaries suggest that he certainly would have revealed his relationship prior to kissing her or she would not have allowed it.[12]

Upon meeting Jacob at the well, Rachel runs to her father to tell him about the visitor. Since in the prior story, Laban's sister Rebekah goes instead to her mother to tell her about the visitor and proposal (Gen. 24:28), the rabbis conclude that Rachel and Leah's mother must have been deceased.[13] These commentaries create a picture of the sisters' life before Jacob's arrival. Leah, the pious and responsible elder, stayed home and presumably took on the duties of the woman of the house. Rachel, the young, beautiful, and carefree shepherdess, was destined for romance and adventure.

The Wedding Night Deception

In several ways, the biblical text foreshadows the duplicity that is to come on Jacob's wedding night. Commentaries take note of the repetition of Jacob's familial status within the text as well as the erroneous statement that Jacob was Laban's brother when, in fact, he was his nephew. While the simple nuance of "brother" could signify a clansman, the rabbis find significance in the redundancy as well as the terminology used:

> "*Rachel, daughter of Lavan, the brother of his mother.*" The words "*the brother of his mother*" appear three times in this verse. Apparently, Rachel told Yaakov first that her father was a swindler, and that it would be a mistake on the part of Yaakov to live in his house. Yaakov replied to her that seeing that her father was a brother of his mother, he was aware, and would know how to protect himself against trickery on the part of her father.[14]

Another hint of the future deception is found in Gen. 29:18, when Jacob seeks Rachel's hand in marriage: "*Jacob loved Rachel; so he answered, 'I*

will serve you seven years for Rachel, for your daughter, the younger one."[15]
This formulation is reminiscent of the *Akedah* story, in which God tells
Abraham, "*Take your son, your favored one, Isaac, whom you love*" (22:2).
Just as the multiple descriptors in the *Akedah* story are ripe for midrash,
this description of Rachel also begs for interpretation:

> "*for Rachel, thy daughter, the younger one*"—What reason was there
> for mentioning all these detailed descriptions of Rachel? Because
> he (Jacob) knew that he (Laban) was a deceiver. He said to him, "I
> will serve thee for Rachel": and should you say that I mean any other
> Rachel out of the street, therefore I say "your daughter." Should
> you say, "I will change Leah's name and call her Rachel," I say "your
> younger one." In spite of this, however, all these precautions did not
> avail, for he did actually deceive him.[16]

According to midrash, in order to thwart Laban's possible treachery, Jacob
and Rachel worked out secret signs so he would be assured it was her, and
not Leah, on their wedding night. However, when the night approached.
Rachel realized that her sister would be shamed if the deception was
exposed and so she participated in the ruse by providing Leah with the
signs.[17] Just as it was to Leah's credit that she had "weak eyes" from crying
about her intended marriage to Esau, it also was to Rachel's credit that
she saved her sister from such a fate by allowing her to wed Jacob first.

The rabbis offer additional explanations as to how Jacob could have been
deceived on his wedding night. Although Leah and Rachel are described
as "greater" (elder) and "smaller" (younger), there is a minor thread in
midrashic literature that Leah and Rachel were twins, which helps explain
why Jacob could not tell them apart.[18] It is also suggested that the entire
community was complicit. Jacob's presence brought blessings to the community, and they wished Jacob to remain among them, so they helped
trick him into marrying and working for both women by getting him so
drunk during the wedding feast that he could not tell the sisters apart.[19]

While most sources describe the wedding night swap as Laban's machi-
nation to foist his unwanted elder daughter upon Jacob, *Or ha-Ḥayim* (by

Rabbi Hayyim ben Moshe ibn Attar) paints a different picture of events. According to this depiction, Laban could have argued that Jacob knew about the local customs and that Laban acted out of love for both of his daughters:

> He, Laban, had taken it for granted that Jacob would first stay with him long enough to conform to the local custom and marry Leah. When Jacob had said: "give me my wife!" Laban had naturally understood that Jacob referred to Leah. After all, the local customs were no secret. Laban rejected the accusation that he had acted with subterfuge. Should Jacob be of the opinion that Laban differentiated between his two daughters, this was not so. He loved both equally and treated them both equally. To prove this, he would not ask a higher price for Rachel than he had been willing to accept for Leah. If Jacob was indeed so enamoured of Rachel that he could not wait another seven years, he would show his understanding by letting him have Rachel in another week, as soon as the wedding festivities in honour of Leah had been concluded, i.e. when he had completed a week with this wife.[20]

Few commentators consider Leah's own perception of her wedding night. *Or ha-Ḥayim*, speaking of the humiliation Leah must have experienced, offers the possibility that Leah may have been forced or coerced into going along with the deception, noting that Laban "*took*" Leah to Jacob (Gen. 29:23).[21] In contrast, Ramban asserts that even though Leah may have obeyed her father dutifully, nonetheless, she should have alerted Jacob to her true identity.[22]

While the biblical text states that Leah is hated (Gen. 29:31), the rabbis found it unseemly that the Jacob would hate the mother of his children and therefore provide numerous rationales for that sentiment. According to some sources, upon seeing Leah on the morning after his wedding night, Jacob asks her to explain the deception, and she proceeds to scold him for being a trickster himself, having deceived his own father to gain Esau's blessing. Just as Jacob had responded when his father, Isaac, mistakenly called him Esau, Leah answered Jacob when he called her Rachel. One midrash explains that this scolding causes Jacob to despise Leah.[23] Alternatively, other commentaries suggest that Jacob does, in fact, love Leah, but because his love for Rachel is so much greater, it only appears as if he hates Leah by comparison.[24] Still other sources offer that it is not Jacob but rather others who hate Leah after hearing of her deception:

> All hated [i.e. abused] her: sea-travellers abused her, land-travellers abused her, and even the women behind the beams [used in the crushing of grapes] abused her, saying: "This Leah leads a double life: she pretends to be righteous, yet is not so, for if she were righteous, would she have deceived her sister!" R. Judah b. R. Simon and R. Hanan said in the name of R. Samuel b. R. Isaac: When the Patriarch Jacob saw how Leah deceived him by pretending to be her sister, he determined to divorce her. But as soon as the Holy One, blessed be He, visited her with children he exclaimed, "Shall I divorce the mother of these children!"[25]

According to this midrash, despite the fact that her father Laban dictates her actions, Leah's reputation is sullied, and she is despised for deceiving her husband and cheating her sister. Hated by her husband and shunned by the community, Leah's existence surely would have been miserable. God takes pity on Leah and opens her womb, ensuring that Jacob will not divorce her. And thus, Rachel and Leah's battle for babies begins.

Sibling Rivalry

Though Leah may have been unloved by her husband, she is amply compensated by the fruitfulness of her womb. According to the chronology of the biblical text, Rachel does not become jealous of Leah until the birth of her fourth son. Commentators speculate that the matriarchs, known to be prophets, foresaw that there would be twelve tribes. If Leah, Rachel, and their two handmaids equitably bore those children, each would give birth to three sons. However, once Leah gives birth to her fourth son, Rachel becomes jealous because she has more than her fair share.[26]

Rachel's jealousy is unquenchable even though she is the favored wife and Jacob sleeps with her most often.[27] According to midrash, Rachel's bed had always been next to Jacob's bed, and after she dies, he moves Bilhah, Rachel's handmaid, next to him.[28] Rachel's growing desperation for a child strains her relationship with an unsympathetic Jacob, who becomes angry when she threatens that she will die without children (Gen. 30:2). Her handmaid Bilhah becomes her surrogate. Then Leah's handmaid Zilpah becomes Leah's surrogate, and the birthing contest continues.

Growing ever more frantic, Rachel trades a night with Jacob for mandrakes, presumably an aphrodisiac, collected by Leah's son Reuben. That proves to be a fateful choice, as Leah bears two more sons, while Rachel remains barren.

The rabbis ascribe merit to both Rachel and Leah for their desire to have children in fulfillment of the marital mitzvah and the future they have divined. After making their trade, Leah assertively goes out to meet Jacob and insists on the agreed-upon marital relations: "*When Jacob came home from the field in the evening, Leah went out to meet him and said, 'You are to sleep with me, for I have hired you with my son's mandrakes*" (Gen. 30:16). While that may seem brazen, the commentaries suggest that Leah's intention is to spare Rachel the embarrassment of having Jacob go into her tent and then be redirected. Her consideration for her sister outweighs her audacious behavior, and she is rewarded with yet another son.[29]

While her desire for children is to her credit, the rabbis also criticize Rachel for relinquishing her night with Jacob to Leah, and thus forgoing the opportunity to conceive one of the twelve tribes. Because she gives up the privilege of lying with Jacob that night, she loses the privilege of lying with him for eternity:

Our sages in Bereshit Rabbah 72,3 were so convinced of this that they attributed the fact that Rachel was not buried in the cave of Machpelah with her husband Yaakov to her forgoing his company for even one night. By volunteering to miss that opportunity to conceive a child from Yaakov on the night she made the deal with

Leah about Reuven's *dudaim* (the aphrodisiac plant Reuven had found) she was punished. She should have treasured Yaakov's company more. On the other hand, we are taught in that same Midrash that Leah who did treasure the company of her husband bore two more sons for Yaakov as a result of the deal she made. Issachar was born to Leah as a reward for her giving Rachel the *dudaim* of her son Reuven in order to secure an extra opportunity to conceive a child from her husband.[30]

As the contest between the women winds down, Leah has yet another child: a daughter, Dinah. The rabbis speculate about the phraseology. The text does not mention her first becoming pregnant, as do all the descriptions of Leah's prior births; here, the text simply states "*Last, she bore him a daughter, and named her Dinah*" (Gen. 30:21). The nuance of the word "*last*" (*aḥar*) is ambiguous and could connote "afterward." Read that way, a legend holds that Leah and the handmaids pray for the child to be a girl, and then "afterward" Dinah is born. They feel pity for Rachel's circumstances, knowing from their prophecy that only two more sons will be born. Since each of the handmaids already has given birth to two sons, it would not be right for Jacob's favored wife to give birth to fewer sons than the handmaids, so they pray for this child of Leah's to be a girl, allowing Rachel to give birth to the final two sons of Jacob. Due to their compassion for Rachel, their prayers are answered. In some variations of this midrash, the child's gender is switched while still in Leah's womb. In other versions, both Leah and Rachel are pregnant, and the male and female babies are miraculously switched between their two wombs:

> *And afterward she bare a daughter*, and called her name Dinah; for she said, Judgement is from before the Lord, that there shall be from me a half of the tribes; but from Rahel my sister shall go forth two tribes, even as they shall proceed (in like manner) from each of the handmaids. And the prayer of Leah was heard before the Lord; and the infants were changed in their wombs; and Joseph was given to the womb of Rahel, and Dinah to the womb of Leah.[31]

The second son born to Rachel's handmaid Bilhah is named Naphtali: *"And Rachel said, 'A fateful contest I waged with my sister; yes, and I have prevailed.' So she named him Naphtali"* (Gen. 30:8). This child's name captures the pathetic competition among the sisters for Jacob's love and progeny.[32] The sisters compete for Jacob's affection, for their matriarchal status, and for the blessing of motherhood.

Ultimately there seems to be a rapprochement among the sisters, as seen in the previously mentioned midrash related to the birth of Dinah. Leah is satisfied, having given birth to more than her share of the clan, and Rachel finally has her sons by Bilhah and her son Joseph.

Interestingly, after Joseph's birth, the sisters begin to act in unison. At this point in the biblical narrative, Jacob seeks to separate from Laban and take his growing clan and herds back to his homeland. When he conveys his intention to his wives, they respond with one voice: *"Then Rachel and Leah answered him, saying, 'Have we still a share in the inheritance of our father's house? Surely, he regards us as outsiders, now that he has sold us and has used up our purchase price. Truly, all the wealth that God has taken away from our father belongs to us and to our children. Now then, do just as God has told you"* (Gen. 31:14–16). Their use of the plural forms "we" and "us" suggests a shift in their relationship from lifelong rivals to a united front—a sign that the two have reconciled and may have finally found harmony in sisterhood.

Sadly, Rachel dies giving birth to the last of Jacob's sons, Benjamin, and is buried en route. Leah's death goes unmentioned; she is presumed to have been buried in the cave of Machpelah, based on Jacob's deathbed statement (in Gen. 49:31) that he had buried Leah there. (Rebekah's death similarly is not recorded, though a reference in 35:8 to the death of her nurse, Deborah, is presumed to be a reference to Rebekah's own death.) In fact, Leah is not mentioned in the narrative after Rachel's death. The matriarchs live on through the deeds of their descendants, and the midrash lauds the meritorious lineage of each of the mothers of Israel:

"Now Laban had two daughters"—like two beams running from end to end of the world [interpreting *banoth* (daughters) as *bonoth* (builders): from them the world of Israel was built up]. Each produced captains, each produced kings, from each arose slayers of lions [David, descended from Leah, and Samson, descended from Bilhah], from each arose conquerors of countries [Moses and David, from Leah; Joshua and Saul from Rachel], from each arose dividers of countries [Moses and Joshua, who divided the country among the tribes].[33]

AUTHOR'S COMMENTARY: *A Tale of Two Sisters*

Most of the rabbinic literature about the matriarchs Leah and Rachel see them from the lens of their male relations: Laban's daughters, Jacob's wives, the twelve tribes' mothers. The biblical text does provide insights into their relationship through their complicity in the wedding night scheme and in their jealous competition for Jacob's affection and for children. Overall, however, the traditional texts do not consider the sisters' complex, long-term relationship. By contrast, the focus of this midrash, "Leah's Eulogy," is the intense, deep, and nuanced relationship between the two sisters, from Leah's point of view, as she reflects upon the tragic loss of her younger sister.

Numerous themes found in rabbinic commentaries are woven into the creative midrash, such as the presumption that Leah and Rachel were twins, although clearly Leah behaves and is treated as the elder of the two. As an older twin herself, the author relates to this dynamic; despite being twins, certain birth order roles nonetheless get assigned and behaviors adjusted accordingly. As the elder, Leah may have resented the freedoms allowed her younger sibling, yet also felt protective of her. In this depiction, Rachel appears to be the youthful, carefree, and adventurous sister, while Leah dutifully tends the home, does as she is told, and is devoted to her marital duties. These are typical and opposing archetypes, similar to the portrayals of Jacob and Esau, in which Esau is the carefree adventurer, a "man of the field," while Jacob is happy at the hearth, dutiful, and obedient to his mother.

It is noteworthy that the biblical text and rabbinic literature repeatedly refer to Jacob's love for Rachel, but the reverse is not explicitly stated. We are left to wonder if Rachel loved Jacob as much as he loved her. According to the rabbis, Rachel is complicit in Jacob's wedding night deception due to her devotion to her sister and, perhaps, obedience to her father—yet the biblical text is silent as to whether Rachel willingly relinquished her marital bed. Did she silently acquiesce? By contrast, later in the text, Rachel makes her feelings clearly known, first demanding that Jacob give her a child and then insisting that Leah give her the aphrodisiac mandrakes. Is it possible that when it came to marrying Jacob, Rachel was ambivalent? Could she have feared being forever bound in marriage and felt (at least partially) relieved that her older sister was willing to step in for her?

In criticizing Rachel for trading a night with Jacob for the mandrakes, the rabbis allude to this imbalance in their relationship. In fact, her willingness to forgo her marital duty is presumed to be the reason Leah, and not Rachel, lies with Jacob in the cave of Machpelah. Jacob's love is not enough for her; she does not desire Jacob as much as she desires to have what Leah has: children.

While "Leah's Eulogy" does not delve into Rachel's feelings, we do see Leah questioning the sincerity of her sister's love for their husband—a reflection of the bitterness Leah must have felt knowing that Jacob loved Rachel more than her.

Jacob is clearly smitten and passionately in love with Rachel from their first kiss at the well, and thus the biblical text reads as a love story. The rabbis seem never to consider the possibility that the patriarch's love is not fully requited by Rachel, but perhaps by Leah instead. Turning the biblical love story on its head, "Leah's Eulogy" gives voice to Leah's feelings as part of a love quadrangle: four women, two of them sisters, sharing Jacob's bed. Given this reality, the relationships among the women are bound to be complex. While the biblical text takes note of the envy and jealousy that occur around their childbearing, the deeper nuances of the relationships between the women and their individual relationships with Jacob are left to the imagination and addressed here in this midrash and a second one on Bilhah's relationship with Jacob and the children (see chapter 4).

Inasmuch as Leah exhibits and seeks sympathy in her own retelling, Leah also seems rigid, judgmental, and, sadly, unloved, just as she is described in the biblical and rabbinic tradition. Both Leah and Rachel have cause for bitterness and jealousy: Leah for being unwanted and unappreciated, and Rachel for being childless and having her primary role usurped. Despite their differences, when they resolve to leave their father's home, they have a chance, finally, to form their own household, free of the trappings of their past. In setting their sights on the future, they begin to speak with one voice. Together with their children in tow they will face the dangers of their journey and forge a new clan in a new land.

This allusion to unity provides a hopeful image of the sisters reaching a point in their lives when they can find joy and companionship in their sisterly bonds. It is comforting to imagine Leah and Rachel growing wise with age and experience. If they can eventually reconcile, then perhaps we, too, can move past the disappointments and wounds of our past and find satisfaction with our place in life before the end of our days.

When Rachel gives birth to Benjamin, the biblical text references an unnamed midwife (Gen. 35:17). "Leah's Eulogy" assigns this role to Leah, which is a logical assumption since the family was traveling on the road at the time and not in a town where a midwife was likely to be present. Having the midwife's assurances and comfort at a tender moment come from Leah reinforces the notion of their reconciliation and Leah's compassion for her sister.

At the end of Genesis, Jacob states that he buried Leah in the cave of Machpelah, where he also wishes to be buried, yet nothing in the text indicates how much longer she lived or where or how she died. In never mentioning Leah's life after Rachel's death, the biblical text seems to view Leah solely in relation to Rachel and not as an independent character in her own right, despite the fact that Leah was the elder sister, first wife, and mother of seven of Jacob's thirteen children. Even her role as mother to half of the twelve tribes is largely ignored beyond the fact of her having given birth to them. The biblical account of Leah's story begins with

Rachel's meeting Jacob at the well and ends with Rachel's death. Alternatively, "Leah's Eulogy" uplifts Leah as an essential participant in the Jewish people's story, giving Leah her own deserved character and voice. Yet the modern midrash also imagines Leah's life virtually ending with Rachel's death—the sisters linked together from the moment of their birth to the moment of their death.

Leah's role in Jewish teachings and tradition similarly remains understated and underrepresented. The traditional formulation for listings of the matriarchs in prayer books and commentaries, "Rachel and Leah," consistently lists Rachel first, thus forever elevating Rachel over Leah. I hope that this reimagining of the story through Leah's eyes and experience may give her character the attention and status she deserves.

3

Bat Shua

Judah's Unnamed Wife

BIBLICAL TEXT: *Genesis 38:1–12*

About that time Judah left his brothers and camped near a certain Adullamite whose name was Hirah. There Judah saw the daughter of a certain Canaanite whose name was Shua, and he took her [into his household as wife] and cohabited with her. She conceived and bore a son, and he named him Er. She conceived again and bore a son, and named him Onan. Once again she bore a son, and named him Shelah; he was at Chezib when she bore him. Judah got a wife for Er his first-born; her name was Tamar. But Er, Judah's first-born, was displeasing to God, and God took his life. Then Judah said to Onan, "Join with your brother's wife and do your duty by her as a brother-in-law, and provide offspring for your brother." But Onan, knowing that the offspring would not count as his, let [the semen] go to waste whenever he joined with his brother's wife, so as not to provide offspring for his brother. What he did was displeasing to God, who took his life also. Then Judah said to his daughter-in-law Tamar, "Stay as a widow in your father's house until my son Shelah grows up"—for he thought, "He too might die like his brothers." So Tamar went to live in her father's house. A long time afterward, Shua's daughter, the wife of Judah, died. When his period of mourning was over, Judah went up to Timnah to his sheepshearers, together with his friend Hirah the Adullamite.

I have had many names. I was first known as Bat Shua, the Daughter of Shua. Then I was known as Eishet Yehudah, the Wife of Judah. I have been called the Canaanite Woman, the Mother of Er the Childless, the Mother of Onan the Defiler, the Mother of Shelah the Young. I was briefly the Mother-in-Law of Tamar, the Whore. Now I am the Woman Who Mourns. I am defined only by others; I have no name of my own.

My early life as Bat Shua, the Daughter of Shua's House, was carefree and joyous. I had been born into wealth and privilege, and all around me admired my beauty. I had no mother to teach me the ways of women or to warn me of the importance of modesty and restraint, but my father, a cunning merchant, taught me the ways of negotiation and trade. He was proud of me and regularly showed me off to his many friends and business associates. I didn't mind; I rather enjoyed the attention. I became his partner in business. When he had important dealings, I would entertain the men, pouring wine and encouraging them to let down their guard, priming them to ensure a good deal for Father.

There was one trading partner in particular I looked forward to seeing—our neighbor Hirah. He was not much older than I was and very handsome. He was always deferential to my father, bowing low whenever he entered our home. He was gracious and respectful to me too; whenever I entered the room he would smile sweetly, bowing in a most formal manner. I responded in kind, smiling as I served him the customary meal. Father once told me that Hirah would negotiate a deal for me one day. For me! I imagined myself as the Woman of Hirah's House and blushed at the thought.

I barely gave a thought to the dark young man who joined Hirah for our evening meal one night. Like so many others, his eyes smoldered with lust as I poured his drink. I played along as usual, laughing and smiling, entertaining him to ensure a good trade. When he returned the next day, I continued to ply him with drinks and tempt him with my charm.

Little did I know that this time, I was the deal! Father must have made a good trade—too good to refuse. After all I'd done to manage Father's household and assist him with his business dealings, how could he let me go so easily?

And so quickly! Before I knew it, Father had given me over to Judah ben Jacob, who whisked me away from my home. Just as suddenly, I found myself in Judah's bed.

With no mother or sisters to guide me, I hadn't known much of what happens between a man and woman, but Judah was kind and gentle, and eventually I learned what pleased him. What choice did I have? I now belonged to this stranger and lived among his foreign people, nomads who were constantly moving further away from the House of Shua.

So I settled into my new role as Eishet Yehudah—Judah's Wife. While at first his language was strange to me, I recognized some of the words from Father's negotiations, devoted myself to learning his tongue, and eventually was able to communicate with my husband and his tribe. While I'd been used to a stable home and the comforts of wealth, the road was Judah's home, and so I came to accept the nomadic life. I did look forward to the occasions when Judah's brothers and their wives briefly pitched their tents with us, even though that never lasted long enough to make real friendships among the wives.

Still, Judah's tent became my home, so whenever it was erected, I situated our few possessions in our space in the same way to make it feel familiar each time we moved. Perhaps that's also why Judah built stone markers wherever we traveled. He told me it was to claim the land for his god, but I think it was to establish something enduring . . . to leave behind a memory of our having been in that place.

As the months went by, our loneliness drew Judah and me closer, and our tent became our refuge. Judah's lust evolved into affection and companionship—perhaps even love. For a long while his sleep had been disturbed by strange dreams and memories that riddled him with guilt, and I tried my best to soothe his troubled spirit. Eventually he came to trust me, whispering the dark secrets of his lost brother and tormented father into his pillow to purge his soul. And soon Judah was beaming with pride as my ripe belly proved his virility.

But how things changed when our first son was born! Judah named him Er—which sounded like an evil portent to me. And then, eight days later, Judah drew ritual blood from my baby boy's most private flesh! While the men of the household cheered and celebrated, I shrieked in agony along with my child. As I soothed his screams, I swore I would protect him forevermore.

I suffered terrible labor pains the second time, so much so that the midwives thought I might die, but both the baby and I came through. And this time, I chose our new son's name—Onan, meaning "the aggrieved." What might have been cause for mourning had instead resulted in the life of this beautiful boy.

On the eighth day, Judah took Onan from my arms for that awful bloody ritual. Just as before, I comforted my son, cried with him, and vowed to myself that I would never let such harm come to him again. But this time I added: *or to any child of mine in the future.*

Judah and I grew apart after that. I avoided his visits and began to cringe at his touch, and he came to my bed less often, respecting my privacy and seeking entertainment elsewhere. He traveled often with our old family friend Hirah for weeks at a time. The rest of the tribe stayed put while Judah was gone, and I devoted my attention to our sons and to managing the household. This suited me—I began to feel the self-assurance I had known in Shua's home.

And with Judah away, it was easier to conceal my own dark secret: I had surreptitiously begun practicing some of the rituals of my youth. I found comfort surrounding myself with figurines like those I'd had as a child and reciting charms in the language of my people. I formed shapes out of soft stones to represent my father's gods and goddesses and offered small sacrifices to them. Of course, I couldn't be seen bringing in goats or sheep from among our herds, as we had done in Father's home, so I used water and grains; being scarce and therefore valuable, these seemed sufficient tokens for my prayers. I offered supplications for the well-being of my sons. I prayed to see my father once more. And I entreated the gods to ensure that I would not be discovered, for in Judah's clan this crime was punishable by death.

By the time I realized I was with child a third time, Judah had been away for several months. Hoping to forestall a repeat of his bloody custom, I decided not to send word to him and pleaded with my gods for a female child. I was heartsick when my third son was born!

I named him Shelah, "the calm one," since this birth was so much easier than Onan's, and vowed to never again lie with my husband. I sent word to Judah that when the eighth day came, I would fulfill his god's command in his absence, but instead I secretly cut myself and displayed my blood as the ritual sacrifice in place of my child's. Since Judah and his companions were away, I was the head of the household, and there was no one with greater authority to question me.

From then on, I had to make sure that no one else would ever see the truth of my deception. I kept Shelah close to me always. We were inseparable.

When Judah found a bride for Er, I did not object. It was the right time for him to wed and take his place as the first-born, ensuring that he would be head of the clan one day. And I looked forward to meeting Tamar, who, like me, was an outsider. While no one had eased my way into a strange household, I could embrace Tamar and teach her the customs of the clan. Tamar could share the daily work. Maybe she would be like my own daughter, and I could be like the mother I never had.

At first it seemed so. Young and inexperienced, Tamar welcomed my guidance and wisdom. We fell into an easy routine, each responsible for our own tent and dedicated to our proper roles as the wives of the current and future heads of the tribe.

Everyone waited with great anticipation for an heir to strengthen our clan and safeguard our future, but Tamar failed to produce a grandchild. Judah grew impatient and irritable, stomping around the tent and pestering Tamar and Er to get to it more quickly. I had given him three children so quickly that he expected the same for our son. With all the hounding, my once joyous child became despondent. He shriveled into himself as if he wanted to disappear. I feared that the gods were punishing us for mutilating Er's manhood.

And then, suddenly, he breathed his last.

Tamar and I were both bereft. I, at least, had my other two sons, but Tamar was terrified of being a widow at such a young age. We clung to one another through the period of mourning.

One day, as she wept inconsolably, I felt I had to do something to comfort her. I took her by the hand, led her into my tent, and revealed to her my secret stone gods. After a glance at her face showed nothing, I began reciting incantations and making offerings for her well-being . . . but she quickly jumped up and knocked over my altar! As her mouth opened wide to scream, I slapped her horror-stricken face before she could alert anyone. Grabbing her tight, I hissed into her ear that revealing my secret would mean death for both of us. If she told anyone, my gods would strike her down, and I made her vow to keep silent.

After that, Tamar and I kept our distance. I no longer trusted her, and I could tell she looked down on me, acting as if she belonged to the clan more than I.

And then the unthinkable happened—Judah gave our second child to Tamar. How could he shackle Onan to this same, cursed woman for the sake of Er's legacy?

To delay the marriage, I convinced Judah to allow Hirah to escort me back to Father's home, where I would seek consolation in my grief for Er. I was so happy to see Father again! I ran to hug him, but he cringed at the sight of me. I was no longer the youthful beauty who'd stood by his side and entertained his associates. I had become Eishet Yehudah, Judah's Wife, a tent dweller dusty from the road, smelling of wet wool. I no longer belonged in Shua's home.

Despite my hurt, I had a mission to attend to. I sought out oracles and sorceresses among my people to learn how to protect my middle child and appease the angry gods. Once armed with that knowledge, I let Hirah bring me back to my tent.

Then I explained to Onan how he could prevent Tamar from bringing forth a child. Onan obeyed his father and married Tamar, but he also obeyed me and refused to give his seed to her.

As Tamar grew increasingly desperate for a child, I privately rejoiced. I knew it was unkind, but she'd brought it on herself, by turning her back on our gods. And it had to be this way, to keep my second-born safe.

But then my dear Onan drew his last breath!

It had to be my fault. My gods were not powerful enough to protect Onan, and Judah's god had punished me to prove it. His was a vengeful god—a spiteful god.

By then, even Judah began to doubt the wisdom of allowing Tamar to remain in our camp. He sent her back to her father, but not before pledging that one day she would wed Shelah to fulfill his brotherly duty on behalf of Er and Onan. I couldn't believe it!

I was devastated. My first two sons were dead, and Shelah would be dead too, once he married that evil woman. Everything I tried had failed. My gods had failed me. The wisdom of the oracles had failed me. Judah ignored my pleas to spare our son his fate. I even offered my bed once again, but he had lost his appetite for me. He blamed me for the loss of our sons, echoing his father and brothers, who told him he never should have married a foreign woman. I became a virtual outcast, abandoned by my husband, rejected by the clan, grief-stricken and alone.

There was nothing left to do. I bundled up young Shelah, gathered up my stone gods, and in Hirah's company, journeyed back to Shua's home. Father took us in, reluctantly. Even he believed the gods must have been angry at the union he had made.

Shelah thrived in his grandfather's home. He learned the trade and took up my old place at Shua's side. He looked up to Hirah, who had remained Father's trusted partner. But even as Shelah prospered and blossomed into a young man, I would not allow him to leave our home to travel the trade routes with Hirah.

Judah never came for us. Was he relieved to be rid of me? Was he grateful that Shelah was out of Tamar's reach? Or did he simply forget about us altogether?

As for me, I took to my bed. Though my dear Shelah was now safe, I had lost everything else—my husband, my two sons, my daughter-in-law, my station in life, and my place as Woman of Bat Shuah's House.

When my end drew near, I called Hirah to my side and poured out my soul to him. I confessed that I had loved him in our youth, but when Father arranged my marriage to Judah, I became a dutiful wife to his friend. I admitted that I had schemed to keep Shelah's manhood intact, and I defended my actions—I only did what any mother would do to protect her children. I tried to honor my husband's ways, but still I had remained faithful to our gods, though they had abandoned me. I begged Hirah to protect my beloved Shelah and keep him from Judah and Tamar, lest he, too, be struck down.

Hirah said nothing, but as I looked into his eyes I saw a tear—perhaps he too wondered what might have been?—and he sweetly squeezed my hand. Assured that Shelah would be safe with Hirah, I closed my eyes and breathed my last.

CLASSICAL COMMENTARY AND MIDRASH:
Judah's Family Misfortune

The brevity of the biblical story is astounding. Judah and Bat Shua meet, have and raise three sons, marry and bury two sons, and delay the marriage of their third son, and then Bat Shua dies, all within a scant twelve verses. We also know that Judah sojourned with his friend Hirah, and during their visit he met and became infatuated with a Canaanite woman, Bat Shua, but beyond the fact that they wed and had three sons, two of whom died, we know nothing about her personality, about her married life with Judah, about how she raised her sons, about how she felt about their marriage to Tamar—and most poignantly, about the anguish she must have felt at the loss of her children.

The rabbinic commentary on this section is similarly minimal. In fact, the rabbis largely view these events as background: setting the stage for the subsequent and much more significant story of Judah's own unknowing union with Tamar and the birth of Perez, through whom the Davidic and messianic line will emerge. As we will see, the commentaries draw numerous lessons from the unfortunate marriage of Judah and the daughter of Shua but say little about the woman herself, which provides a rich opening for midrashic exploration.

Placement of Bat Shua's Story

This storyline oddly interrupts the Joseph narrative. It immediately follows the tale of Judah and the other brothers selling Joseph into slavery and their father Jacob's mourning for his beloved son, who is presumed dead. After this interlude, the Joseph narrative continues with Joseph being taken to Egypt and sold into slavery. The peculiar placement of this section invites linkages between Judah's story and the passages before and after, which influence the rabbinic understanding of the storyline.

The rabbis take note of the language used to introduce this section, "*About that time Judah left* [literally: *he went down from*] *his brothers*" (Gen. 38:1). Noting that the same Hebrew verb for "*going down*" (*vayeired*) is utilized in the previous passage, when Jacob refuses to be comforted and exclaims "*I will go down*" (*eireid*; 37:35) to Sheol in mourning, as well as in the very next section, as Joseph is "*brought down*" (*hurad*; 39:1) to Egypt, they explain that Judah's "*going down from his brothers*" signifies a decline in his position among his brothers, as they blame him for causing his father's "*going down*" in grief at the loss of Joseph. Some sources suggest that Judah's brothers excommunicate him. Although Judah had in fact saved Joseph's life by suggesting they sell him rather than kill him, his brothers hold him responsible for their father's despair, since they followed his advice:

> They said: "When you told us: 'Come and let us sell him,' we listened to you, but if you had told us: 'Come, let us take him back,' we would have listened to you. You are responsible for our father's grief." That is why they excommunicated him. Hence the word *red* ("*get thee down*") implies excommunication.[1]

In presuming that Judah could have convinced them to release Joseph entirely, numerous commentaries also use this passage to teach a lesson about integrity and worthiness and the risks of doing good deeds only partway:

That Judah went down, etc. It was a descent for him, for he buried his wife and his sons. R. Judah b. R. Simon and R. Hanan said in R. Johanan's name: He who commences a good deed but does not finish it, buries his wife and children. From whom do you learn this? From Judah: *And Judah said unto his brethren: What profit is it, etc.?* (Gen. 37:26) now he should have led him home in person to his father. What was the result? He buried his wife and children.[2]

While most commentaries connect Judah's demotion to his participation in the scheme to sell Joseph and deceive his father, others connect his downfall to his marriage to Bat Shua. Linking this text to Malachi 2:11 and 2:14—"*Judah has broken faith; abhorrent things have been done in Israel and in Jerusalem. For Judah has profaned what is holy to [God]—what [God] desires—and espoused daughters of alien gods. . . . Because [God] is a witness between you and the wife of your youth with whom you have broken faith, though she is your partner and covenanted spouse*"—the midrash suggests that Judah's marriage to a Canaanite woman was an abomination and thus explains that Judah was lowered in his rank among his brothers because of his marriage to her.[3]

Bat Shua's Background

According to the biblical text, Judah's wife was the daughter of Shua, a Canaanite (Gen. 38:2). Although she is unnamed, like many other minor female biblical personages, elsewhere in the Bible she is referred to as the "*Canaanite woman*" (1 Chron. 2:3), and most commentaries refer to her as Bat Shua, "daughter of Shua." The book of *Jubilees* (second century BCE, within the Pseudepigrapha) calls her Bedsuel, a variation of Batshua.[4] The *Testament of Judah* (also part of the Pseudepigrapha) refers to her as Batshua the Canaanite, as well as Saba, daughter of Barsaba King of Abdullam[5] and Anan the Canaanite woman.[6] Centuries later, the medieval midrash *Sefer ha-Yashar* speaks of her as Aliyat.[7]

The rabbis were challenged by the idea that Judah would marry a Canaanite woman. In the first book of the Torah, Abraham did not want his son Isaac to marry a Canaanite woman (Gen. 24:3), and by the last book of the Torah, such a union had become forbidden (Deut. 7:3). Early sources, including the Talmud, *Targum Onkelos* (first-century Aramaic translation of the Bible), and numerous commentaries, explain that the term "Canaanite" was actually meant to describe a merchant or trader.[8] Other commentators take the text literally and deem Judah's marriage to a Canaanite woman a violation of custom and cause for his demotion, even though the union was not forbidden at the time Judah lived.[9] *Targum Jonathan*, a later Aramaic translation, reconciles both ideas, suggesting that Shua was a merchant and that Bat Shua converted before Judah wed her.[10] The eighteenth-century *Or ha-Ḥayim* commentary by Rabbi Hayyim ben Moshe ibn Attar provides an overview of the dilemma the rabbis tried to resolve:

> The word "Canaanite" means a trader. Ibn Ezra writes that it is possible that the word Canaanite is to be understood in the usual way, i.e. a local inhabitant of the Canaanite tribes. I maintain that it is impossible to imagine that any of the sons of Jacob would intermarry with the Canaanites, something which their forefathers had so strenuously opposed, as pointed out specifically in *Pessachim* 50. The Torah was careful to say *"the daughter of a Canaanite man,"* meaning that she herself was not a Canaanite woman. This is only possible if her father was a merchant, not an actual Canaanite. Had she been a Canaanite, Yehudah would have been guilty of a great misdemeanour by marrying her. If this had indeed been the case the Torah would have indicated it by writing "he married a Canaanite woman whose father was called Shua," or something similar. It would not even have required an additional word to inform us of that fact. The Torah should not have let us surmise that Yehudah married a Canaanite woman but should have spelled it out clearly.[11]

Several sources associate Judah's friend Hirah with Hiram, the king of Tyre, who lived at the time of King David and Solomon (1 Kings 5:15), acknowledging that he would have to have lived over a thousand years to be the same man.[12] According to these sources, Bat Shua was the daughter of the Adullamite king, who held a banquet in Judah's honor, during which Judah became drunk and libidinous and was seduced by her beauty and the promise of wealth. Had he not been in such a state, he would not have married a Canaanite woman. In the *Testament of Judah*, this depiction of Judah's marriage to Bat Shua is used as a cautionary tale to warn against the evils of wine, promiscuity, and avarice. These are presumed to be Judah's last words to his children while on his deathbed:

> And I knew that the race of the Canaanites was evil, but youthful impulses blinded my reason and when I saw her, I was led astray by the strong drink and had intercourse with her. . . . For I said to my father-in-law, "I will confer with my father and then I will take your daughter." But since he was unwilling to delay, he showed me a measureless mass of gold which was in his daughter's name. He decked her in gold and pearls, and made her pour out wine for us in a feast. The wine perverted my eyesight; pleasure darkened my heart. I longed for her and lay with her; thus I transgressed the Lord's command and that of my father when I took her as my wife. And the Lord repaid me according to the rashness of my soul, because I had no delight in her children. . . . And now, my children, I command you not to love money or to gaze on the beauty of women. Because it was on account of money and attractive appearance that I was led astray to Bathshua the Canaanite. And I know that on account of these two things my tribe is doomed to wickedness.[13]

Outside of the question of whether Shua was an actual Canaanite or just a merchant, the rabbis have little to say about Shua. He would not have been of interest, as he is not part of the Israelite story. Bat Shua herself is only of passing interest as lead-in to the Tamar narrative, which is where the line of Judah begins.

Bat Shua and Judah's Sons

After Judah and Bat Shua wed, she gives birth to three sons in short order. Since all three of their names are unclear and unusual, the rabbis offer creative and often divergent meanings. Some suggest Er means "childless" or "awakening." Others play on his name Er (*'-r*) to suggest his name foreshadows his death, explaining that "he was poured out from the world" (*she-hu-'ar*).[14]

The name Onan (*'-w-n-n*) could come from the Hebrew root meaning "vigorous" (*'-w-n*) or the Hebrew root for "complaining" (*'-n-n*), which is the verb used to describe the Israelites' bitter grousing in the wilderness (*mitonenim*) (Num. 11:1). Many rabbis associate Onan with *aninut*, from the Hebrew root related to grief or mourning (*'-n-h*)—an allusion to his father's later mourning for him or to his mother's near death from hard labor.[15]

The Hebrew root of Shelah's name (*sh-l-h*) typically means "quiet" or "ease," but it can also have the nuance "to extract" or "draw out"; the same root is used for "afterbirth." Some commentators connect his name to the meaning of "*Chezib*" (*kh-z-v*), the name of the town where Judah was at that time, which has the nuance of "deception" or "ceasing." Given these possible derivations, many commentators explain that his name signifies that Bat Shua was unable to bear more children after his birth.[16]

Curiously, the text states that Judah names Er, while Bat Shua names both Onan and Shelah. To explain this unusual description, numerous sources surmise that it must have been customary in ancient times to alternate the naming of children between the husband and wife. If that was the case, however, Judah should have named their third child, so the rabbis remind us that the text explicitly states that Judah is away, and therefore Bat Shua has to name their third child in his absence (Gen. 38:5).[17]

When it comes time to find a wife for Er, Judah arranges a marriage with Tamar (who, according to the commentaries, is a descendant of Shem and therefore a permissible bride). Er commits an unnamed offense and is struck down, whereupon Judah demands that his second son Onan marry Tamar to ensure his brother's name will continue. This is the first example of levirate marriage,[18] through which the first-born child of Onan and Tamar would be considered Er's progeny and entitled to Er's first-born share of the inheritance, thus diminishing the inheritance of any future children born to Onan.[19] Once wed to Tamar, Onan commits the sin of "wasting his seed," presumably to prevent Tamar from having a child, and he, too, loses his life.

While the text clearly states Onan's offense, we are left to wonder about Er's punishable behavior. Most commentaries presume that since the text says that God "also" took Onan's life, the two brothers' offenses must have been the same.[20] Because these sins took place within the privacy of the marital bed, they were not public crimes but rather offenses only *"in the eyes of God"* (Gen. 38:7). Discussing the nature of Er and Onan's sexual crimes, the rabbis imagine "unnatural" forms of intercourse, masturbation, and coitus interruptus—essentially any sexual act that cannot result in pregnancy. A few commentaries note the Er's name (*'-r*) spelled backwards means "evil" (*r-'*). They also note that this same Hebrew word for "evil" is used in conjunction with Onan's actions as well as with the people of Sodom (13:13) and conclude that the same sin was committed in each of these cases.[21]

While levirate laws might explain why Onan committed his offense, there was no inheritance-related reason for Er to want to prevent Tamar's pregnancy. Some commentators suggest he wanted her to retain her beauty before she swelled with child.[22] Others assign blame to Bat Shua, who wanted her sons to take wives from among her Canaanite people and therefore poisoned them against Tamar and encouraged them to leave her childless.[23]

A few sources suggest that Er and Onan were struck down as punishment for Judah's crimes against Joseph: Judah had to be made to feel the loss of a child just as he had made Jacob feel the loss of his beloved Joseph.[24] However, Ramban rejects that perspective:

> Scripture does not specify the nature of [Er's] wickedness as it did in the case of his brother. Instead, it simply states that he died for his own sin. It informs us that this was not by way of punishment of Judah for his role in the sale of Joseph, since the saving of Joseph's life by Judah compensated for his role in the sale. There was no case of death of a child in the house of the patriarchs except this one who

was wicked in the sight of the Eternal, since the race of the righteous is blessed.[25]

According to the biblical text, after his first two sons are struck down, Judah is reluctant to give his third son to Tamar in marriage, so he sends her back to her father's home until Shelah will come of age: "*Then Judah said to his daughter-in-law Tamar, 'Stay as a widow in your father's house until my son Shelah grows up'—for he thought, 'He too might die like his brothers.' So Tamar went to live in her father's house*" (Gen. 38:11). Noting that Jewish law prohibits superstition, the rabbis explain that Judah's fears were not founded on a belief in bad omens, but rather reasonably based on an observable pattern.[26] Others suggest that Judah hoped Shelah would marry and have children with another woman before fulfilling his duty to Tamar.[27] According to the *Testament of Judah*, Bat Shua secretly wed Shelah to a Canaanite woman, for which she was cursed by Judah and subsequently died.[28] Alternatively, some suggest that Judah merely wanted Shelah to mature so that he would not be awed by Tamar's beauty and compelled to commit the same sin as his brothers. According to Rabbi Jacob ben Asher in the *Tur ha-Arokh*:

> Shelah was perfectly suitable to be the husband of Tamar in a levirate marriage, but his father did not want him to marry Tamar while he was still young [immature], so that he would not commit a sin similar to those committed by his brothers. They died in their youth precisely because they were too immature, neither of them being even 12 years of age. When Shelah would reach maturity and therefore be obedient to his father's moral and ethical instructions, he would be quite prepared to have him marry Tamar. At the time of Onan's death, he was not even 10 years old.[29]

Bat Shua and Tamar

The early literature of the Pseudepigrapha in *Jubilees* and the *Testament of Judah* provide the most detailed characterization of the relationships between Judah, Bat Shua, and Tamar. In these sources, Judah regrets his impulsive marriage to Bat Shua and turns away from her and toward his own tradition in guiding his sons. The relationship between Bat Shua and Tamar is presumed to be one of contempt and rivalry. Bat Shua wishes her sons to marry women among her own Canaanite people and uses her influence to dissuade them from procreating with her. The *Testament of Judah* relays that after the death of her first two sons, Bat Shua secretly marries off Shelah before he, too, can be tied to Tamar.

As time passes, Tamar realizes that Judah does not intend to fulfill his promise. And once Bat Shua dies, Tamar knows that Judah is himself free to fulfill the levirate obligation.[30] Thus, in the next part of Judah's story, he himself will become the father of Tamar's twin sons and progenitor of the messianic line.

AUTHOR'S COMMENTARY: *A Tragic Tale of Lust and Loss*

Traditional sources use the Bat Shua narrative as an opportunity to provide several moral lessons. Judah's downfall after his hasty marriage is a warning against illicit unions and the risk of being led astray by intoxication, lust, or greed. The deaths of Er and Onan are so deeply associated in Jewish and Christian theology as an admonition against "unnatural" sexual relations that the term "onanism" has entered our lexicon.

However, when considering this story from the female characters' perspectives, these do not seem to be the primary themes. If we envision the biblical story from Bat Shua's vantage point, we might instead learn valuable lessons about processing grief, bereavement, and loss. We could explore familial dynamics and even, perhaps, engage in conversation about how different rituals and customs are melded within interfaith families. Modern midrash provides an opportunity for today's readers to wrestle with such matters.

"The Woman Who Mourns" attempts to fill in some of these gaps by embellishing upon the few commentaries that reference Bat Shua. Whether the daughter of royalty or a merchant, this midrash imagines her as raised in luxury, attendant to her father, independent within the confines of her station, cunning like her father, and perhaps a bit imperious and self-important.

The biblical text provides no information about the relationship between Bat Shua and Judah. In filling in the details of their married life, there are no heroes or villains in this midrash. Bat Shua feels resentful as she is thrust into a rustic life among strangers, yet she accepts her fate and endeavors to be a good wife and mother. Being raised by her merchant father, she loves her sons as best she can but is more transactional than maternal—her children would secure her status and add to the strength and security of the clan. Judah is depicted here, as in rabbinic literature, as lascivious and impulsive; he is most at home when wandering with his mates and the herds and free to do as he pleases. Nonetheless, he provides for his family, looks after their welfare, and is a sensitive husband (when he is home). Bat Shua and Judah are both imperfect characters, yet they each have redeeming qualities as well.

Although the rabbis anachronistically presume that Bat Shua "converted" to Judaism before her marriage, nothing in the text suggests that she had any preparation for the life she was thrust into within in Judah's clan. As such, in the modern midrash, absent any grounding in the beliefs and rituals of her new community, Bat Shua clings to the beliefs and customs of her youth to provide a sense of stability. While the rabbis find her Canaanite heritage significant as a rebuke to Judah, when viewed from Bat Shua's perspective, the familiar Canaanite traditions of her childhood become her means of comfort, solace, and hope in coping with harsh losses in her life. In this light, perhaps we might acknowledge or sympathize with Bat Shua's attempts to protect Onan from the fate of Er, even by resorting to her childhood gods despite knowing that her husband's Israelite law forbids idol worship.

This serves as a reminder of the importance of ongoing support and preparation for those new to the Jewish community even today. Some may find it challenging to navigate unfamiliar customs and ceremonies, and they may miss the comfort of their former traditions. We can support them in this process through education, empathy, and understanding.

This midrash also seeks to address some of the emotional issues that the (male) rabbis never thought to consider but seem logical and natural for us to weigh today. It should not be surprising that Bat Shua would blame Tamar and Judah for her sons' demise and that they, likewise, would blame her or each other. The grief over the loss of a child is immeasurable, and the loss of two children incomprehensible. For those faced with such inconsolable pain, it is natural to seek a cause and focus for blame. Few families can endure such suffering, and for Judah and Bat Shua, this is their point of separation. These events also come to define Bat Shua, who in this creative rendering of her story becomes known as the Woman Who Mourns.

In many ways, Bat Shua is a victim of a society that commodifies women. Her father uses her to advance his commercial endeavors and then gives her to Judah when that transaction is sufficiently beneficial. Judah values Bat Shua for her childbearing, but when she ceases having children, she is of no more use to him; he moves on to fulfill his legacy through Tamar's offspring.

Yet in this midrash, Bat Shua has agency as well. She names both her second and third sons, and her naming of Shelah portends a special relationship between her and her third son. She refuses to sleep with Judah, to prevent the birth of another son, and deceives him regarding Shelah's circumcision. She derives the comfort and hope she needs in her life by praying to her Canaanite gods and seeking out the advice of oracles. In the end, she is able to protect her youngest son by stealing him away from Judah and guaranteeing his protection in her father's home under Hirah's watchful eye. Whether or not all of these are laudable actions, Bat Shua uses her limited power to try to achieve a better outcome for herself and her children.

Curiously, neither the text nor the commentaries tell us what happens to Shelah after his brothers die, although he is included in genealogical lists of the Israelites in the wilderness, and notably 1 Chronicles 4:21 records that Shelah's eldest son is named Er, presumably an homage to his departed elder brother. While this modern midrash imagines Shelah as sojourning with and safeguarded by his mother in her childhood home until she passes on the responsibility for his protection to Hirah, Shelah's story, like his mother's, is begging to be further explored through midrash.

The minor character of Hirah appears at the outset of the Judah—Bat Shua saga when, according to the rabbis' interpretation of the biblical text, Judah, who is traveling with Hirah, falls passionately in lust with Bat Shua and impulsively weds her. Many years later, immediately after Bat Shua dies, Judah travels with Hirah again, this time to join the sheepshearers after his period of mourning ends. Thus, Hirah's appearances as Judah's traveling companion essentially frame the love story of Judah and Bat Shua. The rabbis express some curiosity about Hirah's identity but otherwise don't take note of this interesting literary device. By contrast, in this new retelling of the story, Hirah appears as a friend and companion not only to Judah, but to Bat Shua as well. Hirah forms a connection with Bat Shua early in her life that ends on her deathbed—or perhaps even beyond, by continuing to protect her only remaining son. Hirah makes yet another appearance in the continuation of the saga after Judah has a liaison with his daughter-in-law Tamar while en route to the sheepshearers, believing her to be a prostitute. Judah sends his friend to seek out and pay his pledge to Tamar, though she is not to be found. In assisting Judah in his affairs with Tamar, was Hirah also fulfilling his pledge to Bat Shua to protect Shelah? Metaphorically, Hirah provides a bridge between Judah and Bat Shua and the cultures they represent.

Bat Shua is a flawed character, but in this telling, there is much more to her as a human being—both good and bad—than just being "that Canaanite woman" whose marriage to Judah led to misfortune. Her actions are not always meritorious as she does her best to shape the events that are within her limited control. And in the end, she succeeds in her most important task—to see to the survival of her son Shelah, who will march out of Egypt one day with his clan.

4

Bilhah

The Loving Handmaid

BIBLICAL TEXT: *Genesis 50:15–17*

When Joseph's brothers saw that their father was dead, they said, "What if Joseph still bears a grudge against us and pays us back for all the wrong that we did him!" So they sent this message to Joseph, "Before his death your father left this instruction: So shall you say to Joseph, 'Forgive, I urge you, the offense and guilt of your brothers who treated you so harshly.' Therefore, please forgive the offense of the servants of the God of your father's [house]." And Joseph was in tears as they spoke to him.

MODERN MIDRASH: *A Letter to My Beloved Son Joseph*

My dear, beloved Joseph,

With this note, I send you the saddest of news. Your father, Jacob, has passed on.

I share your grief and pray that you may find comfort in your loss, surrounded by your wife and children, by the abundance of wealth you enjoy, by your enormous success and high station, and by memories of a happy childhood when your mother, of blessed memory, was still with us. Allow me to hold you to my bosom once more and give you the love and comfort she would offer if she were here. You know that I loved your mother dearly, and there was no one closer to her than me, so let me now be that source of motherly comfort to you.

Your father, too, speaks through me now. I was there for him through his life's many joys and challenges, and there is no one—not even your mother—who knew him as I have known him. I celebrated with him the birth of each child. I consoled him upon the passing of each beloved wife. I stood up for him and provided a buffer when he confronted your Uncle Esau, and I struggled through famine and drought with him. I comforted him in his grief when we thought you had perished, and I cried with him at the joyous news of your miraculous survival. I journeyed with him to this forbidding land of narrow places and have cared for him in his hoary age. So I know, better than anyone, the wisdom he would share with you now.

He would tell you that *there is nothing more important at the end of one's days than the ability to forgive*. It is the most important gift we can give to ourselves and to our loved ones as we prepare for our final journey. It is the gift of a soul at peace, ready for its eternal rest.

I assure you that your beloved father was, finally, at peace. He had forgiven all those who had wronged him—including you, my son—and he forgave himself for his own failings. And he would want the same for you.

I, too, have found peace in forgiveness. I offer you my story as proof that forgiveness and healing of the soul are possible.

You know that I was a daughter of your grandfather Laban's household and your mother's handmaid. You knew me first as your auntie, the half-sister to Laban's daughters Leah and your mother, our beloved Rachel. Later I became like a mother to you: comforting you when she died, while I suckled your baby brother Benjamin and, in time, watching with joy as you so playfully chased after my sons Dan and Naftali while they cared for our flocks.

But did you know that I and your Auntie Zilpah are of noble blood? Did you know that our grandfather was a Chaldean nobleman, a member of your great-grandfather Abraham's clan? He was taken in battle, enslaved, and eventually brought to Laban's household. My father and mother were servants, and Zilpah and I were born nothing more than handmaids, but our father never let us forget our heritage. He told us over and over again the stories he had learned from his father of our illustrious lineage, of battles won and lost, of family honor and defeat. To the very end he was angry and bitter. He could not forgive the loss of his station.

I might have been bitter also, if it were not for your mother. She and I were born the very same day. Suckled and weaned together, we grew up together, sharing each other's secrets and loves. We were sisters in every sense of that word. How could I resent the very family that brought my dear Rachel into this world? I would have done anything for your mother, even if I hadn't been her handmaid.

I do have regrets, however. We did not realize that in our devotion to each other we had excluded others, especially Leah, who resented our closeness. I was supposed to be Leah's handmaid, but when Laban switched her for Rachel at the altar, I also was switched. I was thrilled, and so was Rachel—we had been joined at the hip since birth and now we would never be parted. In fact, I suspect Rachel conspired with Laban to secure me as her handmaid, even though by right I belonged to Leah.

Of course, that only made Leah even more angry. How furious she must have felt when I then started bearing children for your mother! She was always competing with Rachel for love and affection from her father, from Jacob, even from me. Just when she had achieved the status of First Wife and had the prestige of giving Jacob so many children, suddenly she had to contend with my progeny, and Zilpah's as well.

After your mother's death—that's when you and Benjamin came to my tent, so I could look after you along with my boys—Jacob and I were both bereft. Though we loved her differently, each of us had lost the center of our world. It was natural that we then clung to each other for comfort. You see, when you were little, your father had had Rachel's bed moved into his tent, but once she was gone, Jacob couldn't bear to be alone. That's when I, as her replacement, filled the empty space in her bed. Eventually, out of our mutual longing for Rachel, we filled the empty space in each other's hearts as well. I believe your mother sent me to Jacob after her death, just as she had sent me to him to bring Dan and Naftali into the world.

But this too brought regrets. Blinded by our own shared grief, Jacob and I were oblivious to the dishonor we brought to Leah and her sons by flouting tradition. We did not see Leah's hurt and despair. Unknowingly, we triggered the very events that would nearly destroy our family.

Your oldest brother Reuben had once been Jacob's greatest joy. His birth assured the family legacy; his destiny was to lead our powerful clan. He loved and honored his parents, yet with each new sibling, he saw his inheritance diminish; just like his mother, he had to compete for a shrinking share of your father's attention. As the eldest, he kept the peace among your brothers and helped to manage our growing clan, but the joy the rest of us felt at the birth of each new child gnawed at him. And he resented you deeply for usurping his place as Jacob's favorite son. Of course, we didn't know any of this then; he suffered each perceived slight against his mother in silence.

Finally, when I moved into Jacob's tent, he felt the insult so deeply, he could no longer contain it. He needed to defend his mother's honor.

It took me a long time to understand all of this. Even longer to find forgiveness in my heart for what he did.

It happened the very same day that you went into the field and your brothers sold you into slavery. After first convincing them to throw you into a pit, Reuben headed home. As soon as he came running in from the field, he saw me emerging from your father's tent. In a split second he turned red-faced, agitated, angry like I had never seen him before. "What is troubling you, my son?" I asked, reaching out to him to offer comfort. Pushing me away, he yelled, "I am not *your* son! How dare you steal my father away from my mother?! You do not belong in his tent. That's *her* place!"

Next he spewed a torrent of insults against me and a litany of perceived offenses committed against Leah and himself, his voice getting ever louder with each accusation. Frightened, I began backing away from him, back into the tent . . . but he followed me, shoving me backward until I fell upon my bed.

Just then Jacob, who had overheard the commotion, entered the tent to witness me upon the bed, Reuben standing over me shaking with emotion, and our eyes locked together. When we both turned to see Jacob we froze, eyes wide, mouths open in a silent scream. I don't think either of us will ever forget the look of anguish on Jacob's face in that moment. Fear, anger, sorrow, pain, disgust, revulsion, loathing. It was enough to extinguish Reuben's frenzy; he took a step back from the bed. I took a deep breath and sat up. None of us spoke. Finally, Jacob whispered, "Get out." It took a moment, but I saw a tear in Reuben's eye as he lowered his head and marched out. I never knew if it was a tear of sadness for what he had done or a tear of anger from his lingering rage now in check. And then, Jacob whispered again, "Get out."

I knew in that instant that something had broken between us. Jacob must have thought we'd committed a sin. Did he think I was at fault? I never found out; neither of us ever spoke of it again.

Many years later I learned that Reuben had immediately regretted his violent outburst. My sons told me that after he calmed down, he returned to save you from the pit, but he was too late. I believe his attempt to save your life that day was an act of contrition to make up for what he had done to me and to your father.

Nothing was ever the same after that day. You were taken from us, and our focus turned to Benjamin's welfare. Your brothers kept to themselves, shamed by what they had done. I returned to my own tent. Jacob remained alone, refusing even to allow Leah or Zilpah into his tent. There was much silence and sorrow during those dark years.

But over time, we each found forgiveness in our own ways. At some point, Reuben explained to Jacob what actually happened in the tent and sought his forgiveness. And Jacob did forgive him, but only to a point. In his final, dying words to your brother, Jacob granted Reuben a share of his inheritance, though he denied him the double portion due the firstborn, as punishment for his actions on that fateful day.[1]

Eventually I, too, was able to forgive Reuben—he had acted out of anger, jealousy, and love for his mother. I could forgive him for his frustration and anger toward me, but it was much more difficult to forgive him for destroying the bond I had with your father. And I also had to forgive Jacob for letting Reuben's anger come between us.

Over the years, your father and I did find our way back to each other. When you, dear Joseph, were restored to our family, it became easier to give, and receive, forgiveness for what came before and simply be thankful for the blessings of our family, our reuniting here in Egypt, and our good fortune. Forgiveness did not come easily, but our family is stronger for it. My child, if I can forgive, you too can forgive your brothers.

So you see, Joseph, I am to blame for the discord between your mother, Rachel, and your Aunt Leah. And because of that, I am also to blame for your problems with your brothers that robbed you of your childhood. I hope you can forgive me for that.

I know they made you feel like it was all your fault. They resented your self-confidence and arrogance. But that's just the way it is with favorites, just as it was with your mother, the most beloved of the wives. If anyone made you feel guilty for revealing those dreams or enjoying that coat, forgive yourself for causing any resentment your brothers had—you don't need to own that.

And, I suppose, I should forgive myself as well. I could not have known that anything bad would come from the love your mother and I had for each other or that it would have such long-lasting consequences for the family. And I can't regret the love I had for your father, even though I am sorry for the bitterness it caused others. The abundance of love with which I was blessed throughout my life requires no apology or forgiveness, and it has far surpassed any misfortunes I suffered along the way.

I hope you, too, might come to know that your good fortune has outweighed the struggles you have endured. As you have received forgiveness for any wrongdoings of your own, I pray that you can offer forgiveness, now, to all those who have wronged you. Their deeds brought you to this place of wealth and influence. The power to forgive is yours. Use it wisely and graciously, and honor your father now by bestowing it generously upon your brothers.

I offer these words of counsel and wisdom to you, my dear Joseph, on behalf of your father and your mother. As they are with me, they are with you also.

Sent with love from your humble servant and loving aunt,
Bilhah

Servant, Sister, Surrogate, Spouse

Given her key role in the biblical tradition as one of the four mothers of the twelve tribes, Bilhah, unlike some of the lesser-known female characters in the Bible, is a personage of interest to the rabbis. The vignette between Bilhah and Reuben in Gen. 35:22 adds to her story line and provides a rich opportunity for rabbinic commentary. Additionally, a strong thread in the midrashic literature connects Bilhah with the Joseph narrative.

Who Was Bilhah?

The biblical text does not provide any background about Rachel and Leah's handmaids, Bilhah and Zilpah, opening the door for commentary and midrash. A detailed lineage for Bilhah and Zilpah appears in the *Testament of Naphtali*, part of the *Testaments of the Twelve Patriarchs* in the Pseudepigrapha, a second-century collection of noncanonical books supposedly written by biblical characters. According to Naphtali's deathbed testament to his children, his mother Bilhah was the daughter of Roetheus, the brother of Rebekah's nurse Deborah. A "God-fearing" Chaldean nobleman within the tribe of Abraham, Roetheus was captured in battle and sold to Laban, who gave him his slave Aina as a wife. Aina gave birth to Zilpah and then Bilhah, on the same day as Rachel was born.[2] Accordingly, Bilhah and Zilpah were of noble blood, though born servants in Laban's household.

In contrast, numerous rabbinic commentaries presume Bilhah and Zilpah to be daughters of Laban through a concubine and thus half sisters to Leah and Rachel. This understanding comes from several textual abnormalities, including an ambiguity in the text, "*And Laban gave to Rachel his daughter Bilhah his handmaid to be her handmaid*" (Gen. 29:29). As written, with no punctuation, the phrase "*his daughter*" could refer to either Rachel or Bilhah.[3] Further in the biblical text, Laban refers to "*his daughters*" in the plural form twice within the same verse, and since nothing is deemed extraneous in the text, Rashi understands this duplication to signify that Laban had "two times two," or four, daughters: Rachel and Leah and the two handmaids.[4]

Noting that the biblical text generally refers to Bilhah and Zilpah with Bilhah's name mentioned first, the rabbinic assumption is that Bilhah was the elder of the two handmaids. That being the case, one might have expected the elder handmaid Bilhah to be given to the elder sister, Leah, and Zilpah to be given to Rachel. Why, then, is Zilpah given to Leah? Rashi explains that Zilpah was in fact the youngest of the four women but that the handmaids were switched as part of the ruse to convince Jacob that he was marrying Rachel; seeing the younger handmaid, Zilpah, reinforced his belief that the younger sister, Rachel, rather than Leah, was in their marriage tent:

> In the case of all Jacob's wives there is mention of their having been with child [i.e. Scripture states *vatahar*] except in the case of Zilpah. This was because she was the youngest of all and quite a child in age so that her being with child was not noticeable [Gen. R. 71:9]. Laban had given her to Leah in order to deceive Jacob—that he might not perceive that they were bringing Leah to him in marriage—for thus was the custom: to give the elder handmaid to the elder daughter, and the younger handmaid to the younger daughter.[5]

The status of Bilhah and Zilpah is unclear; the Bible refers to them alternatively as handmaids, servants, concubines, and wives. To resolve this ambiguity, the rabbis suggest that the two had been concubines to Laban and were then given to Rachel and Leah as servants, or handmaids. Commenting on the shift of terminology in Gen. 30:4, where Rachel gives her servant (*shifḥatah*) to Jacob to be his wife (*ishah*), several commentaries note that in this moment, Rachel frees her handmaid and Bilhah becomes a wife, thus ensuring that her own children will be born free. Leah similarly frees Zilpah upon giving her to Jacob to bear children on her behalf. Once Bilhah and Zilpah gain the status of wives, they are referred to as concubines only when compared, unfavorably, to Rachel and Leah.[6]

The Bilhah and Reuben Incident

The incident between Bilhah and Reuben is mentioned only briefly and cryptically in a single verse immediately after the death of Rachel: "*While*

Israel stayed in that land, Reuben went and lay with Bilhah, his father's concubine; and Israel found out. Now the sons of Jacob were twelve in number" (Gen. 35:22). A common interpretation suggests that Reuben and Bilhah did not have sexual relations; the rabbis simply could not fathom that one of Jacob's sons could commit such an egregious and subsequently forbidden act and still be counted among the twelve tribes listed immediately following the incident.[7] This perception led to the custom that this verse should be read, but not translated, so as not to bring disgrace to the patriarch before common people, who would not understand the nuances of the text.[8] In defense of this interpretation of events, the rabbis also note that sexual sin is not explicitly stated when Reuben receives his father's deathbed blessing (49:4), but rather his offense is referred to euphemistically as being committed against his father's bed.[9] The *Tur ha-Arokh* justifies this reading of the text through linguistic analysis: the Hebrew term for "with" in this verse is *et*, rather than *im*, signifying a lesser form of intimacy and suggesting that Reuven placed his bed *near* Bilhah but did not actually lie *with* her.[10]

These sources presume Reuben "disturbed" her bed, making it only appear as if they had had illicit relations, in order to undermine Bilhah's relationship with Jacob and prevent her from having more children, who would further diminish his inheritance.[11] Indeed, the rabbis note, Jacob did not have any additional children after that incident.[12] Alternatively, Reuben's actions were perceived to be in defense of his mother's honor, given that Leah should have been honored as the primary wife after Rachel's death but was usurped by Bilhah. According to these commentaries, upon Rachel's death, Jacob turned to Bilhah and moved his bed into her tent or, conversely, brought her bed into his tent.[13] In this depiction of events, just as Bilhah was Rachel's surrogate in childbearing, she continued in that surrogate role as Jacob's bedmate following Rachel's death.

Despite this generally accepted interpretation, other commentators acknowledge the simple reading of the text: Reuven did in fact have sexual relations with Bilhah, and because of that, his first-born status was revoked. Many of these commentaries also surmise that he had fully repented, and thus was restored to Jacob's household and legacy. Sforno's commentary on this verse notes that despite this affair, Jacob continued to count Reuven among his twelve sons because he immediately repented.[14] Others claim that Reuven so confessed and repented only after Judah had done so for his own illicit relations with his daughter-in-law Tamar.[15]

An alternative perspective regarding the encounter in the tent is advanced by Rabbi David Kimhi (Radak). Noting the use of the term "concubine" (*pilegesh*) to describe Bilhah in this verse, Radak suggests that Reuven may have thought it was permissible to have relations with her given that status. However, Radak then discounts that such a scenario could have transpired, since an earlier text, Gen. 30:4, refers to Bilhah as a wife (*ishah*) of Jacob, and thus Bilhah would certainly have been off-limits to her stepson. Radak also suggests that after this incident, Jacob spurned all his remaining wives and became a recluse, explaining why he had no additional children.[16]

A common midrashic thread links the Reuben-Bilhah story with the Joseph saga through a creative interpretation of Gen. 37:29, which states that Reuben *returned to* the pit to rescue Joseph, but by then Joseph had already been sold into slavery. Since Reuben was the one who'd recommended throwing Joseph into the pit instead of killing him, a question arises as to where he went afterward, while the other brothers, free of his oversight, proceeded to sell Joseph into slavery. Various midrashim, playing on the alternative nuance of "*returning*" as *teshuvah* (repentance), explain that Reuven had been donning sackcloth and fasting in penitence for his violation of Bilhah.[17]

The book of *Jubilees* offers a slightly different version of this story. Reuben sees Bilhah bathing naked and is smitten. When she is asleep, he sneaks into her bed and lays with her. Once she awakens to see Reuben rather than her husband, she screams and he runs away. Later Bilhah tells Jacob what transpired, and he is so angry about her defilement that he will no longer sleep with her. What follows is a reminder of the laws of incest that prohibit a son from having relations with his father's wife—a crime for which both parties are to be stoned.[18]

Bilhah and Joseph

Numerous commentaries suggest that there was a special relationship between Rachel's children, Joseph and Benjamin, and Bilhah's children,

Dan and Naftali. This is based on Gen. 37:2, which states, *"At seventeen years of age, Joseph tended the flocks with his brothers, as a helper to the sons of his father's wives Bilhah and Zilpah."* Rashi and other commentators explain that Joseph befriended their sons because the other brothers ridiculed them for being sons of handmaids; that was the substance of Joseph's report to his father.[19] The *Tur ha-Arokh* provides an overview of the various rabbinic perspectives regarding the relationship between Joseph and Bilhah's sons:

"and he was a lad keeping company with the sons of Bilhah." Rashi interprets this as Joseph's immaturity, acting childishly. Onkelos interprets this to mean that already from his earliest youth, Joseph preferred the company of the sons of Bilhah who looked up to him and flattered him. Nachmanides writes that the words [*v'hu na'ar—he was a lad*], refer to what has been written previously, so that we have to understand the sequence of the verse as follows: "these are the developments in the house of Yaakov; Joseph, who was a lad of 17 years, used to tend the sheep together with his brothers." Ibn Ezra interprets the verse to mean that because Joseph was still immature at 17, the sons of Bilhah made him their personal valet.[20]

According to midrash, Rachel's handmaid Bilhah raised Joseph and Benjamin after their mother Rachel died.[21] This understanding serves as an explanation for Joseph's dream foretelling that in the years to come his mother and father would bow down to him, since by this time his biological mother was already dead. The rabbis explain that his mother in this dream actually refers to Bilhah, who raised him and was like a mother to Joseph.[22]

The biblical text does not mention the death of Bilhah; hence different sources provide alternative theories. According to the book of *Jubilees*, both Bilhah and Dinah died while mourning Joseph, and both were buried near Rachel's tomb.[23] Rabbinic sources, however, suggest that Bilhah outlived her sisters, traveled to Egypt with Jacob and their sons, and in fulfillment of Joseph's dream, bowed down to him in Egypt. According to this version of her story, Bilhah served as nursemaid to Jacob as he grew old, and she was the unnamed source who informed Joseph that his father was ill (Gen. 48:1).[24]

Continuing the theme of this special relationship, several sources suggest that Bilhah or her children served as emissaries to Joseph on behalf of his brothers after Jacob died (Gen. 50:16). Rashi suggests that Joseph's brothers sent a message through the sons of Bilhah, Dan and Naphtali, to plead on their behalf, lest Joseph still harbor ill will toward them and act on that anger after their father had died.[25] These commentaries suggest that the messengers had to be one of the brothers who were there that day, as they were the only ones who would have known how Joseph had been sold into slavery. Of the brothers, Bilhah's sons would have been the ones most likely to curry some favor with Joseph. However, that assumption discounts the possibility of their mother still being alive and serving as their representative. *Targum Jonathan* and other sources explicitly name Bilhah as the emissary who urges Joseph to forgive his brothers for the crime against him for the sake of family peace:

> R. Simeon ben Gamaliel said, "Peace is great, because the Holy One, blessed be He, has written things in the Torah that did not happen, which are there only because of peace. . . . They are the following: *When Jacob had died* (Gen. 50:15), '*And Joseph's brothers saw that their father was dead, and they said, "Perhaps Joseph begrudges us."*' What did they do? They went to Bilhah and said to her, '*Go in unto Joseph and say to him* (in Gen. 50:16), "*Before he died, your father gave a command saying, 'So shall you say to Joseph, "Please forgive the transgression of your brothers."*'"' Now Jacob never commanded any of these things at all; yet they said this thing on their own."[26]

AUTHOR'S COMMENTARY: *Emissary of Forgiveness*

Like most of the women characters in the Bible, Bilhah is a secondary character in the biblical narrative. Though she is one of the four mothers of the twelve tribes, she seems to be a passive, silent bystander in her own story. She is given to Rachel to be her handmaid, passed along to Jacob to bear children for her mistress, used as a buffer to protect Jacobs's wives and their children from Esau, and (presumably) bedded by her nephew Reuben. These are all things done to her; she is not depicted as an independent actor with her own free will.

The rabbis, however, take note of Bilhah and assign her two roles later in life: as Jacob's caregiver in his elder years in Egypt and as the emissary sent by Joseph's brothers to assuage any ill will he may hold toward them. Combining the classical rabbinic commentaries with creative midrash, "A Letter to My Beloved Son Joseph" allows Bilhah to tell her version of the oft-repeated biblical events in such a way that she becomes the wise observer, trusted counselor, loving guide, and agent of change who is able to interrupt the cycle of family discord by teaching Joseph the art of forgiveness.

The various themes about Bilhah that run through the rabbinic texts—especially her strong connection to Rachel, her half sister born on the same day, with whom, presumably, she was raised—suggests a heartfelt personal relationship skimmed over in the biblical text. The modern midrash imagines the two women as close-knit sisters, deeply connected through their mutual affection and the birth of their shared children. Even after Rachel's death, Bilhah maintains the sisters' loving bond by caring for Rachel's children as well as Rachel's beloved husband, Jacob. Given the length of time that Jacob and Bilhah lived after Rachel's death, it seems reasonable to presume that they eventually developed their own relationship, likely born out of a mutual loss and need for comfort, nurtured by familiarity and shared experiences, and motivated by a desire for companionship. Though neither the biblical text nor the rabbinic literature expounds upon what their relationship might have been, there are sufficient allusions to the ongoing connection between Bilhah and Jacob to allow this portrayal as a reasonable and logical embellishment on the text.

The corollary to the deep relationship between Bilhah and Rachel and, later, Bilhah and Jacob is the impact of those exclusionary relationships on others, particularly on Leah and her children. Favoritism in familial relationships, a common thread in the biblical narrative, often leads to disastrous outcomes. In this case, the resulting jealously provokes the incident between Reuben and Bilhah. While the biblical text itself depicts it as sexual in nature, the actual disposition of the event is ambiguous; we do not know if the story is about a violent rape or an illicit affair. Regardless, the rabbis feel the need to absolve Reuben of the perceived crime, by either presuming his innocence or allowing for his repentance. By contrast, this midrash depicts the event differently than either the simple reading of the text or the rabbinic interpretations, while also giving a nod to the aforementioned family dynamics and the rabbis' determination to relieve Reuben of an unforgivable crime.

After years of feeling rejected by his father, in a fit of violent rage, not passion, Reuben confronts Bilhah. The bed is the location, not the source, of the altercation. While the rabbis tried to redeem Reuben's character by allowing for his repentance, this midrash absolves him of the sin altogether by interpreting his actions as an angry outburst rather than a sexual liaison. Nonetheless, Reuben still has much to regret; when his father catches them at the bed together, Reuben is horrified to think of what his father must be imagining. His anger and impulsive actions lead to the same unfortunate results: Jacob rejects Bilhah and has no more children, Reuben's relationship with his father is diminished along with his inheritance, and by the time Reuben catches up with his brothers, it's too late to save Joseph.

The difference, however, is in how we understand the overarching lessons of the biblical story. The rabbis' version of events, whether depicted as an inappropriate assignation or violent assault, imagines outrageous and scandalous relations between these biblical characters. The equally justifiable interpretation in this modern midrash reveals something much more common: the consequences of familial jealousy, favoritism, and unresolved childhood wounds. These threads run throughout the biblical narrative, from Jacob and Esau's struggles to Rachel and Leah's competition for Jacob's affections (see chapter 2, "Leah's Eulogy"), to Joseph's fraught relationship with his brothers. Reuben and Bilhah are just two more victims of the cycle of family dysfunction that continues from one generation to the next.

The special relationship between Bilhah and Joseph runs throughout the rabbinic commentaries. It is logical to presume that Rachel's handmaid would have had a special relationship with Rachel's children and that she might have taken Joseph and Benjamin into her own tent after Rachel's death. However, how that relationship might have continued later in the saga, once the family is in Egypt—in particular, that Bilhah composed a heartfelt letter to Joseph urging him to forgive his brothers for the sake of family peace—is entirely a midrashic invention. Some early writings presume Bilhah died the moment she heard of her adopted son Joseph's supposed demise, while a minor rabbinic thread does imagine her with the family in Egypt. She is presumed to be the unnamed emissary mentioned twice in the story: the messenger who notifies Joseph of his father's illness and the messenger Joseph's brothers send to him after Jacob's death to seek assurance of his forgiveness. In the former case, the rabbis picture her as being Jacob's caregiver in his old age, and therefore naturally the one to inform Joseph of the sad news. In the latter instance, the rabbis depict her as the loving and wise matriarch, the family peacemaker whose special relationship with Joseph can secure his forgiveness for his brothers' past offenses. "A Letter to My Beloved Son Joseph" concretizes Bilhah's possibly pivotal role in convincing Joseph to forgive his brothers.

Forgiveness is the overarching theme running throughout this biblical narrative. Sisters and brothers feel slighted and hurt. Jealousy leads to anger and violence. Yet, time and divine providence lead to reunion and healing. In the end, the protagonists find their way to forgiveness, even for reprehensible actions. Jacob and Bilhah find their way back to one another. The brothers make peace with one another and find common cause in caring for their clan. Reuben is forgiven too, though he still must bear the consequences. And Joseph grants forgiveness to his brothers, perhaps inspired by his aunt Bilhah's impassioned plea and the example of her own forgiving spirit.

5

Pharaoh's Daughters, Part 1

Potiphar's Unnamed Wife

BIBLICAL TEXT: *Genesis 39:1–19*

When Joseph was taken down to Egypt, Potiphar, a courtier of Pharaoh and his prefect—a [type of] Egyptian official—bought him from the Ishmaelites who had brought him there. God was with Joseph, and he proved highly capable; and he stayed in the house of his Egyptian master. And when his master saw that God was with him and that God lent success to everything he undertook, he took a liking to Joseph. He made him his personal attendant and put him in charge of his household, placing in his hands all that he owned. And from the time that the Egyptian put him in charge of his household and of all that he owned, God blessed his house for Joseph's sake, so that the blessing of God was upon everything that he owned, in the house and outside. He left all that he had in Joseph's hands and, with him there, he paid attention to nothing save the food that he ate. Now Joseph was well built and handsome.

After a time, his master's wife cast her eyes upon Joseph and said, "Lie with me." But he refused. He said to his master's wife, "Look, with me here, my master gives no thought to anything in this house, and all that he owns he has placed in my hands. He wields no more authority in this house than I, and he has withheld nothing from me except yourself, since you are his wife. How then could I do this most wicked thing, and sin before God?" And much as she coaxed Joseph day after day, he did not yield to her request to lie beside her, to be with her.

One such day, he came into the house to do his work. None of the household being there inside, she caught hold of him by his garment and said, "Lie with me!" But he left his garment in her hand and got away and fled outside. When she saw that he had left it in her hand and had fled outside, she called out to her servants and said to them, "Look, he had to bring us a Hebrew to dally with us! This one came to lie with me; but I screamed loud. And when he heard me screaming at the top of my voice, he left his garment with me and got away and fled outside." She kept his garment beside her, until his master came home. Then she told him the same story, saying, "The Hebrew slave whom you brought into our house came to me to dally with me; but when I screamed at the top of my voice, he left his garment with me and fled outside."

When his master heard the story that his wife told him, namely, "Thus and so your slave did to me," he was furious.

MODERN MIDRASH: *Zuleikha, the Prison Mistress*

My earliest memory is a pinch from my mother. As long as I can remember, each day, at some unexpected moment, she would suddenly slap me. Or push me down. Or pinch me. Not hard enough to leave a mark, but enough to make me cry. And there was never any comfort from her afterward—she would just walk away until I soothed myself, and then we would carry on as if nothing happened. As I got older, the slaps got harder and the bruises would come, but never in places where Father would see them. He never would have allowed it.

I know that Mother loved me. We had many joyous moments together. We shared secrets and giggles. We played games, and she taught me the ways of women.

The other mothers were kind to me too. They braided my hair and let me hold their children when I was old enough. I saw they didn't like it when Mother hit me, but they kept their distance and respected Mother's rule that I was not to be comforted.

Once, when I was just old enough to use my words, I asked her why she hit me every day. "Someday, Zuleikha, you will understand," she said.

Years later, when I was almost a woman, I asked her again. Then she said, "Because you are a second daughter, just like me."

Although I still did not understand why she hurt me, I did know what it meant to be the second daughter. I idolized and envied my older sister, Pharaoh's First Daughter. She ruled the household with her moods. Father coddled her. Mother bowed to her. The servants dressed her in fine silks and decorated her eyes with the darkest kohl. Visitors brought her gifts when they paid homage to Father, knowing she was Father's favorite. Everyone said that one day Pharaoh's First Daughter would marry our half brother, the First Son, and together they would rule the land.

When I was young, I had dreams of being like her. I imagined the feel of her soft silks and the jewels on her neck and fingers. One day the servants would bow to me: I would marry the prince of Egypt and rule by his side.

Once I spoke of it out loud. As I cuddled and rocked one of my baby cousins, I whispered, "One day, I will be queen. And you and the other cousins will all bow to me. But don't worry, little one, I will always take care of you. I will order my servants to dress you and feed you. They will do my bidding, and you will be protected." Just then my mother came from behind me. I knew by the look in her eyes that she had heard me. She gently took the baby from my arms and handed her to her mother. Then with one swift motion she slapped me so hard I stumbled backward. "You must never dream like that, child!" she admonished, as she struck me a second time. Then she clutched me to her bosom, squeezing my breath from me, and gently insisted, "You—will—not—be—queen. Do not think of it again." With that, she set me back on my feet, looked me over to make sure I wasn't damaged, and rushed away with the saddest look in her eyes.

Despite her warning, I never stopped dreaming that dream. No matter how hard I tried to block it from my mind, I could not stop it. But I never spoke of it again.

And then one day, I understood what Mother meant about second daughters. Without any warning, Father arranged for me to be married to Potiphar, the man who ran his prison. I was the price to be paid for the man's service to Father, and our union would elevate his stature among

Father's other officers. As a daughter of Pharaoh, I would be his First Wife, though ruler of none. Without a word of farewell, the servants bundled my clothing and a few trinkets and sent me away with this stranger.

I had been instructed about the marriage bed, but I did not expect the brutality of it. When he called me to him, I never knew what he wanted, and I never seemed to please him.

Mother's training suddenly made sense. She had hardened me to the sting of undeserved slaps; she had prepared me to accept Potiphar's unpredictable rages and not to question the blows that came as a nightly ritual. And she had given me the gift of knowledge that the pain would pass and life would go on.

Less than a year after I came to Potiphar, Hathor, the goddess of motherhood, blessed me with a daughter. But the moment my beloved Asenath was born, she was removed from my arms to be reared in the palace in which I grew up. I ached for her but was grateful at least that she would be spared my husband's attentions. Mother and the other women of Pharaoh's court would care for her, and as a granddaughter of Pharaoh she would know luxury and privilege. Father would not allow even a second daughter's child to be raised within prison walls.

Occasionally I was able to accompany Potiphar when he visited the palace, and I brought Asenath gifts and charms so she might know her mother loved her. I insisted she always wear an amulet that had once been a gift to me from Father; it would ensure her lineage would be remembered and she would be appropriately honored. And when the time came for her to be matched, I wanted to be sure Father remembered the service and sacrifices I performed to ensure my husband's loyalty.

Once my obligation to provide an heir was fulfilled, Potiphar no longer took interest in me. My life became easier, though I was desperately lonely. I could not befriend the other women of Potiphar's household, who were considered beneath my station. As the minister's First Wife and mother to his heir, I retained my own rooms and would not be sent to the harem, but my life was not so unlike the poor souls chained in the dungeons below my feet. I was a prisoner within the upper chambers of the house.

My days grew tedious. The servants ran the household, Potiphar ran Father's prison, and I was left to myself. My only respite from the drudgery was gazing out my window and dreaming of imagined adventures and the life I might have had, had I only been born first.

At night the sounds from Potiphar's chambers brought chills. On some nights there were sounds of merriment—music and laughter, the jangling of bells on the dancers' wrists and ankles, the stewards bringing in food and wine and slaves—but on those other nights the sounds were terrifying: bodies crashing against walls, furniture breaking, muffled cries and screams. Even Mother's slaps had not prepared me for this existence. I retreated further into my dreams until I barely knew what was real and what was imagined.

The arrival of the annual River Festival brought distraction and renewed energy. I watched from my window as merchants delivered their silks and slaves. Father must have been particularly generous to my husband that year.

A week later, one of the new servants delivered my morning meal. He was a slight, strange-looking boy. I presumed he was from the north—he had lighter skin than the servants from the south. He never spoke. Every morning he would serve my meal, shuffling in and then backing out. Although I could barely see his downcast eyes, I recognized the terror in them and realized: *he must be afraid of me*. What an odd sensation to be feared rather than afraid! I felt a new kind of power.

I wielded that power with all the pent-up pain and anger of my upbringing. Around this servant boy I was no longer meek, no longer a victim. My voice became harsh. Each day I scolded him for the slightest misstep, then dismissed him with a wave of my hand.

I felt supremely entitled in those moments. This young boy was tending to me, obeying my orders without question, just as my childhood dreams had foretold.

We went on that way for months, until one morning he looked up at me, smiled, and muttered something I barely understood: "*Blessings God.*" I scowled and he immediately lowered his gaze and backed away, but the next morning, he tried again: "*Blessings God, Master.*" I didn't know whether to be angry at his impertinence or amused at his attempt to speak our language. Didn't he understand that I was the daughter of Pharaoh, himself among the gods of Egypt?

Yet he greeted me each day with a smile and, in time, in our language: *"May God bless you, Mistress."* By then I was so lonely I did not care that he was but a servant. I was grateful for his kindness. And so, we began speaking every morning. I helped him learn new words and advised him on how to please the master of the house.

As he grew more confident, I saw that despite his youth he had a quiet wisdom about him. He seemed to understand me, anticipating my needs and moods and attending to me effortlessly. Even when he advanced in his station, becoming head of the household, he continued to bring me my morning meal each day.

Yosef became my best friend. I woke each day eager to hear whatever little he knew about the world beyond my walls. He was always kind to me. He never hurt me or reproached me. I thought this was love. And I thought he felt it too.

Over time, Yosef invaded my dreams. I imagined him sitting beside me on the throne of Egypt, governing with confidence and kindness, admired by people from all over who came to seek his advice. They brought me gifts as well. I was adorned with jewels even grander than my sister's.

One day I worked up the courage to reach out to him. Taking his hand, I tugged him in the direction of my bed. Suddenly his eyes grew wide with fear. He blurted, *"No, mistress, we cannot!"* and bolted out the door.

Yosef's words were like a knife to my heart. Of all the slaps and kicks I had endured, the pain of his rejection was the most excruciating.

But after my tears dried, I grew angry. How dare this slave deny me, daughter of Pharaoh, mistress of the house, mother of a princess of Egypt? I planned to confront him the next morning, but another servant boy brought me my morning meal. I screamed at him and threw him out of my room, refusing to eat.

As the days passed, my anger turned to longing. I missed Yosef terribly, but he never returned. I was so alone.

Gazing out my window I saw the household preparing for the River Festival once again and realized an entire year had gone by since Yosef first came to us. Tomorrow the house would be empty—Potiphar would be at the festival, and most of the servants would be at the market. And then it struck me—Yosef and I would be alone in the house!

The next day, after the other servants left, I called for assistance, knowing Yosef was the only one there to respond. When he entered my chamber, I grabbed him and pulled him toward me, but he abruptly pushed me aside and left the room, leaving me grasping only his empty cloak. I called out after him, urging him to return, begging him to love me. I cried and screamed in a tempest of despair, anger, and longing.

And just then the servants returned! They found me crumpled on the floor, sobbing and cradling Yosef's garment. I imagined what would happen next: Potiphar would find out, and he would finally kill me, ending my misery. I should have let it happen.

But something deep inside urged me to survive. My mother's training took over like instinct—for the first time, the victim was not going to be me. So I lied. Through my tears, I accused Yosef of attacking me and showed them Yosef's cloak as proof.

When Potiphar returned and saw my distraught state, he had no choice but to defend my honor, though I could tell he did not really believe me. Yosef was sent to Potiphar's prison, and I was forbidden to leave my chambers, even to visit Asenath at the palace. He said it was for my protection, but I knew it was really to punish me. Betrayed by his wife and Yosef, his most trusted steward, Potiphar directed his anger toward the servants, especially those he had just purchased during the River Festival. The screams from his chambers were relentless. Eventually, the sweet dreams of my beloved Yosef turned into guilt-ridden nightmares as I imagined my beloved Yosef suffering in the prison below, with me as his tormentor.

The servants feared me after that. Instead of bringing my meals to me, they left them at my door. From that point on I saw no one, except through my window. This new loneliness was even more excruciating than before. Years of solitude passed by, and there were no more dreams to bring relief.

One day, when I could no longer bear my loneliness, I made a final decision. I'd never had control over my life, but that day I would, finally, take control. I would simply step onto the window ledge and end my pain.

As I approached the window, I heard a commotion. Surely it was not time for another River Festival? Servants were scurrying about, and my husband was dressed in his finest attire. A royal entourage was approaching—could it be Father? Would Asenath be with him?

Now a man was emerging from the royal carriage. He was so beautiful; he glowed with a light so bright it was blinding. It was not Father, but something about him was familiar . . . It was Yosef! My beloved Yosef!

He was wearing royal robes and a golden chain around his neck. A pendant dangled from the chain. It looked like . . . could it be? It was the amulet I had given Asenath!

But how? Why?

And then, suddenly, it all became clear. My visions had come true after all—but for her, not for me.

CLASSICAL COMMENTARY AND MIDRASH:
Potiphar's Wife in the Joseph Narrative

The story of Joseph is a key element in the biblical narrative, serving as a segue between the early tales of the patriarchs in the land of Canaan and the Israelites' servitude at the hands of the Egyptians.

According to the biblical text, after his brothers, the sons of Jacob, sell Joseph to Ishmaelite traders, Joseph is brought to Egypt and sold to Potiphar, a minister to Pharaoh. Captivated by his beautiful appearance, Potiphar's (unnamed) wife becomes smitten with Joseph and seeks to seduce him. She tries to entrap him into an illicit liaison, and when her attempts fail, she grabs a piece of his garment as he flees from her advances. Afraid of being found out, Potiphar's wife uses the piece of cloth as evidence to falsely accuse Joseph of attempted rape, whereupon he is sent to prison for twelve years. Eventually, his reputation as a dream interpreter brings Joseph to Pharaoh's attention. His vision and wisdom in managing the ensuing famine earn him a station of wealth and power, which he will later use to rescue Jacob and his brothers and bring them to Egypt, where the clan will sojourn until their eventual enslavement under a new pharaoh.

Understanding Potiphar's Wife

The biblical narrative says nothing of the relationship between Potiphar and his wife or her backstory. Who was she, and what would compel a minister's wife to seek the company of a foreign slave?

Potiphar, too, is scarcely developed in the Bible. The text refers to him as a minister, or "prefect," to Pharaoh, yet his specific role is not clear. The Hebrew phrase *sar hatabaḥim* (Gen. 39:1) is ambiguous and may be translated as "chief steward" or "chief executioner."[1] The first-century Jewish historian Josephus depicts Potiphar as the chief cook; however, other early sources, including the book of *Jubilees* in the Pseudepigrapha, the Talmud, and *Targum Jonathan* (an early Aramaic translation of the Bible), place him in charge of the prison.[2] The interpretation of Potiphar as prefect of the prison, a common theme in later commentaries, suggests a particular cruelty to his character. As Rabbeinu Bahya comments, "The person described as [*sar hatabaḥim*] was the man who was appointed to execute all those prisoners who had received a death sentence. He was a physically strong specimen and a cruel person such as Nebuzaradan who occupied that position in the army of Nebuchadnezzar as we know from Jeremiah 39,13: 'he (Nebuchadnezzar) dispatched Nebuzaradan the chief executioner, etc.'"[3]

A simple reading of the biblical text would suggest that the wife of a minister of Pharaoh must have been of some high station, if not noble birth. As a wife, she would have had a higher status than other women in the household, including servants and concubines. While the commentaries and midrash provide little in the way of background, a few sources offer some insight into her character.

One strand in the midrash considers her to be gifted with future vision, just like Joseph: "R. Joshua b. Levi said: She [Potiphar's wife] saw by her astrological arts that she was to produce a child by him [Joseph], but she did not know whether it was to be from her or from her daughter."[4] Rashi references this midrash in explaining the placement of the Judah-Tamar story immediately prior to this story, so that it interrupts the Joseph narrative. To him, the juxtaposition of Tamar, who tricked Judah into fathering her child, with Potiphar's wife indicates that both women's actions were meritorious, having been motivated by foreknowledge of their maternal destiny.[5]

Another midrashic motif suggests that Potiphar was a sexual predator who purchased Joseph for carnal purposes. As punishment, Potiphar was made a eunuch, which is how some sources translate *seris par'oh* ("*courtier of Pharaoh*"; Gen. 39:1). According to Genesis Rabbah, "A Eunuch [*seris*] of Pharaoh. This intimates that he was castrated, thus teaching that he [Potiphar] purchased him [Joseph] for the purpose of sodomy, whereupon the Holy One, blessed be God, emasculated [Potiphar]."[6]

This portrayal of Potiphar provides a bleak image of the household into which Joseph was sold. His master bought him with the intent to force illicit relations, even though divine intervention would prevent Potiphar from doing so. Other commentaries affirm that Potiphar was unable to have sexual relations with his wife, which helped explain her sexual appetites. The combination of commentaries that portray Potiphar as particularly cruel and his wife's sorrow at being childless paint a picture of a very unhappy mistress.

Joseph's Year of Servitude

The commentaries calculate that Joseph resided in Potiphar's household for twelve months.[7] During that time he was continually promoted due to the success of his efforts. His rise within Potiphar's household is described in detail in the eighteenth-century *Or ha-Ḥayim* commentary:

> *He stayed in the house of his master, etc.* The Torah described how G'd arranged for a variety of promotions Joseph experienced while in the service of Potiphar. At the beginning Joseph performed menial labour outside the home of Potiphar. When he did so successfully he was promoted to work inside the home. He then became a guard in the home. Eventually, he performed all his duties only indoors. . . .

Still later he became Potiphar's personal valet. . . . This made Joseph's life comfortable. Still later Potiphar appointed Joseph as the general manager over his entire household. . . . Eventually, Potiphar left every initiative to Joseph, not even bothering to ask him to account for what he was doing.[8]

The only exception to Joseph's complete run of the household is noted in the biblical text: "*[Potiphar] left all that he had in Joseph's hands and, with him there, he paid attention to nothing save the food* [literally: *bread*] *that he ate*" (Gen. 39:6). The classical midrash presumes "bread" is a euphemism for his wife.[9] Rashi concurs with this interpretation, noting also that in verse 9 Joseph evades Potiphar's wife, saying, "*He has withheld nothing from me except yourself, since you are his wife.*"[10] And, of course, the one thing forbidden to Joseph is what tempts him.

At this point in the story line, the text offers a sidebar about Joseph's good looks, stating "*Now Joseph was well built and handsome*" (Gen. 39:6). As a rather unusual comment that seems out of context, it provides fodder for midrashic explanation. According to Rabbi David Kimhi (Radak), the rationale for including the description of Joseph's good looks was simply to explain why a woman of Potiphar's wife's status would seek the attentions of a foreign-born slave.[11] However, numerous commentators think there is more to it, noting that there would be no reason to comment on his good looks at this point in the story except to signify a change of some kind. They suggest it was not just his natural good looks that appealed to her, but that Joseph began to primp and glorify himself as he was elevated to higher stations within the household. Rashi, citing *Midrash Tanḥuma*, offers this description: "As soon as he saw that he was ruler (in the house) he began to eat and drink and curl his hair. The Holy One, blessed be God, said to him, 'Your father is mourning and you curl your hair! I will let a bear [Potiphar's wife] loose against you.'"[12] Similarly, Sforno (ca. 1475–1550) suggests, "After Potiphar had entrusted him with all these important tasks Joseph found time to make himself look handsome, having no longer to perform demeaning physical labour assigned to most slaves."[13]

Whether because of Joseph's personal grooming efforts, his natural beauty, or both, Potiphar's wife was definitely smitten. The commentaries variously describe her as lusty, vulgar, and aggressive or besotted, lovesick, and entranced. *Midrash Tanḥuma* depicts how Joseph mesmerized not only Potiphar's wife but other Egyptian women as well:

> Our sages inform us that on one occasion Potiphar's wife assembled a number of Egyptian women so that they might see how very handsome Joseph was. But before she summoned Joseph she gave each of them an ethrog [citron] and a knife. When they saw Joseph's handsome countenance, they cut their hands. She said to them: "If this can happen to you, who see him only once, how much more so does it happen to me, who must look at him constantly." Each day she strove to entice him with words, but he suppressed his evil inclination. Whence do we know this? From what we read in the section: *His master's wife cast her eyes upon him* (Gen. 39:7).[14]

The medieval midrash *Sefer ha-Yashar* presents a variant of this story in which Potiphar's wife's friends lose their wits and bloody themselves. In this midrash, Zulycah (or Zuleikha, which is also how she is known in the Qur'an and other non-Jewish sources[15]) is so desperately obsessed with Joseph, she is at the point of death:

> And Zulycah was very ill through her desire for Joseph, and her love sickness weighed heavily upon her, but the people of Zulycah's household, and her husband knew nothing of the matter and that Zulycah was sick out of her love to Joseph. And all the people of her household asked her: Why art thou so emaciated and sick whereas thou lackest not the least thing? And she said unto them: I know not the illness that is growing upon me day after day. And all the women and her friends came to visit her daily and they spoke unto her, saying: This is certainly caused through thy love for Joseph; entice him then and use force against him, peradventure he will listen unto thee and remove thy impending death. And Zulycah

became more seriously ill and she grew poorer with every coming day until she had no more strength in her to stand up. And one day, while Joseph was attending to his work in the house, Zulycah came in secretly and threw herself suddenly upon him, and Joseph used force to free himself from her and he cast her to the ground. And Zulycah wept before him on account of the passion within her heart, and she entreated him, and tears gushed down her cheeks, and she spoke unto him in weeping and supplication, saying: Hast thou ever seen, or heard, or known of a woman more beautiful or better than myself, that she would speak unto thee day after day and become so reduced by sickness through love to thee, and ready to bestow all these honors upon thee, and still thou dost not listen unto my voice? And if thou be afraid of thy master, that he might punish thee, as the king liveth no harm shall befall thee in this matter. Do then listen unto me and gratify my desire for the honor which I have shown thee, and free me from this disease; for why should I die on thy account? And when she ceased speaking Joseph answered unto her saying: Get thee from me and leave that matter to my master.[16]

Day after day for a year, Joseph resists Potiphar's wife's persistent advances. Commentaries describe the many ways Potiphar's wife tried to seduce him and the various ways he avoided her. He feigned ignorance of the Egyptian language and pretended not to understand his mistress.[17] He tried looking away; she fitted him with a metal brace around his neck to force him to look at her. He argued that she was married; she replied that her husband could not fulfill his marital duties, and therefore their marriage was null and void. He explained that Hebrew men were not permitted to have relations with Egyptian women, and she threatened him with prison, to which he proclaimed his steadfast faith that God would provide his release. In *Da'at Zekenim*, a collection of commentaries from the twelfth to thirteen centuries, many of these midrashic threads are pulled together:

During the 12 months that Joseph was in Potiphar's house, he was exposed to those tactics by Potiphar's wife on a daily basis. When the Torah speaks of these ongoing attempts at seduction (verse 10) as occurring "every day," this must be considered as if Joseph had withstood a year's temptation. . . . He would literally have to take evasive action, such as covering his face, practically shrinking to the ground. She would use instruments in order to force him to resume his normal posture. She would use the argument that she was not really married to Potiphar; he was a homosexual and had never consummated the "marriage." He had to explain to her that the Hebrews were not allowed to have sexual relations with Egyptian women even if the latter were unmarried. She would threaten him with having him consigned to jail. Joseph would reply that his G-d had means of freeing him from jail. She would threaten to have him blinded, to which he replied that his G-d could make the blind see.[18]

Several commentators wrestle with the seeming redundancy in the biblical phrasing of Gen. 39:10, "*And much as she coaxed Joseph day after day, he did not yield to her request to lie beside her, to be with her.*" The simple meaning of the text would suggest she implored Joseph to engage in sexual relations with her, but since nothing is deemed extraneous in the text, the rabbis wonder how the two phrases "*to lie beside her*" and "*to be with her*" are to be understood differently. According to the Talmud, the redundancy teaches that if he were to "*lie beside her*" in this world, he would "*be with her*" in purgatory for eternity in the world to come.[19] Ibn Ezra suggests that "*to lie beside her*" simply meant to sit together, fully clothed, in idle conversation, while Rashi cites both of these possible explanations.[20]

Joseph's refusal to accommodate his mistress is considered a sign of his moral integrity. He would not even lie next to her without touching, lest he give in to temptation and betray his master. While he was obligated to do his mistress's bidding, he had a higher duty to his masters—both Potiphar and God.[21] The moral grounds suggested in midrashic sources include Joseph's obeisance to laws forbidding adultery, laws prohibiting consorting with foreign women, and, all the more so, prohibitions on consorting with married foreign women.[22]

What is to Joseph's credit is to Potiphar's wife's discredit. The *Tur ha-Arokh* summarizes these views:[23]

> "I would commit a sin against G'd." Rashi explains that basic legislation about incestuous relations including adultery applied universally, not only to Jews. Nachmanides writes that he finds it difficult that Joseph mentioned the sin of adultery against his own master Potiphar, which is secondary, before mentioning the sin against G'd, which is primary. He answers this problem by saying that women do not perceive matters in that order. They relate first and foremost to their visible masters, their husbands, and are only marginally concerned with their sins against the Creator, who remains invisible both to them and to their husbands.[23]

Many of the aforementioned themes come together in an early text of the Pseudepigrapha, the *Testaments of the Twelve Patriarchs*, which refers to Potiphar's wife as an "Egyptian woman of Memphis" who had no male child and thus treats Joseph like her own son before seeking to seduce him.[24] An additional plotline depicts the Ishmaelites as leaving Joseph in the care of a shopkeeper, who grows wealthy through Joseph's interventions. Both Joseph's success and beauty come to Potiphar's wife's attention, and she sends her eunuchs to purchase him. Doubting Joseph's explanation of his servitude, Potiphar, the prison keeper, proceeds to beat and imprison him, but his wife takes pity on him and intercedes to save him from her husband's abuse.[25] As she comes to adore him, she tries many ruses to tempt him, such as seeking instruction about his God and offering to kill Potiphar in order to marry him. When Joseph deflects each of these temptations, Potiphar's wife grows increasingly depressed and despondent, eventually threatening to kill herself. Joseph convinces her not to do so for her children's sake, but she confuses his concern with love for her.[26]

After a year of relentless pursuit, Potiphar's wife conceives a plan to force Joseph into a liaison once and for all. She will catch him alone in the house on the day of the Nile festival.[27] The biblical narrative sets the stage for the entrapment: *"One such day, he came into the house to do his work. None of the household being there inside"* (Gen. 39:11).

In the Talmud the rabbis debate Joseph's intentions in entering Potiphar's house. Given the biblical text, some rabbis presume Joseph entered the house innocently to do his usual work, while others suggest Joseph had finally relented and entered what he knew was an otherwise empty house for an assignation.[28] If the latter, why, then, did Joseph demur at the last moment? *Midrash Tanḥuma* suggests that he did, in fact, attempt to fulfill his sexual desire, but he was unable to do so; hence "there was no man" in the house.[29] Rashi and other commentators advance a different explanation found in the Talmud: while no other man *of the household* was present, there was nonetheless another presence not of the household—a vision of Joseph's father Jacob, who appeared to Joseph to appeal to his honor.[30]

Those who presume Joseph's innocence offer an alternative depiction of the fateful day. The fact that it was daytime serves as evidence both of Potiphar's wife's vulgarity and Joseph's innocence regarding her intent, since, according to that view, sexual activity took place only at night:

> "It was on a day no different from any other day;" this short phrase has been inserted here as in praise of Joseph, the righteous person, and as condemnation of the cursed person. In a cultured society, marital intercourse is an activity reserved for the night, to be performed in darkness; the wife of Potiphar demanded from Joseph that he engage not only in infidelity to his master and to G-d, but that he do so in broad daylight. Seeing that Joseph could not have foreseen such a demand by his mistress, he can certainly not be faulted to have gone about his daily routine on that day just as on any other day. Regardless of this, she tried to disrobe him.[31]

Commentators have asked why Potiphar allowed Joseph to live if he believed Joseph had attempted to rape his wife. Most suggest that Potiphar did not, in fact, believe his wife, but that he had to punish Joseph nonetheless to save face.[32] The Zulycah narrative found in *Sefer ha-Yashar* offers a divergent, miraculous explanation: as the angry master beats Joseph, Potiphar's eleven-month-old child, a witness to what really transpired, speaks up, asserting that Joseph has been wrongly accused.[33] The goodness of the baby shames both Potiphar and his wife and saves Joseph from a terrible beating and death.

Joseph and Asenath

Numerous sources associate Potiphar with Potiphera, Joseph's father-in-law, who appears later in the saga after Joseph has earned Pharaoh's gratitude: "*Pharaoh then gave Joseph . . . for a wife Asenath daughter of Poti-phera, priest of On. Thus Joseph emerged in charge of the land of Egypt*" (Gen. 41:45). If this priest of On is also Potiphar, then Asenath's mother must be Potiphar's wife, and the union would fulfill her earlier vision; she would not bear Joseph's children, but they would nonetheless be of her bloodline. However, if, according to other midrashim, Potiphar was a eunuch, how could he father a child? How does Jewish tradition reconcile the lineage of two of the twelve tribes of Israel, Ephraim and Manasseh, as having come from an idol-worshiping Egyptian woman? And what is the linkage between Joseph's marriage to Asenath and his emergence in charge of all of Egypt? From this single verse there arises an entire strand of midrash around Asenath, Joseph's wife.

A well-known midrash addresses several of these questions by suggesting that Potiphar adopted Asenath and that she was actually the daughter of Joseph's half sister Dinah, born as a result of Dinah's alleged rape by Shechem.[34] According to *Pirkei de-Rabbi Eliezer*, Asenath is cast out so as not to disgrace the family, but before she is left under a bush (a play on her name '-*s-n-t* and *seneh*, the Hebrew word for thornbush), Jacob gives her a protective charm indicating her parentage. Miraculously, an angel carries her to Egypt, where she is adopted by Potiphar and raised in his household. After Joseph's ascension to power, as he parades through the streets of Egypt, maidens enraptured by the light emanating from his beauty longingly throw flowers and jewels at him to draw his attention.

He ignores them all, until he sees the amulet written by his father, which Asenath has thrown to him, leading to their marriage. Later in the story, in presenting their children, Ephraim and Manasseh, to Jacob for blessings, Joseph reveals this charm to prove to Jacob with his own handwriting that their lineage is pure.[35]

Other commentaries ask why Joseph would marry the child of his nemesis and consider several political motives. According to the thirteenth-century commentary *Ḥizkuni*:

> If Joseph had married someone of higher rank, he was afraid that his children would be claimed by his former master as slaves, seeing he had owned their father as a slave. When he married his former master's own daughter, he [Potiphar] would be ashamed to say that her children were slaves. A different exegesis: he married her to prove that he had never slept with her mother as claimed. Still another interpretation: Joseph's wife was called: "the daughter of Potiphar," only because he had raised her. There was no biological connection with Potiphar.[36]

An entire book of the Pseudepigrapha, *Joseph and Asenath*, is devoted to tales of their romance and court intrigue about them. In this retelling of the story, Asenath is the daughter of Pentephres the priest of Heliopolis, Pharaoh's chief counselor. She is "tall as Sarah and handsome as Rebecca and beautiful as Rachel."[37] At eighteen she is a such a beauty that all the men, including Pharaoh's own son, seek her hand in marriage. Like Joseph, she rejects all suitors. Even when her father suggests Joseph as a match, she refuses him sight unseen—but once she sees him in all his royal finery, she immediately regrets her haste. Joseph dismisses her because of her idol-worshiping ways, but she casts idol worship aside in order to marry him. Pharaoh's son, determined to have her for himself, conspires with Joseph's brothers to kill Joseph and kidnap Asenath. When Benjamin steps in to defend his sister-in-law, he wounds Pharaoh's son, who dies of his wounds, after which his father, Pharaoh, also dies of his sorrow—and thus Joseph, *because of* his marriage to Asenath, becomes the ruler of Egypt.

A Name and Narrative for Potiphar's Wife

The modern midrash "Zuleikha, the Prison Mistress" is the first in a trilogy about Pharaoh's daughters, Egyptian women who are seen as minor characters in the chronicle of the ancient Israelites, yet play significant roles in advancing the biblical narrative. In this chapter, Potiphar's wife's intrigues eventually lead to Joseph's rise to power in Egypt. In the chapter 6 midrash "The Sacred Sisterhood," the midwives' heroism saves the Hebrew children from Pharaoh's decree. And in chapter 7's midrash, "Amat-Bat-Ra, the Servant Savior," the rescue of Moses by Pharaoh's daughter and her servant sets the stage for the grand saga of the Exodus from Egypt.

Given Potiphar's wife's pivotal role in the narrative, one might have expected the midrashic literature to have filled in some of her background, as it does for Abraham and Sarah and other biblical personages whom we "meet" later in life. Yet the rabbis are interested only in her character as it relates to her interactions with Joseph, and for that she needs no name or history. *Sefer ha-Yashar* is an exception, offering a creative depiction of her storyline.

Going even further than *Sefer ha-Yashar*'s fanciful portrayal, this midrash attempts to resolve numerous questions that arise logically from the text that the rabbis largely ignored. "Zuleikha, the Prison Mistress" considers what would have motivated a woman of high station to degrade herself, first by pursuing a servant and then by behaving so cruelly to that servant. It renders the prison she lives in as not only physical, but emotional and spiritual as well. It gives weight to the depth of fear and trauma she likely experienced in being married to a cruel man with licentious sexual appetites. While her wretched life does not excuse her behavior, it may elicit some sympathy and compassion for her situation. If we read only the biblical text, with no consideration of what may have preceded or motivated her actions, we might, like the rabbis, presume she was an evil woman, driven by lust, and insignificant other than in her character's role in transitioning Joseph from Potiphar's home to the prison, where his story continues. Yet by simply asking the question of what may have transpired previously, we discover much more depth to her character. Underlying her story are power relationships that constrict her life, damage her psyche, and corrupt her moral compass. Being a victim of abuse perverts her understanding of love, yet despite this we see inclinations toward kindness in her unique friendship with Joseph.

Although a minor thread in the classical midrash does consider the possibility of Joseph entertaining the idea of a liaison, none of the rabbis imagine a mutual friendship that sadly and inevitably comes to a regrettable conclusion. In this depiction of events, Potiphar's wife is a tragic character whose childhood hopefulness is relentlessly beaten out of her, leaving her with loneliness and despair. The conclusion is an intentionally ambiguous cliff-hanger: just as she is about the leap to her death, she sees the fulfillment of her childhood dreams in the life her daughter will now lead with Joseph, the new prince of Egypt. Whether this knowledge strengthens her resolve to go on living or to end her life is left to the reader's imagination.

The theme of dreams runs through the Joseph narrative. In this modern midrash, Zuleikha's childhood dreams of grandeur parallel those of the younger Joseph and result in a similar backlash. Several elements from the Joseph-Asenath legend also appear in this midrash. Joseph's legendary beauty and glow draw Asenath to him, just as it drew Zuleikha to him. However, rather than Asenath's amulet coming from her grandfather Jacob to prove her parentage, in this midrash it comes from her grandfather Pharaoh, to ensure her place in the Egyptian court—a much more logical flow for the story.

Finally, a word about names. In this retelling of the story, Joseph is referred to with the Hebrew pronunciation Yosef, which highlights the language differential between him and his mistress, as well as his foreign upbringing, which makes him intriguing to Zuleikha. It also underscores the cultural differences they overcome in forming their unusual friendship. A derivation of his name is used for his descendant, Yosefa, in chapters 6 and 7. Initially this author planned to invent a name for Potiphar's wife that would reflect her newly imagined backstory, but research showed that she was known by the name Zuleikha not only in *Sefer ha-Yashar*, but also in the Qur'an and in Arabic, Persian, and Christian sources. To give her a new, fictitious name rather than using the one already ascribed to her felt like usurping her identity and denying her history. Hopefully, through this new midrash her name will be restored to us as well.

6

Pharaoh's Daughters, Part 2

Puah, Shiphrah, and the Sacred Sisterhood

BIBLICAL TEXT: *Exodus 1:8–22*

A new king arose over Egypt who did not know Joseph. And he said to his people, "Look, the Israelite people are much too numerous for us. Let us deal shrewdly with them, so that they may not increase; otherwise in the event of war they may join our enemies in fighting against us and rise from the ground." So they set taskmasters over them to oppress them with forced labor; and they built garrison cities for Pharaoh: Pithom and Rameses. But the more they were oppressed, the more they increased and spread out, so that the [Egyptians] came to dread the Israelites.

The Egyptians ruthlessly imposed upon the Israelites the various labors that they made them perform. Ruthlessly they made life bitter for them with harsh labor at mortar and bricks and with all sorts of tasks in the field.

The king of Egypt spoke to the Hebrew midwives, one of whom was named Shiphrah and the other Puah, saying, "When you deliver the Hebrew women, look at the birthstool: if it is a boy, kill him; if it is a girl, let her live." The midwives, fearing God, did not do as the king of Egypt had told them; they let the boys live. So the king of Egypt summoned the midwives and said to them, "Why have you done this thing, letting the boys live?" The midwives said to Pharaoh, "Because the Hebrew women are not like the Egyptian women: they are vigorous. Before the midwife can come to them, they have given birth." And God dealt well with the midwives; and the people multiplied and increased greatly. And [God] established households for the midwives, because they feared God. Then Pharaoh charged all his people, saying, "Every boy that is born you shall throw into the Nile, but let every girl live."

"I'm going this time," Shiphrah said, as she donned her cloak.

"No, *I'm* going! It's *my* turn!" I cried, rushing to the door.

"You went last week," Shiphrah countered, shoving me aside.

"So did *you*!" I cried as I pushed her back.

"In the name of Yosefa, stop bickering! You can both come with me," Mother said, feigning anger, though I knew she was pleased by our eagerness to follow in her footsteps.

Mother was one of the most sought-after midwives in all of Egypt. Trained by her mysterious grandmother, Yosefa, for whom Mother herself was named, she had brought more of Pharaoh's children and grandchildren into the world than any other midwife. Shiphrah and I always debated whose turn it was to attend her for one of these royal births. There were always wine and sweets to celebrate the joyous occasion . . . but even more, we loved watching Mother at work. She was calm and confident, in control, always knowing what to do. Patient, yet stern. Especially kind when there was sad news to deliver. But on her watch, that happened much less often than with other midwives.

Shiphrah, who was older by just one year, bossed me around, but she also protected me from the other girls, who were jealous of our craft. From our early age, Mother had begun to teach us how to tend to women on the birthing stool: how to comfort them and ease their suffering, how to clean them and their babies afterward. We helped during simple births and observed difficult ones from a distance. Soon we would learn the special skills that only the greatest of midwives knew: how to stop Anubis, the god of death, when he tried to claim a child, calling on Hathor, goddess of women and fertility, to intercede and bring the child to Ra, king of all the gods and creator of life, instead. Mother had learned special incantations from Yosefa with which she called upon the gods of our ancestors to the north. She also possessed an amulet imbued with the magic of the gods, which had been passed down from mother to daughter for generations; Shiphrah and I were already vying to inherit it one day. With that added power, Mother was the most successful among the sacred sisterhood of midwives.

Shiphrah and I grew up among the women of Pharaoh's court. We never knew our father, who had been a trusted advisor to Pharaoh, from a long line of trusted advisors. After he died, Mother was protected and allowed to retain her position of honor in the palace—not only because of Pharaoh's friendship and respect for our father, but also because the wives of his ministers insisted on keeping her close. They depended on her and trusted her to ensure their own well-being.

Because we were not of royal blood, we did not fret about our futures like the other girls of the palace, whose marriages were bartered to confer political advantage to their families. We were also allowed more freedoms, such as traveling to the marketplace with Mother to learn about herbs and remedies for our trade. We knew from an early age that someday we, too, would be initiated into the sacred sisterhood.

One day, Mother was summoned to the home of a minister in the outskirts of the city. She gathered her supplies and told us to join her. As we journeyed much farther from the palace than ever before, we passed fields and workers making bricks. We had heard of the great pyramids being built for Pharaoh's final rest, but now we saw them with our own eyes. What wonders!

We had no time to stop and stare, though, as we were ushered immediately into the chambers of the wife of the Master of the Builders, who was suffering terribly. Local Hebrew midwives from among the foreign workers were tending to her, but our young mother-to-be preferred Mother's presence, trusting that an Egyptian midwife would know the proper ways to call upon Hathor. Mother assured her that everything had been done properly up to that point, but now she would take charge, and she dismissed the other women. While Mother and Shiphrah were busy instructing the servants, I was stunned to overhear the older midwife whisper Mother's special incantation as she stared at Mother's amulet before they were sent back to their work in the fields. I thought only my mother and great-grandmother Yosefa knew those secret spells.

Mother, Shiphrah, and I immediately went to work, and eventually a son was born. After the feast that followed, it was too late for us to return to the palace, so the Master Builder's servants made accommodations for us there. As we settled for the night, I told Mother what I'd heard. She immediately sent for the two women to discover their secrets. Among the sacred sisterhood of midwives there was no rivalry or jealousy. One woman learned from another, and each shared what she knew generously, with the singular goal to bring new life into the world.

When the foreign midwives Yocheved and her daughter Miriam arrived at the Master Builder's home, escorted by Miriam's older cousin Elzaphan, they were timid and reserved, bowing like servants and clearly worried about why they had been summoned. Mother smiled to make them more comfortable and asked Yocheved about the incantations, which were so similar to her own. In turn, Yocheved commented on Mother's amulet, and the two fell into a long conversation about their families and their trade. Yocheved (now Yochie to us) was herself with child and anxious to learn as much as possible from such an experienced midwife.

While Mother and Yochie traded stories and techniques, Miriam and I chatted away effortlessly, as if we'd been friends our whole life. A little older than Shiphrah, Miriam had a quiet confidence about her, just like Mother. Shiphrah joined us half-heartedly, constantly glancing at Elzaphan, who stood outside the chamber but kept a watchful eye on his aunt and cousin. I noticed that he, too, looked her way occasionally, with a slight grin. I teased Shiphrah for being so obvious, and she pinched me to keep me quiet. As dawn approached, we sent our new friends back to their labors, while we stole a few hours of sleep before the journey home.

After that, life returned to normal, but I couldn't stop thinking about my new friend, Miriam. She was kind and sweet, and a bit exotic. I begged Mother to tell me more about her Hebrew people and how they came to Egypt, and Mother relayed what little she knew—mostly tales from her grandmother Yosefa about a time of great suffering when many foreigners journeyed from the north, south, east, and west. Pharaoh had been blessed with abundance and allowed those who were hungry to come and settle in our land. I was fascinated by these stories, but Shiphrah was not interested; she could not stop talking about the handsome Elzaphan, who suddenly filled her dreams.

A few months later, Mother determined that the time of our apprenticeship was at an end, and Shiphrah and I were ready to be initiated as full members of the sacred sisterhood. She gathered together all the local midwives who were not currently attending births, and one by one they asked us questions about how we might handle the challenges we would face: long labors, frail mothers, large babies, feet first, tangled cords, and finally, what to do when babies were born cold and snatched by Anubis before they emerged. Mother had prepared us well, and we answered each question to their satisfaction. Finally, they declared us ready. They surrounded us and huddled close so each one could lay their hands upon our heads, and together they prayed that Hathor would bless us and our healing hands. As the warmth of their blessings flowed over me, I felt immense pride to be a member of this sacred sisterhood of wise, caring women dedicated to bringing life into the world.

I'll never forget the first time we attended a birth without Mother. We were both terrified! The minister's home was near the palace, so Mother could be summoned at a moment's notice. "No arguing, you two!" Mother said, as she assured us that we were ready and all would be well.

When we arrived, all the attendants turned to us for guidance, and we knew we had to appear calm and self-assured, as Mother always was. I paused for a moment to let Shiphrah speak first, but she just looked at me with wide, panic-stricken eyes, so I took a deep breath and suddenly found my voice. As Mother had promised, when the time came, I was ready. Somehow, from deep within, I simply knew what I had to do.

I immediately instructed the servants to prepare clean water, cloths, the birthstool, and fans, and then I comforted our frightened young mother-to-be. Shiphrah was relieved to take direction from me, and to my surprise, she was efficient and thorough and did exactly what I asked. It was a fast delivery, and soon the new mother was cooing blissfully as she cradled her beautiful daughter in her arms.

From then on, whenever Mother was not available, Shiphrah and I were sent together to attend the women of the court. Even when there were complications, we were up to the challenge. We worked effortlessly as a team and soon became well regarded in our own right. Shiphrah eventually gained confidence; she was as capable as I was but less self-assured, so she continued to defer to me, especially for difficult births. Our roles had reversed: although she was older, I was the one in charge.

One day, as Shiphrah and I made our way to the market to collect herbs, Shiphrah gave me a sudden jab with her elbow. I followed her gaze, and there was Elzaphan carrying a heavy load of bricks for the Master Builder. When Elzaphan saw Shiphrah coming toward him, he nearly dropped his bundle. I saw the look of panic in his eyes and heard his silent scream, "Stop!"

I grabbed Shiphrah's cloak just as he turned away and held her tightly until he was out of sight. When I finally let go, Shiphrah turned to me with an angry, pained look on her face. "Why did you stop me?!" she cried, giving me a shove. Then she ran away, leaving me alone in the market.

For a moment I was confused—not really sure what had just transpired, but something was not right. I was also a bit frightened, since I had never been at the market alone. But it was a familiar street and I knew the vendors, so I continued to collect the supplies we needed.

After completing my purchases, I turned to head back to the palace, but from behind the stall something caught my eye . . . something familiar. And then I remembered: it was the cloak Miriam had worn the night the Master Builder's wife gave birth! Miriam gave a quick half-wave and just the slightest of motions that no one else could see, indicating that I was to follow her down a side street where the smaller vendors sold their goods. I was nervous venturing into an unfamiliar part of the market, but my curiosity was stronger than my fear, and I so wanted to see my friend again! So I followed her through the winding paths of the bustling market streets, up and through the smaller and cheaper stalls off the beaten path. Eventually we came to a small courtyard between the stalls, where suddenly she stopped and threw her arms around me.

"Oh, Puah!" she cried. "It brings me such joy to see you! You look well! Have you been initiated yet? How are Yosefa and Shiphrah?"

After I shared all that had happened since we last met and Miriam told me about her mother and Elzaphan, I asked her about the secrecy surrounding our rendezvous. "We have to be careful because of the decree," she said. "What decree?" I asked. When she told me about Pharaoh's edict, about the hard labor her people were forced to endure, and about the danger brought by her mother's pregnancy, I felt foolish and naïve. How could I have been so oblivious to what was happening outside the palace? Why had Mother not told us this? And when I heard the worst of it—that the Hebrew midwives were forbidden to ply their trade and forced to let the Hebrew boys perish—I was horrified. Such cruelty was simply unimaginable. How could our sacred sisterhood allow it?!

Miriam would not speak further about it. She feared we had been together too long already, so she led me through the winding paths back to the main road. Before she left, I gave her all the herbs and medicines I had just purchased and hugged her close to me. "Be strong, my friend," I whispered to her. "I will help you if I can."

I made my way back to the palace, fighting to control my tears of anger and sorrow, but relieved that Shiphrah was there. When she came toward me, still angry about my stopping her from speaking with Elzaphan, I pushed her aside and went straight to Mother. "Do you know about the king's order?" I blurted out. "Do you know what's happening to the Hebrew babies? How could you not tell us? How can we allow this?!" "Quiet!" she hissed under her breath. Then she grabbed Shiphrah and me and led us to a quiet chamber where no one would hear us.

"What's going on?" Shiphrah asked, her anger turning to curiosity and then fear as she sensed some terrible news approaching. I told her what I had learned from Miriam but kept my eyes on Mother, silently condemning her for her complicity. Mother let me finish, and then, very quietly, she told us where she had been all those times when Shiphrah and I had been called to a delivery instead of her. She had been with Yochie and Miriam, secretly birthing and hiding Hebrew children. Under Hathor's protection, members of the sacred sisterhood were defying Pharaoh's outrageous decree, remaining loyal to their calling to bring life.

"My daughters," Mother said, "you are now old enough to know these things. And to choose for yourselves. Join me, if you will, but know this—if you are caught disobeying Pharaoh, it could bring death or prison to you and our household. Our sacred sisterhood must now become a secret sisterhood."

Without a moment's hesitation, I threw my arms around her, crying. My tears were a mix of fear and relief, pride and terror. Shiphrah joined in as well. She was anxious at first, but she too had spent her entire life preparing to join the sacred sisterhood. She would not, could not, abandon our mission, even if it meant defying the gods.

Just as we began planning, Kebu, one of the palace eunuchs, came running toward us, out of breath. "Kebu, what's wrong?" Mother asked her old friend, startled to have been discovered so far away from our chambers.

"Yosefa, I've been looking all over for you! The king commands you—all three of you—to come to him. Hurry! Now!"

"I will go alone," Mother said.

Kebu seemed startled by her defiance of the king's order, but he knew his place and kept silent. With a flick of her wrist, Mother sent us back to our rooms as she followed Kebu to the royal residence.

After what seemed like hours, Mother returned to us, ashen, flustered, more shaken than I'd ever seen her before. We sat her down, brought her a cool drink, and pelted her with questions while she just sipped her drink and tried to take stock. At last she took a deep breath. "He knows we disobeyed him," she said. "I explained that the Hebrew women live too far away for us to arrive in time for the births and that they have their own midwives and do not always call us. I reminded him that it was the will of the gods. But nothing appeased him. Had I not brought his own son into the world, I fear he might have killed me right then."

"The king is frantic," she told us. He had paced around the room, muttering about everyone being against him. "He's determined to thwart Hathor's will," she continued. "I fear our king will incur the gods' anger. What he has planned is unthinkable."

With that, she looked up at us from her seat, calmly took each one of us by the hand, and said, "I am sorry, my daughters, to place such a burden on you. But our work is more important than ever. The king knows we will not comply, so now he has ordered every person in the land to commit this horrible act. The children are to be cast into the Great River. We must do what we can to save them. I myself can do nothing, as the king no longer trusts me. He has decreed that I cannot leave the compound, except for royal births, and even then, Kebu must escort me. So now it is up to you."

And so, we began planning. Just as Shiphrah and I had worked side by side since our first birth together, now we would work together, joining the secret sisterhood to save the Hebrew children, and so fulfilling our sacred calling.

Yocheved's child would be our first.

CLASSICAL COMMENTARY AND MIDRASH:
The Subversive Midwives

The first chapter of Exodus, filled with pathos and intrigue, sets the stage for the Israelites' dramatic journey to freedom following their enslavement and suffering at the hands of their Egyptian taskmasters. The midwives' heroic resistance against Pharaoh's decree and protection of the Hebrew children is a key element of this chapter. While minor biblical women rarely are named, Shiphrah and Puah's defiance of Pharaoh's order to kill the Hebrew babies merits both names and the promise of great rewards in the future.

Nothing is revealed about these two women in the biblical text, and many questions arise from the story. Who were the midwives? Why did Pharaoh scheme to kill only the Hebrew male children and do so surreptitiously through the midwives? What compelled the midwives to defy Pharaoh, and how did they manage to disobey the most powerful man in Egypt and survive? And, finally, what happened to them after these events unfolded?

A fundamental question that several commentaries consider is whether Shiphrah and Puah were Egyptian or Hebrew women. Just as in English, the Hebrew phrase "Hebrew midwives" is ambiguous and could mean either midwives who were themselves Hebrew women or midwives who tended *to* the Hebrew women. This linguistic ambiguity, coupled with the illogic of Pharaoh expecting Hebrew women to kill Hebrew children, leads several commentators to presume that the midwives were actually Egyptian women.[1]

One clue to discerning their nationality is found in the derivation of their names. Modern biblical scholar Nahum Sarna points out that while the names may be Semitic in origin, they are not necessarily Hebrew names. The root letters of Shiphrah (*sh-p-r*) can mean "to be beautiful" in Hebrew and other Semitic languages, and the name also appears in ancient Egyptian slave lists. The name Puah is found in Ugaritic literature, where it means "a girl."[2]

A common midrashic interpretation of these verses suggests that Shiphrah and Puah were actually Jochebed and Miriam, respectively. Alternatively, some commentators associate them with Jochebed, Moses' mother, and Elisheba, Aaron's wife. To explain why the biblical text would refer to Jochebed and Miriam (or Elisheba) by the names Shiphrah and Puah, the rabbis suggest various wordplays on the names:

> "Shiphrah" is Jochebed; and why was her name called Shiphrah? Because she straightened [*meshappereth*] the limbs of the babe. Another explanation of *Shiphrah* is that the Israelites were fruitful [*sheparu*] and multiplied in her days. "*Pu'ah*" is Miriam; and why was her name called Puah? Because she cried out [*po'ah*] to the child and brought it forth. Another explanation of *Pu'ah* is that she used to cry out through the Holy Spirit and say, "My mother will bear a son who will be the saviour of Israel."[3]

An additional derivation of the name Puah is related to the Hebrew term for insolence (*hofiy'ah panim*). Using this play on her name, the midrash suggests that Puah-Miriam rebuked Pharaoh, who became angry and sought to kill her. Alternatively, the name is a reference to another well-known midrash in which Miriam chastises her father Amram for divorcing Jochebed upon hearing Pharaoh's decree, in order to avoid having more children, because his actions went further than Pharaoh's decree, which prevented the birth of only boys. After Miriam's rebuke, Amram remarried Jochebed, and then they had Moses.[4]

Several commentaries note that there could not have been *only* two midwives for all the Hebrew women. Numerous questions arise from this: why were just these two selected, and how would Pharaoh have known any of the Hebrew midwives to begin with? Ibn Ezra answers both of these questions. He estimates that there would have been more than five hundred midwives to serve the population of six hundred thousand Hebrews. He asserts that Shiphrah and Puah were the administrators of all the midwives, tasked with collecting taxes for Pharaoh on the midwives' earnings.[5] Hence Pharaoh or his finance ministers would have known them, and they would have been in a position to convey and enforce the decree to all of the other midwives. Sforno also wrestles with this question, suggesting that these two were Egyptian midwives serving the Hebrews based in the capital, which had fewer Hebrews, and thus two would have been sufficient. The king presumed that if these midwives were unable to carry out his plan, then those from regions where Hebrews were more prevalent would certainly not do so. Rather than pursuing the plan further, Pharaoh issued his second decree to the entire population to kill all the male babies.[6]

Why Did Pharaoh Involve Midwives in His Murderous Plan?

According to midrash, efforts to suppress the Hebrew population involved not only the rigors of servitude, but also attempts to prevent the Israelites from procreating by separating the men and women. Yet the women found means to arouse their husbands and thwarted Pharaoh's plans.[7] Only when these efforts failed did Pharaoh resort to his more drastic scheme.

The eighteenth-century *Or ha-Ḥayim* commentary notes that up until this point, the Hebrew text utilizes the plural form to describe the

Egyptians' oppression of the Hebrews, suggesting a communal consensus to these actions. For example, the text of Exod. 1:11 reads, *"So they set taskmasters over them to oppress them with forced labor."* In shifting to more draconian measures, Pharaoh acted alone and privately, as signified by the singular form in Exod. 1:15, *"The king of Egypt spoke to the Hebrew midwives."*[8] His choice to enact secret measures may have sprung from his concern that the Egyptian people might have demurred or, alternatively, because the Hebrew women would hide their pregnancies if they knew about the decree.

An obvious question arising from the text is why Pharaoh issued multiple decrees. In Exod. 1:16, Pharaoh calls upon the midwives to kill every Hebrew boy on the birthstool but to let the girls live. Yet later, in verse 22, Pharaoh decrees that the entire populace is to throw every newborn boy into the Nile and let every girl live. The latter decree is somewhat ambiguous and could have applied to just the Hebrew babies, as one might expect, or to all male babies born in Egypt, though the logic of the broader reading is illusive.[9] If Pharaoh had the power to command the murder of the Hebrew boys, why did he initially conspire with the midwives in secret? And if he wanted Egypt to be rid of the prolific Hebrews, why didn't he simply command their death from the beginning? And why did he dictate the death of just male babies rather than order the Egyptians to kill or exile all of the Hebrews? Certainly, there must have been more going on here than a simple reading of the text allows.

The *Tur ha-Arokh* offers several explanations for Pharaoh's reluctance to kill the Hebrews outright:

> Neither Pharaoh nor his servants wanted to do violence to the Israelites, as it would have been a major act of betrayal to commit genocide against an innocent nation that had settled in Egypt at the request of the previous king. He was afraid that even if he were to give an order to destroy these people his subjects would not obey that order. Moreover, the descendants of Ephrayim and Menashe possessed considerable influence in the highest governmental circles, and the very number of the Israelites would have made open warfare

against them a highly dangerous undertaking. The Israelites would surely resist any attack upon them by violent means. Therefore, he imposed a form of taxation upon that nation, a common practice in those days. When this did not have the desired effect, he resorted to instructing the midwives who assisted the Jewish women at birth, to kill the male babies before the mothers had held them in their arms. This was done clandestinely, so that even the mothers were unaware that they had given birth to a male baby. When this proved impossible to carry out, he issued the decree to drown all male babies.[10]

Fear that the Israelites were growing too numerous and could join forces with Egypt's enemies explains why only the male children were targeted, since only the males would fight against the Egyptians.[11] Another explanation is that the Hebrew women would marry Egyptian men out of necessity, since there weren't enough Hebrew men, and thus the peoples would become intermingled and Egypt would no longer have a fifth column within its ranks.[12] As a corollary benefit, the Egyptian men would have more women at their disposal for marriage and sexual relations.[13]

Several commentaries suggest that killing only the male babies was particularly devious. Allowing some babies to live and snatching life from the boys at their moment of birth allowed the midwives to evade suspicion. They simply declared some babies stillborn before the mothers even knew the gender, and it would take some time before the Hebrews would realize that only girls had been born.[14] According to numerous sources, Pharaoh had instructed the midwives how they would know which babies were male or female even before they actually emerged from the womb; if the baby was facedown, it would be male, and faceup would be female.[15]

Numerous midrashic sources reveal a legend that serves as yet another explanation as to why only the male babies were to be killed. Pharaoh had a premonition that a boy would be born who would usurp his power. He had a strange dream about the land of Egypt on one side of a scale, outweighed by a sickly lamb on the other. His astrologers interpreted the dream as signifying that soon a Hebrew boy would be born who would lead his people to rise up and destroy Egypt. Hence a plan was devised to eliminate all Hebrew males from being born. Variants of this legend suggest that the astrologers did not know if the child would be Hebrew or Egyptian, and thus Pharaoh extended his decree to include all males born in Egypt.[16] Other variants explain that the astrologers foresaw that the child would die by water, and thus the decree was for drowning. The midrash notes that Moses' death did in fact come about by water, since Moses was condemned to die in the wilderness because of the incident at Meribah in which he struck rather than ordered the rock to produce water as God had instructed (Num. 20:1–13).[17] This legend, reminiscent of a common motif found in ancient Near Eastern mythologies, such as the Oedipus tale, is found in numerous early sources and picked up by later commentaries as well.[18]

Finally, some commentators note that by employing the midwives, Pharaoh was evading responsibility and making them the guilty parties, so he himself would not fear divine retribution.[19] But it was precisely because the midwives feared God that his plan failed. Similarly, with the second decree as well, the Egyptians were charged with drowning the infants, not Pharaoh himself. And, as we will read in the next chapter of Exodus, because not all Egyptians were willing to comply, that decree also failed.

The Midwives' Defiance

The biblical text offers a simple explanation for why the midwives defied Pharaoh's order. *"The midwives, fearing God, did not do as the king of Egypt had told them; they let the boys live"* (Exod. 1:17). Their fear of God might lend weight to the interpretation that they were Hebrew, not Egyptian women. However, the Hebrew for *"God"* used in this verse is *Elohim* (literally "the gods") rather than *YHVH*, which could allow an alternative interpretation that the Egyptian midwives feared their own gods.[20] Whether Hebrew or Egyptian, the simple reading suggests they were women of moral character who would not commit that heinous act even at the pain of death.[21]

Yet a redundancy in this verse begs interpretation. If the midwives did not do as Pharaoh commanded, then it is clear that they let the boys live, and therefore that point did not need to be repeated—unless there is additional information to be inferred. Of the several explanations within the Talmud, one suggests that the first statement, *"the midwives . . . did not do as the king of Egypt had told them* [dibeir aleihen]," refers not to the decree about the male babies, but rather to a solicitation of sexual favors (derived from a play on the word *aleihen,* a term used elsewhere in the Bible to infer sexual relations). Another explanation is that the second statement, *"they let the boys live,"* suggests that the midwives not only allowed them to live, but also kept them alive, providing food and water for their young charges.[22]

The midrash goes even further, suggesting that the repetition is intended to reinforce the God-fearing nature of the midwives:

It is only to add praise to praise; for not only did they not fulfil [*sic*] his command, but even went beyond this and did deeds of kindness to them. For those who were poor, the midwives would go to the houses of the rich to collect water and food and give them to the poor and thus keep alive their children. . . . Some children are liable to be born lame or blind or cripples, or require the amputation of a limb so that they may come out safely. So what did they do? They would pray to God thus: "Thou knowest that we have not fulfilled Pharaoh's command; for it is Thy command that we wish to fulfil. Lord of the Universe! Let the child come out safely, so that Israel find no occasion to accuse us by saying: 'Behold, they have come out crippled, because they sought to slay them.'" God at once hearkened to their prayer and they were born safe and sound.[23]

The Midwives' Reward or Punishment

Here again, redundancies in the text invite exploration. First, in Exod. 1:20 we read, *"And God dealt well with the midwives; and the people multiplied and increased greatly."* In what way did God reward them? Is there a connection between God dealing well with the midwives and the people multiplying? The next verse, *"And [God] established households* [batim] *for the midwives, because they feared God,"* repeats their God-fearing attribute, which is redundant, since we already know this from verse 17. The actual meaning of the word *batim* is also unclear. Furthermore, while this verse would seem to more explicitly indicate the nature of the reward referenced in the prior verse, the rendering is not conclusive, leading to the question: is this the same reward noted in the previous verse or an additional reward somehow connected to the midwives' God-fearing nature?

Varying interpretations of Exod. 1:20 seek to resolve the possible redundancy. In the preceding verse, the midwives lied to Pharaoh, explaining that the Hebrew women were "*vigorous*" and able to give birth before the midwives could get to them. Reading verse 20 in conjunction with verse 19, "*God dealt well with the midwives*" may suggest that the rewards God conferred were the miracle of Pharaoh's belief in their deception along with the Hebrew wives' ability to continue procreating.[24] Other sources propose different divine interventions, offering elaborate explanations of how pregnant women hid their pregnancies or gave birth in the fields, which miraculously opened up and hid their children underground.[25]

Still other commentaries suggest that the two verses reference two different benefits and explain how the internal logic of each verse provides a connection between the reward and the corollary phrase within that verse. In Exod. 1:20, God "*dealt well*" with the midwives by making the people multiply—in other words, God made them successful in their midwifery endeavors, and therefore the population grew. An alternative explanation is that God gave the midwives an abundance of wealth, which allowed them to provide food and water for the Hebrew children (as described in the aforementioned midrash), and thereby the population grew. According to these readings, "*dealing well*" with the midwives meant that God granted them the tools to accomplish their part in the divine plan, thus allowing the Israelites to increase.[26]

In contrast, in Exod. 1:21, God actually grants the midwives a personal gift as a reward for their piety. Although the translation of the word *batim* is uncertain, one might presume that it somehow relates to their faithfulness, which is referenced in the latter part of the verse. Generally, *batim* translates as "houses," but its usage is unusual in this context. Most scholars propose that the nuance here refers to a dynasty, or their legacy, suggesting that the midwives were destined to have many children and be the progenitors of great "*households,*" or clans.[27]

Coupled with the classical midrashim that associate Shiphrah and Puah with Jochebed and Miriam, the rabbis look at the Hebrew women's lineage as their reward. In Jochebed's case, her fear of God merits the gift of Torah, given through her son Moses; in Miriam's case, she is the foremother of Bezalel, builder of the Tabernacle, who was known for his wisdom.[28] Alternatively, Jochebed was destined to be the progenitor of the priestly clan through Moses and Aaron, and Miriam would be the foremother of the royal dynasty through David.[29]

Yet other commentaries take the word *batim* to literally mean "houses," suggesting their reward was to be given grand homes. Still others point out the ambiguity of the primary actor in the verse. While most translations presume God is the party conferring the reward, it could also refer to Pharaoh—in effect, "Because the midwives feared *Elohim*, Pharaoh made them houses."

How would we then understand the verse? The *Tur ha-Arokh* shares several possibilities related to such a rendering:

> Other commentators understand this as relating to the line . . . "*when, due to the midwives being in awe of G'd*, and Pharaoh's decree therefore becoming futile, Pharaoh placed pregnant Jewish women in houses surrounded by Egyptians so that their neighbours would know when they would be likely to give birth." These women were forbidden to give birth anywhere else but in these houses. Still a third way of interpreting this verse is that the "*houses*" were jails in which the midwives would henceforth be kept. The word *bayit* does appear in this sense in Genesis 40,14 Joseph saying to the chief of the cupbearers . . . "*so that you will bring me out of this jail* (the jail being called a house)."[30]

According to this alternative reading of the text, Pharaoh is angry that the midwives fear and obey the Hebrew God (*Elohim*) instead of him. Rather than a reward from God, the "houses" are a punishment by Pharaoh, who either locks them up or severely restricts their movements so they can only perform their duties in designated houses where they can be watched carefully—or, alternatively, where the Hebrew women coming to them to give birth can be readily observed by the Egyptians.[31]

Whether perceived as Hebrew or Egyptian women or presumed to be Jochebed and Miriam or others, the simple reading of the text is that these midwives remained true to their sacred task of bringing life into the world. Strengthened by their moral certitude, they defied the greatest human power in the known world to do what they believed to be right. Their true fate may remain unknown, yet their names, unlike those of most biblical-era women, live on to inspire future generations to value human life, to defy evil, and to risk their own lives for a just cause.[32]

AUTHOR'S COMMENTARY: *The Midwives' Tale*

The modern midrash "The Sacred Sisterhood" is the second segment of the midrashic trilogy "Pharaoh's Daughters," about non-Hebrew biblical women who play pivotal roles in advancing the narrative of the ancient Israelites. Potiphar's wife (chapter 5), the midwives Shiphrah and Puah, and subsequently Pharaoh's daughter (chapter 7) are seminal characters without whom the story of the Exodus from Egypt might not have taken place. Yet, because they are not part of the Jewish people's family tree, within Jewish lore these protagonists have been, at worst, maligned and, at best, neglected and ignored.

That said, uniquely, the midwives' names are preserved, and they are lauded for their act of defiance. They are possibly the first recorded practitioners of civil disobedience.

Yet there is little in the rabbinic tradition to amplify their story or to "fill in the blanks," as midrash often does with other biblical figures. There is a dearth of classical texts to help us know who these women were and what motivated them to take their ethical stand. If our tradition finds their actions honorable, then we should want to know more about them and perhaps even imagine what we, ourselves, might have done in their sandals. How would we have responded to the king's brutal order if we faced the threat of punishment or death? Through this modern rendering of their story, "The Sacred Sisterhood" attempts to provide these heroines with a voice and a story of their own. Imbued with a moral imperative to preserve life, to which certainly all midwives must subscribe, how could they have acted any differently?

The simple nuance of the text requires seeing these women as Egyptian. As numerous commentators noted, it makes no sense that the king would have expected Hebrew women to kill Hebrew babies to advance his plan or that he even would have known any Hebrew midwives he could call by name. With that understanding, the backstory constructed for Shiphrah and Puah places them in Pharaoh's purview and provides a rationale for the degree of independence and assertiveness they exhibit. They also are depicted as sisters, allowing for the introduction of the character of their mother and, through her, the link way back to their ancestor, Yosef (Joseph), who famously rose from humble beginnings to become vizier of Egypt (see chapter 5). The sisters' familial connection to Yosef can be intuited by their mother's and grandmother's name, Yosefa, and the special incantations of their ancestors "from the north."

That the midwives' lineage is loosely linked to Yosef is a natural segue for the ongoing narrative of the Hebrews' sojourn in Egypt. In addition, the reference to the amulet links this midrash to both the traditional commentary and the creative midrash about Joseph's (Yosef's) wife, Asenath. According to the classical midrash, Asenath, the child of the illicit union of Dinah and Shechem, is given the amulet by her grandfather Jacob to prove her family lineage before being cast out. She miraculously finds her way to Egypt, where Potiphar adopts her. The amulet she carries is a sign to Joseph that they are kin and thus permitted to marry. Later, Joseph uses this amulet to prove their sons' pedigree when seeking Jacob's deathbed blessings for Ephraim and Manasseh.[33] In a variation of this legend, the amulet in "Zuleikha, The Prison Mistress," in "Pharaoh's Daughters, Part 1" (chapter 5), is a gift from Asenath's mother Zuleikha, who had received it from her father, the Pharaoh.

A great deal of commentary addresses the Pharaoh *who did not know Joseph*" (Exod. 1:8). How could the people of Egypt have forgotten the vizier of Egypt, who, according to some rabbinic calculations, lived just one generation prior to the Exodus story? The assumption underlying "The Sacred Sisterhood" is that there had been more than one intervening generation between Joseph and the midwives. They are close enough to allow for carryover of historical names and some family customs, yet distant enough that the individual characters do not have personal memories or relationships with the characters of the Joseph narrative. Both scholarly literature and some midrashic calculations allow for this understanding. Traditional midrashim also suggest that Joseph's descendants continued to have political attachments to the Egyptian court, so the midwives' family placement within Pharaoh's court is within the scope of traditional midrashic understandings.

Though the classical midrash associates Shiphrah and Puah with Jochebed and Miriam (or Aaron's wife, Elisheba), this midrash does not co-opt their story and replace the Egyptian midwives with Israelite women. The essence of their heroism and the power of their example are not to be found in personal vested interests, but rather in their integrity, bravery, moral fortitude, and strength of conviction. For that reason, the association with their own Egyptian heritage is reinforced through references to traditional Egyptian gods and names. Similarly, some classical commentaries allow *elohim* to be read as "the gods" of Egypt and consider the midwives' fidelity to their own gods, rather than the God of Israel, as their motivation. Nonetheless, the rabbinic association with Hebrew foremothers is such a prevalent motif throughout the traditional midrash that elements of it are incorporated in this midrash, such as the inclusion of Jochebed and Miriam within the storyline as midwives, associates, and collaborators. The midrashic interpretation of Puah's name, which can mean "insolence," along with the well-known midrash that connects the midwife to Miriam, provided the source material for the personality here crafted for Puah. The classical midrash depicts Miriam's disposition as outspoken, assertive, and wise. For that reason, Puah became the narrator of this saga, with some of those characteristics ascribed to her.

While the storyline of "The Sacred Sisterhood" tracks with the chronology of the biblical verses, filling in details and giving color to their adventure, creative license has been taken in inventing several characters, who will also be found in the third segment of the "Pharaoh's Daughters" trilogy, "Amat-Bat-Ra, the Servant Savior" (chapter 7). As noted earlier, given the linkage of their names, it seems logical to consider Shiphrah and Puah as sisters; in fact it is somewhat surprising not to find such a depiction in the rabbinic literature. If one considers the midwives' to be sisters, then the idea of a parental role model who instilled altruistic values within them feels natural, though the character of Yosefa is entirely invented. These heroic women acted out of a deeply rooted sense of integrity, humanity, and moral courage; from where did those qualities emerge if not from their mother?

In another departure from the simple reading of biblical text, Yosefa, rather than Shiphrah and Puah, has a face-to-face meeting with Pharaoh. While the text says, *"The king of Egypt spoke to the Hebrew midwives, one of whom was named Shiphrah and the other Puah,"* this rendering interprets that verse as two separate statements. The first clause, *"The king of Egypt spoke to the Hebrew midwives,"* refers to the meeting with Yosefa and perhaps other midwives. The second clause, *"one of whom was named Shiphrah and the other Puah,"* is understood as an aside: the narrator notes that these were the names of two of the midwives, but not necessarily the only two or the ones who met with Pharaoh. While that may be a stretch, such linguistic deconstruction is a permissible midrashic technique. This creative interpretation allows some distance between Pharaoh and Shiphrah and Puah, who are depicted as young, yet brave, novices. Perhaps this is the author's literary maternal instinct trying to protect them.

Other minor characters have been invented as compatriots of the conspirators. Elzaphan is in fact the name of a cousin of Miriam, according to the biblical family tree. A descendant of Levi, Elzaphan was the grandson of Kohath, Amram's father. He was thus a nephew of Amram and a cousin of Aaron, Miriam, and Moses. Later he became a leader of the Kohath tribe in the wilderness (Exod. 6:22). Intimating a special connection between Elzaphan and Shiphrah is intended to provide a bit of color to her character, as well as additional motivation for her participation in the scheme. Kebu, a minor character in "The Sacred Sisterhood," will have a greater role in the continuation of the tale in "Amat-Bat-Ra, the Servant Savior," in "Pharaoh's Daughters, Part 3" (chapter 7).

The unusual use of the word *batim* ("houses") in Exod. 1:21, which is used to describe the reward given to the midwives, is noteworthy in classical midrash. The translation of *batim* as "*households*" and the assumption that this is an allusion to the midwives' future legacies, either as Egyptian clans or through the priestly lineage of Jochebed and Miriam, is widely accepted. Nonetheless, some sources interpret the term *batim* literally as "houses," giving rise to different understandings of the verse. Similarly, the alternative reading that Pharaoh, not God, delivered this reward (or punishment) is equally striking. In these commentaries, the word *batim* is understood to mean prisons, either for the midwives or the Hebrew women they served, a nuance found elsewhere in the biblical text. Picking up on that thread, Yosefa, representing all of the midwives in the cabal of the "sacred sisterhood," is called to stand before her angry king and answer for her disobedience. She accepts her punishment, knowing it could have been so much worse. An allusion to the legend of the astrologers' prediction that a male adversary is about to be born, leading to Pharaoh's excessive agitation, is also incorporated into this storyline. This conclusion to "The Sacred Sisterhood" helps set the stage for the third part of the trilogy (chapter 7), in which our heroines, Shiphrah and Puah, will continue to conspire with Jochebed and Miriam to save baby Moses, joined by none other than Pharaoh's own daughter.

7

Pharaoh's Daughters, Part 3

The Princess and the Slave Girl Who Rescue Moses

BIBLICAL TEXT: *Exodus 2:1–9*

A certain member of the house of Levi went and took [into his household as his wife] a woman of Levi. The woman conceived and bore a son; and when she saw how beautiful he was, she hid him for three months. When she could hide him no longer, she got a wicker basket for him and caulked it with bitumen and pitch. She put the child into it and placed it among the reeds by the bank of the Nile. And his sister stationed herself at a distance, to learn what would befall him. The daughter of Pharaoh came down to bathe in the Nile, while her maidens walked along the Nile. She spied the basket among the reeds and sent her slave girl [*amatah*] to fetch it. When she opened it, she saw that it was a child, a boy crying. She took pity on it and said, "This must be a Hebrew child." Then his sister said to Pharaoh's daughter, "Shall I go and get you a Hebrew nurse to suckle the child for you?" And Pharaoh's daughter answered, "Yes." So the girl went and called the child's mother. And Pharaoh's daughter said to her, "Take this child and nurse it for me, and I will pay your wages." So the woman took the child and nursed it. When the child grew up, she brought him to Pharaoh's daughter, who made him her son. She named him Moses, explaining, "I drew him out of the water."

"Amat-Bat-Ra, come quickly! Your mistress needs you!" The palace eunuch Kebu grabbed me and pulled me along toward her chambers. It seemed that no matter where I was, I was needed somewhere else. "Fetch water," Bat-Ra, my mistress, would command. "I'm too hot—come here and fan me." "Amati, where's my fresh water?" "Where have you been? Help me to my bed."

I was born to be a servant, and with the blessing of Ra, god of the sun and the supreme power of the universe, I'd been selected to serve the royal house.

Bat-Ra was Pharaoh's First Daughter. She was kind to me, and our relationship was the closest thing to friendship I'd known. After several years as her servant, I'd learned to anticipate her needs, and we'd found a comfortable rhythm, until this latest pregnancy, which caused her such anguish. Now, nothing I did could ease her suffering.

"What is it, Kebu?" I gasped, trying to catch my breath as we rushed through the palace.

"Her time has come," he said. "Go, attend your mistress, and I will fetch the midwife."

I stopped in my tracks. "Now? It can't be! She has many months before the time comes!"

"Go!" he screamed as he pushed me forward and then ran to find the midwife.

Not again. My heart sank for my mistress. It was far too soon; surely this child too would not live.

This was the third time Kebu called for the midwife; already, two children had been lost. With each loss my mistress had grown more anxious and short-tempered, pushing away her friends and family and frightening the servants. She grew weaker and more depressed as well. How would she ever recover if she lost this child too?

Once the midwife and her daughters Puah and Shiphrah arrived, Puah and I gathered all the needed supplies and then sat by Bat-Ra's side, wiping her face and arms with cool wet cloths and cooing softly to try to calm her. It was over very quickly. The midwife sent Kebu to bring the news to Pharaoh and the prince, though there was nothing to give to the royal embalmer. Shiphrah cleaned and put fresh gowns on my mistress while the midwife made a soothing tea to make her drowsy. Finally, Bat-Ra's sobs quieted, and with a few final heaves she rolled onto her side and fell into a fitful sleep.

I stayed by Bat-Ra's side for days, trying to make her comfortable, bringing her food that she never ate. She just stared out the window overlooking the Great River, with a pale, dim expression and an occasional whimper. Each day she seemed to become weaker, and finally I asked Kebu to take me to the midwives' chambers, hoping they would know a cure for her melancholy.

Puah was there. When I asked for her help, she sighed. "There are many grieving mothers in Egypt now. Ever since the king ordered that male babies be thrown into the Nile, many homes know this sorrow."

Horrified, I blurted out, "Why would the king order such a thing? And who would throw their own child into the Great River?"

Puah ignored my outburst. "Come with me, Amat-Bat-Ra," she said with a sigh. "Since the edict, fewer women seek our services—they hope they can hide their babies before the king's officers take the boys away. I have more time now to go to the market with you to get healing herbs for your mistress."

Kebu gave me leave to go, and I practically had to run to keep up with Puah as she wound her way through the stalls buying, to my surprise, food and general supplies. Finally, she came to an herb vendor at the edge of the main marketplace, who nodded when he saw her. "Remain here!" Puah told me as she strode away into the smaller market, her packages grasped firmly in her hands. Several minutes passed. When she finally returned, her packages were gone. When I asked where she had been and what had happened to her purchases, she ignored me as she gathered the needed herbs, and we headed back to the palace.

The herbs seemed to help Bat-Ra, and she began to eat and grow stronger. Yet her eyes remained dull and lifeless, and she rarely spoke. Her body was healing, but not her spirit. Once, as I brushed her hair, she took my hand—maybe to thank me, or perhaps just because she was lonely. The midwife had instructed the prince to stay away until she healed, and the other servants kept their distance, fearing the cloud of death hovering about her. Kebu and a few of the other eunuchs continued to attend her, but I was her constant companion. I know we were not really friends, but perhaps allies, trying to get through each day as best we could.

Now each week I accompanied Puah to the market to replenish our supplies of fresh herbs. Each expedition was the same: she bought food and supplies, left me with the herb vendor, went off on her own, returned without her packages, and bought more herbs, and we headed home.

I grew more and more curious until one day I followed Puah as she zigzagged through the maze of alleyways and stalls, stopping in a small courtyard. In the shadow of a nearby doorway, I watched as she hugged another woman about our age and gave her the packages. I heard snippets of their whispered conversation: "How much longer?" Puah asked. "Send Elzaphan with word to Kebu. Shiphrah and I will try to come."

Right then, as Puah turned to leave, she caught sight of me in the shadows.

"What are you doing here, Amat-Bat-Ra?!" she hissed, her eyes flashing with anger and then panic as she grabbed me and whisked me back to the herb vendor.

All I could think of was how much trouble I'd be in when she told Kebu that I disobeyed. I would be beaten. Or I would be banned from the market. Or we would no longer be friends. I so wanted a friend!

As we slowly walked back to the palace, my fear took hold and I started to cry. Puah finally stopped and looked at me. "I'm sorry I yelled at you, Amat-Bat-Ra. You must never tell anyone what you saw or heard. If you do, we could both be sent to the prison or even killed."

"I'm so sorry!" I cried. "I didn't mean to spy on you. I was just so curious. Who was that girl? Who is Elzaphan?"

"I am sorry, but I put you at great risk. You must forget what you heard."

"Please, Puah. I want to know. If you're in trouble I want to help. Aren't we friends? Maybe my mistress can help."

And then it all poured out of her like the Great River when it rises over its banks. The bitter lives of the Hebrew slaves. The Egyptian midwives who were defying the king's order that all the Hebrew boys be killed—and not only sparing the babies' lives, but bringing food to their suffering families. The king's discovery that the midwives had not been carrying out his order—including her own mother, the palace midwife, who had since been confined to her chambers except for royal births. The king's new edict that every Egyptian had to throw the male babies into the river. The Hebrew women's desperate attempts to hide their pregnancies, sneak away into the fields to give birth, and conceal the boys. And, since their mother's confinement, Puah and Shiphrah's decision to become defiant midwives too. With Kebu's knowledge, the two were sneaking out of the palace to help the Hebrew women in their labor. The woman I'd spotted at the courtyard was their friend Miriam, whose mother, Yocheved, was pregnant again. Everyone was worried. If Yocheved gave birth to a boy, how could they save him?

What Puah told me was terrifying and thrilling at the same time. Kebu and the midwives dared to defy the king! Yet I shared Puah's distress at the brutality of the edict. Bat-Ra had suffered so at the loss of her children; I could only imagine the pain of the Hebrew women. With the sorrow of so much loss in the palace, how could our king impose such cruelty on others, even if they were only slaves like me?

Once Puah confided in me, I became part of the grand conspiracy—the midwives, the Hebrew slaves, Kebu, and now, me. I stood guard for Puah and Miriam when they met in the market and helped Kebu dispatch messages to Shiphrah and Puah or sometimes Elzaphan, Miriam's cousin, whom Shiphrah secretly loved. I believed it was what my gods would have wanted.

Meanwhile, Bat-Ra continued to grieve at the loss of her children. Most days she stood on her balcony looking out onto the Great River. I wondered what she was thinking as she watched the river flow. When I looked at the river, I could only imagine drowning babies and the suffering of their mothers. And I feared that someday Hathor, the god of motherhood, would have her vengeance.

As we looked out the window one morning, I saw Elzaphan in the garden below. Sensing something was afoot, I made excuses to Bat-Ra and went to meet him. "Tell them it's time," he whispered and then hurried away.

I knew what he meant: Miriam's mother was about to have her child! I found Kebu, relayed the message, and prayed to my gods to save that child!

"What happened?" I asked Puah two days later, as soon as we left the palace grounds on our way to market. "So far it's been . . . a miracle," she said. "We were afraid when we saw it was a boy, but suddenly Miriam's home was filled with light, and somehow we knew the gods were looking down upon this child. Like your mistress, the child came very early, but he is healthy and strong. They are doing their best to hide him, hoping he will not cry out. There are inspections all the time, and one never knows when the guards will come."

"If they hear a cry, how do they know it is a boy, and not a girl?" I asked. "Surely there are girl babies born to the Hebrews, and they are permitted."

Puah suddenly stopped walking, and I could see her thinking. "Amat-Bat-Ra, you're brilliant! We just need to make sure there are other babies there. If all the babies cry, no one will suspect there is a hidden child. Miriam and Yocheved know the Hebrew women who gave birth to girls, and there are Egyptian women who help hide and protect the boys. Some have even adopted them when their own births have gone badly. Surely there are enough mothers in Egypt to protect Miriam's baby brother. I know this can work!"

I immediately thought of Bat-Ra and wondered if she would adopt another woman's child after losing her own. It seemed out of the question, but the thought nagged at me. She was still so sad, it made my heart ache for her. Maybe there was a way to help both my mistress and Puah's friends?

I told Puah what I was thinking.

"It's a big risk," she replied, "but still . . . we should explore it."

I knew exactly how I would approach my mistress. Her spirits had lifted a bit, and she seemed less ill-tempered, so the next time we stood together on her balcony overlooking the Nile, I summoned the courage to speak to her without her permission.

"My mistress, what do you see when you look at the Great River?"

She seemed startled to hear my voice, but not angry. She actually smiled, looked back at the Great River, and said, "I think about how nice it would be to feel the cooling waters on my body. I dream that Hapi, who causes the Great River to rise, will wash over me and make me fertile again, like he washes over our land and makes our fields green. And when I emerge cleansed and pure, Hathor will forgive me for whatever I did to displease her, and she will bless me with a child."

Her words were whispered as if she were praying, and we just stood silently together for several moments. And then she turned to me and uttered the very question I had hoped she would ask of me: "Amati, what do you see when you stand beside me on this balcony?"

"Mistress," I said, very softly and carefully, "it is not just what I see, but also what I hear. When it is very quiet, and the wind blows a certain way, I hear the cries of women upstream. Can you hear them? I fear that the Great River is bringing not life, but death."

"Death? No, Amati, the Nile brings life to our people. We eat of its bounty, and its healing waters give life to the trees and the fields that grow our food. I have not heard any such cries. What is going on upstream?"

I took a deep breath. "Children are drowning, My Lady," I said ever more softly. "The Hebrew babies are being cast into the Great River . . . on you father's orders. The mothers scream . . . I feel so sad for them, as I have for you . . . I cannot help but remember your cries when you lost your own children . . ."

"How dare you speak of that!" she retorted, her voice rising sharply. "And how dare you compare me, Pharaoh's daughter, to a Hebrew slave! Someday I will have a son who will be the king of Egypt. Leave me now, before I can no longer contain my anger!"

I ran out of the room crying. What had I done! Had I made a fatal error?

In the days that followed, I quietly continued my duties, hoping my mistress might forgive my indiscretion.

One day, as she stood on her balcony, she called me to her. I could see that she had been crying.

"Amati," she whispered, "I hear them now. I cannot stop hearing them. My heart aches for them, and for me, and for all the children. I keep looking for the babies in the Great River as it flows by . . ."

With that she threw her arms around me and began sobbing.

I held her until her heaving subsided. And then I took a deep breath and steeled myself to ask her that dangerous question that just maybe could help ease her pain and also help Yocheved and Miriam and Elphazan and Puah and Shiphrah find a way to save that one, special Hebrew child.

"Do you want one?"

"What? Do I want one? What do you mean?"

"My Lady, please do not be angry. I have heard that there are women who, like you, have known the loss of a child. And they have taken Hebrew children to raise as their own, saving them from Hapi's waters . . ."

I stopped mid-sentence. What a risk I was taking! If she protested, I would be exposed, and Puah and Shiphrah's lives would also be endangered. But now, my mistress's cries were not only for herself and her own suffering, but also for the pain of all those other mothers. For her, as for me, the Great River was contaminated by death. Still, would she be willing to defy her own father's order? I had to find out.

". . . and I believe I can get a baby for you if it would please you and bring you comfort."

I was astonished by how quickly my mistress embraced the idea. "If such a child is taken from the river," she pondered, "then Father's decree will still be fulfilled. He did not exactly say that the boys must drown, only that they must be sent into the water. And if we receive a Hebrew child from the water, then it is a gift from Hapi that must be accepted. Surely that would please Hathor . . ."

Then she turned to me. "But how can we keep a baby from drowning before we are able to reach him?"

My heart was singing! This must be what the gods wanted of us.

Puah and I made our plans. Two days hence, Miriam and her mother would place the baby in a dry basket at the river's edge not far from the palace. Miriam would keep watch to make sure it stayed afloat. Bat-Ra and I would go to the Great River at the designated time and "find" the basket.

The gods were indeed with us. On the date we had set, the khamsin winds were blowing strong, so no one would question Bat-Ra's desire to cool off by the river. We insisted that Bat-Ra's other servants join us so they could "witness" our miraculous discovery. While they strolled along the shore, we kept our eye on the water. Suddenly Bat-Ra stretched out her arm and pointed to a basket floating not far from us. "Amati, look! There's something in the water. Retrieve it for me now!"

I plunged into the cool waters with a leap of faith and hope, fetching the basket as she had commanded. Peering inside, she loudly exclaimed, "Hapi, the god of the Nile, has delivered a child to the princess of Egypt!"

Just then, Miriam stepped out from the reeds where she had been hiding and offered to find a wet nurse for the child, just as we had rehearsed, so the other servants would hear and corroborate our story.

Before Miriam ran off to get Yocheved, who would be able to nurse her own son, she whispered, "May you be blessed by your gods and mine, My Lady. My people shall call you Bat-Yah, for surely you have done the will of Yah, the God of my people, as well as your own. May the blessing of paradise be your reward for the great mercy you have done on this day."

CLASSICAL COMMENTARY AND MIDRASH:
Princess, Protector, Prophet

In the beginning chapters of Exodus, the Israelites' miraculous redemption from slavery starts with the dramatic tale of the birth of Moses. The Egyptians have enslaved the Hebrews, and Pharaoh has decreed that their male infants should be killed. After the midwives disobey Pharaoh's command, Pharaoh orders all Egyptians to see to it that the male children are thrown into the Nile, though it is unclear whether this edict is meant to apply to all children born in Egypt or just to the Hebrews. When Moses is born, he is delivered from the river by none other than Pharaoh's daughter.

While there are ample commentaries that discuss aspects of Moses' birth, his parents Amram and Jochebed, his siblings Miriam and Aaron, and his childhood ordeal, very little has been written about Pharaoh's daughter or her servant, his unnamed saviors. We are left to wonder who they were, how they came to be at the river at just the right moment, and why they defied Pharaoh to save a Hebrew child.

Although the classical midrashim surrounding Moses' birth, his family, and his early concealment are not directly related to the character of Pharaoh's daughter, a quick review of the classical commentaries surrounding his birth will provide insight into the rabbinic view of his surprising rescue by the princess of Egypt. At the beginning of Exodus 2, the text states that Amram marries Jochebed, who is not yet named, and they have a son, whom they keep hidden for three months because of Pharaoh's decree that male infants are to be killed. Fearing his discovery, his mother sets him adrift in the Nile under the watchful eye of his sister, Miriam, to see what will befall him.

A well-known midrash asks why the text says Amram married and had a son when we already know that he and his wife had two children, Miriam and Aaron. One would presume the two were already married and that the text should have said he had "another" son or that it would have referenced all the children. The midrash suggests that Amram and his wife had Miriam and Aaron, but then, due to the decree, Amram divorced his wife so as not to risk having a son who would be killed. The other Israelites followed suit. A wise and outspoken Miriam chastised her father, reminding him that Pharaoh's decree applied only to the male babies, whereas Amram's actions would prevent the birth of girls as well and thus was even more severe. Thereupon Amram remarried Jochebed, and they had another son, Moses.[1]

Numerous rabbinic sources depict the difficulty in hiding the Hebrew children. According to midrash, Egyptians raided Hebrew homes and schemed to discover hidden babies.[2] For example, Egyptian women would take their own babies to Hebrew homes and make them cry, whereupon the hidden children would also cry and be reported to Pharaoh.[3]

Despite these challenges, Moses was successfully hidden for three months. To explain how that was possible and why for only three months, some rabbinic sources suggest that Jochebed had been three months pregnant when she and Amram remarried, but the Egyptians presumed her pregnancy did not begin until the consummation of their second marriage.[4] Other sources speculate that Moses was born three months premature, and therefore the Egyptians were not looking for him during that time.[5] Nonetheless, at birth, Moses was sturdy and strong as if he had been born full-term—and, miraculously, already circumcised.[6] The idea that Moses was born circumcised provides an explanation for how Pharaoh's daughter knew that he was a Hebrew child, even though in the biblical text there is no clear reference to him being circumcised.

Like other mythic figures from various cultures, Moses was said to be born glowing with a blazing light and with extraordinary qualities, including healing powers.[7] Scholars have noted the similarity of Moses' birth story to ancient mythologies about heroes from numerous cultures, including Akkadian, Sumerian, Greek, Roman, Persian, Indian, and Asian folklores. Common ancient literary motifs include special qualities of beauty and light, miraculous survival and rescue from water, adoption by a queen or princess or the reverse—a royal baby recovered from the water and raised by commoners, only later to ascend to the throne as a matter of rightful destiny.[8]

Why Was Pharaoh's Daughter at the Nile That Fateful Day?

We know little of Pharaoh's daughter from the biblical text itself, other than that she was bathing in the Nile, saw and retrieved the basket, or ark, and decided to adopt Moses, allowing him to be nursed by his own mother. She is such an important character, however, that the commentaries do fill in some elements of her story.

While the book of Exodus refers to her only as "Pharaoh's daughter," the Talmud associates her with a named daughter of Pharaoh referenced in 1 Chron. 4:18: "*And his Judahite wife bore Jered father of Gedor, Heber father of Soco, and Jekuthiel father of Zanoah. These were the sons of Bithiah daughter of Pharaoh, whom Mered married.*" Hence, throughout rabbinic literature the woman in the Exodus saga becomes known as Bithiah—or, more commonly, Batyah, meaning "daughter of Yah [God]."

Earlier non-rabbinic sources provide alternative names for Pharaoh's daughter. Both Josephus and the book of *Jubilees* offer a variation of the biblical story in which Pharaoh's daughter is called Thermuthis.[9] These and other sources also suggest that Pharaoh's daughter was barren, which helps to explain why she would adopt a Hebrew child.[10] However, that explanation is inconsistent with the depiction in 1 Chronicles, which lists numerous children to the woman named Bithiah. The commentaries explain this discrepancy by suggesting that all the listed names refer to her single adopted son, Moses, who was known by many names based on his different characteristics.[11]

In the 1 Chronicles verse cited above, Pharaoh's daughter is married to a man who is not a prince of Egypt, and she is referred to as a "*Judahite*" (*hayehudiyyah*) woman, which begs the question of how Pharaoh's daughter transformed into a Jewish woman. The rabbis explain that she gave up idol worship and converted to the Israelite faith. Her bathing in the river was, in effect, an immersion in a *mikveh*, by which she cleansed herself from the idol worship of the palace.[12] Because she showed mercy to baby Moses, she was among the few permitted to enter paradise while still alive.[13]

As might be expected, most of the traditional commentary is reserved for the moment in which Pharaoh's daughter rescues Moses. The verse is parsed at length, with each phrase explored for its deeper meaning: "*The daughter of Pharaoh came down to bathe in the Nile, while her maidens walked along the Nile. She spied the basket among the reeds and sent her slave girl* [amatah] *to fetch it*" (Exod. 2:5).

Several questions logically arise from the text. Why was she bathing publicly in the Nile, which would be an unusual thing for a princess of Egypt to do? Why were her maidens walking along the Nile rather than remaining with the princess? How did she see the basket when, presumably, no one else saw it? Who was the slave girl, and why wasn't she with the other handmaids who were walking along the river? Also, in that last phrase, the Hebrew word *amatah* is ambiguous and the subject of a great deal of commentary, discussed later.

As noted, a common strand in the midrash associates Pharaoh's daughter's dip in the river with a *mikveh*, explaining that she had joined the Israelite faith and went to the Nile to cleanse herself from idol worship. Alternatively, numerous sources propose that Pharaoh's daughter was plagued with leprosy and sought the healing waters of the Nile. Moses was presumed to have special healing powers, and she was cured the moment she rescued him from the water.[14] Still others declare there was a heat wave; hence the unusual circumstance of a princess bathing so publicly in the Nile.[15] Sforno refutes the notion that she would have been bathing in the Nile; instead, he suggests, she was not "*in*" but rather "*above*" the river, in her bedchamber overlooking the water. This is based on a literal translation of the Hebrew phrase *al ha-y'or* ("*on*" or "*over*" the river) instead of *b'ha-y'or* ("in" the river).[16]

Biblical commentators wrestled with the image of the princess's maidens abandoning her at the shoreline to stroll (walk) along the riverbank. By way of explanation, several sources associate the Hebrew word for "*walking*" with "heading toward death," a nuance found elsewhere in the biblical text. According to this talmudic interpretation, the maidens tried to dissuade their mistress from saving the child, arguing that it would be unseemly for the king's daughter herself to disobey the decree. As punishment for trying to prevent the rescue of Moses, the angel Gabriel struck them down:

"*And her maidens walked along,* [holekhot] *etc.*" [Ex. 2:5] R. Joḥanan said: The word for "*walk*" means nothing else than death; and thus it says, "*Behold, I am going* [holekh] *to die. And she saw the ark among the reeds.*" [Ex. 2:5]. When [the maidens] saw that she wished to rescue Moses, they said to her, "Mistress, it is the custom of the world that when a human king makes a decree, though everybody else does not obey it, at least his children and the members of his household obey it; but thou dost transgress thy father's decree!" Gabriel came and beat them to the ground.[17]

Yet if this interpretation of the text is correct, how was it that a slave girl remained with her mistress in order to fetch the child? One explanation offered is that the angel spared one servant in deference to the princess, who, by virtue of her station, should not be left alone and who, due to her compassion, deserved to retain at least one attendant.[18] A related explanation is that the remaining servant was the senior servant, who had stayed with her mistress while the others departed to give the princess more privacy.[19]

Further parsing Exod. 2:5, the classical sources consider the phrase "*She spied the basket among the reeds*," speculating as to why the princess alone saw the basket. The talmudic text quoted above infers that she intended all along to rescue the baby, whom she knew to be a Hebrew child. However, the twelfth-century French commentator Rabbi Shmuel ben Meir (Rashbam) provides a simpler explanation—the ark was visible only to one who was actually in the water; the reeds hid it from those walking along the bank. Hence, only the princess and the servant standing with her could see it, while the maidens could not.[20]

The Servant with the Outstretched Arm

In the continuation of the talmudic text, the rabbis debate the meaning of the Hebrew word *amatah* in Exod. 2:5, which JPS translates as "*her slave girl*." In this context, it is ambiguous: it could be translated either as "*she sent her slave girl* [amatah] *to fetch it*" or "*she stretched out her arm*." The use of this particular Hebrew word is puzzling as well since the other women in the entourage, who also may have been servants, are referred to by a different Hebrew word, *na'arot* ("*maidens*").

Conducting a grammatical analysis, Rashi concurs with the view that the word means "servant." However, he also explains that those who believe it refers to her arm are playing on the Hebrew word *amah*, meaning "cubit," suggesting that miraculously her arm extended several cubits in order to reach the ark and save the child.[21] In explaining the use of a different term for this particular servant, Sforno notes that it was providence; this servant was special and could be trusted, whereas one of her usual handmaids might have thrown the baby back into the water.[22]

The text of Exod. 2:6, which states, "*When she opened it, she saw that it was a child, a boy crying. She took pity on it and said, 'This must be a Hebrew child,'*" also can be interpreted in different ways. Most commentaries presume "*she*" refers to Pharaoh's daughter, yet a simple reading of the text could refer to either the slave girl who was sent to fetch the basket or Pharaoh's daughter. Those who say it was Pharaoh's daughter are left to explain why the princess opened the basket instead of her servant. Some commentaries consider it to her credit that she, a princess, would send away her only remaining servant, in order to open the ark herself in private and ensure that the child inside would be safe.[23]

This verse also contains a redundancy: "*she saw that it was a child* [yeled]*, a boy* [na'ar] *crying.*" Since nothing in the text is deemed to be extraneous, the commentaries propose various meanings to each phrase. "*She saw it*" refers to his glowing countenance, or the *Shekhinah* (Divine Presence).[24] He was "*a child*" in age, but the strength of his voice made him sound like "*a boy*" crying.[25] Alternatively, "*a child*" refers to Moses, while "*a boy*" refers to Aaron, his older brother, who had been wrapped up along with Moses in the ark and was the boy who was crying.[26]

Pharaoh's Daughter, the Prophet

Identifying Moses as "*this*" Hebrew child, Pharaoh's daughter is presumed to have had foresight that he was the child that Pharaoh's astrologers had divined would overthrow him one day. Their prediction that the usurper would die by water had led to the decree to drown all the male babies.[27] The moment Jochebed placed him in the river, she fulfilled their prophesy and the astrologers no longer saw their vision, since he was presumed to have drowned. Consequently, the order was lifted that very day. According to legend, Pharaoh's daughter envisioned all that, and since the ruling was no longer in effect, she knew she would not be violating her father's order and she would be able to adopt the baby and raise him in the palace.[28]

Having identified the child as a Hebrew baby, Pharaoh's daughter sets about to find a wet nurse for him. There is no logical reason for the wet nurse to be a Hebrew woman, so the midrash offers an explanation. Numerous women volunteered to nurse the child on the princess's behalf, but Moses would not suckle from a non-Hebrew breast; only then does Miriam step forward and recommend trying a Hebrew wet nurse.[29] When Miriam brings Jochebed to Pharaoh's daughter, the princess commands her to "*take* [heilikhi] *this child.*" Playing on the Hebrew word's similarity to *ha shelikhi*, meaning "this is yours," the Talmud and commentaries read this as another example of her unwitting prophesy. Thus, even though she had not been informed, Pharaoh's daughter knew Moses was Jochebed's child.[30]

If Pharaoh's daughter was indeed a prophetess, is it possible that she could foresee not only that the child would challenge her father, but also the dramatic events that would transpire in Egypt? Could she have imagined that her act of mercy would bring plagues upon her people, including death of the firstborn, including perhaps herself? Did she know, and intend, for her act to lead to a revolution and freedom for the Hebrews? Did she know that the gods of Egypt would be no match for the God of the Hebrews? Or was she simply a woman, driven by her own despair, moved by the cries of an innocent child, heartbroken by the world's cruelty, and compelled to act out of mercy and integrity? Regardless of her motivations, throughout rabbinic literature, Pharaoh's daughter is deemed to have acted honorably, and the reward for her kindness is paradise.

AUTHOR'S COMMENTARY: *A Conspiracy of Women*

The "Pharaoh's Daughters" trilogy (chapters 5–7) looks at three stories of Egyptian women: Potiphar's wife, the midwives Puah and Shiphrah, and Pharaoh's daughter. Each tale gives voice to non-Israelite women who play pivotal roles in the Exodus narrative but are understated, unnamed, or underappreciated in the biblical text. These modern renderings do not "convert" them, as the rabbis often did, in order to connect them to the Jewish people. Rather, the women are envisioned within their own Egyptian settings, interacting with the Israelites' narrative as a result of their own moral character instead of divine intervention.

Finding connections between adjacent narratives is a standard midrashic technique, and it seems logical to connect the story of Moses' birth and his rescue by Pharaoh's daughter to the previous story of the midwives' conspiracy ("The Sacred Sisterhood," chapter 6). Several characters overlap in both tales, including the midwives Puah and Shiphrah and two invented minor characters, the servant Kebu and the Israelite slave Elzaphan, both of whom are friends and collaborators in the conspiracy to save Moses. Numerous elements of the classical midrash are woven into this version of events, including the association of Puah's name with her "cooing" to soothe the women in labor, the midwives' meritorious acts in not only saving the Israelite babies but also providing food and other support, the lengths to which Israelite women went to conceal their infants, and the idea that Pharaoh imprisoned the midwives for their disobedience.[31] These ideas are more fully explored in chapter 6.

Jewish tradition gives great weight to the power of names, and considerable thought was given to naming unnamed biblical women in this midrash. As mentioned, rabbinic sources associate Pharaoh's daughter with the woman named in 1 Chron. 4:18 as *Bithiah daughter of Pharaoh*." Later commentators refer to her as Batya or Bat-Yah, "daughter of God" (*Yah* is an abbreviated form of *YHVH*, the Hebrew name for God), and suggest that she threw her lot in with the Israelite people, rejecting idol worship and converting to the Israelite faith. In contrast, this midrash depicts her as the biblical text says she was—an Egyptian princess, an idol worshiper, and a woman who nonetheless adopted a Hebrew child, whom her father had condemned to death. Given all this, the name Bat-Ra (daughter of Ra) seemed a more appropriate moniker for the presumed daughter of the Pharaoh Raamses. Since Ra was the Egyptian god of the sun and creator of all life, Bat-Ra would be the Egyptian equivalent of Bat-Yah—a mirroring of the name given to her in the classical midrash—which is emphasized in Miriam's blessing at the end of the modern retelling of her story.

Similar consideration was given to naming Pharaoh's daughter's unnamed servant. The name Amat, or Amatah, in Arabic means "slave" or "servant" and is typically coupled with the name of the god or the individual served. Here it is used both as her name and as her role. Her mistress refers to her as Amati, which means "my servant," while others refer to her as Amat-Bat-Ra, "the servant of Bat-Ra."

In creating the character of Amat-Bat-Ra, this midrash lifts up one of the many unnamed woman in the Bible. Though a mere servant, she is the actual rescuer of baby Moses, and yet rabbinic literature simply overlooks her, ostensibly because she is not deemed worthy of a second thought. Nonetheless, some translations offered for the ambiguous text of Exod. 2:5–6 do amplify the servant's role, suggesting that it was the slave girl, and not Pharaoh's daughter, who retrieved the ark, opened it, recognized the Hebrew boy within, and took pity on the child. As discussed, the rabbis note that the obscure Hebrew phrase "*vatishlaḥ et amatah*" (Exod. 2:5) could mean either "*she sent her servant*" or "*she stretched out her arm*," but there is a third interpretation the rabbis do not consider: "*she sent Amatah*," using the name of her servant.

Once named, Amat-Bat-Ra suddenly became a person of interest, practically begging to have her character discovered. Who was she, and why was she there? What was her relationship with the princess she served? Why was she the one to fetch the ark?

Elements of the classical midrash are incorporated into this retelling of events in numerous ways. References to the glowing light emitted from Moses, Pharaoh's daughter's room overlooking the Nile, and the heat wave that drove her to take a dip in the Nile River are all found in rabbinic sources. In considering what might have motivated her to save a Hebrew child, the explanation offered in several early sources that she was barren and longed for a child seemed logical and becomes a primary feature of this midrash.

This midrash turns on its head the commentaries describing the lengths to which the Egyptians went to locate hidden Hebrew children by prompting the babies to reveal themselves. In "Amat-Bat-Ra, the Servant Savior," the Egyptian women are complicit, not in betraying, but in protecting the Hebrew babies: they bring their own children to the Israelite homes in order to mask the cries of the Hebrew infants and thus save them from discovery. Similarly, whereas traditional midrash suggests that the princess's entourage tried to dissuade her from rescuing the child, in this retelling, her handmaids serve as witnesses to corroborate the conspirators' version of events.

Furthermore, whereas the classical midrash interprets the Israelite saga as the unfolding of a divine plan, this modern midrash explores the human motivations and personalities that influence both the Hebrew and Egyptian characters. Dismissing the human element, the classical commentaries ignore or fail to recognize the most likely impetus for the heroic actions of the Egyptian midwives, Pharaoh's daughter, and their compatriots: the women's maternal instincts and moral integrity. While the classical sources credit divine intervention for the events leading up to the Israelites' redemption, this midrash depicts direct action by brave women determined to preserve life. The cruelty of Pharaoh and his taskmasters is outdone by the compassion, conviction, and courage of these women.

The author optimistically believes the actions of the women revealed in this modern midrash is more reflective of human nature than what is depicted in the classical midrash. In "Amat-Bat-Ra," as well as "The Sacred Sisterhood," there is an ever-expanding network of women who collaborate and conspire to save the Hebrew children and, in particular, Moses. These women deserve to be named, their stories told, and their heroism celebrated.

8

Shelomith Bat Dibri

The Blasphemer's Mother

BIBLICAL TEXT: *Leviticus 24:10–14*

There came out among the Israelites a man whose mother was Israelite and whose father was Egyptian. And a fight broke out in the camp between that half-Israelite and a certain Israelite. The son of the Israelite woman pronounced the Name in blasphemy, and he was brought to Moses—now his mother's name was Shelomith daughter of Dibri of the tribe of Dan—and he was placed in custody, until the decision of God should be made clear to them. And God spoke to Moses, saying: Take the blasphemer outside the camp; and let all who were within hearing lay their hands upon his head, and let the community leadership stone him.

MODERN MIDRASH: *Testament of Shelomith*

My son! Oh, not my son! Dear God, let it not be so! Let them kill me instead! I'm the one who sinned. I'm the guilty one. Punish me, not my poor boy. Can't you see his innocence? Don't You understand his confusion? It was *my* sin that killed him . . . and *Your* harsh laws. Yes, God, *Your* laws, and Your holier-than-thou Moses. He would kill my only son for the sake of Your name—that is a greater act of blasphemy than my son ever committed.

Yes, my child cursed and used Your name in vain. But You knew his heart. You knew his frustration and his pain. You knew his longing to find a place among our people—a place denied him by the fanatics among us. And yet, You used him to make a point and to set an example, lest others challenge You and Your precious laws as he did . . . as I did.

Now let history record the full tale, not only the crime and the punishment. Let the generations to come consider the deeds *and* the motives, and let the descendants of the executioners judge the Judge.

We were in Egypt for so long. We were hungry and oppressed . . . but You already know that. Suffering was the only world I knew until the day I saw him. The son of the most ruthless taskmaster was handsome and striking in his fine, clean clothes . . . and what confidence and grace he possessed! He was not at all like the Hebrew men working beside me, bent over and beaten into submission. There was a mysterious sadness darkening his features as he watched us work.

At first I thought his father might beat him also, but then I saw that brutal taskmaster put his arm around his son with such warmth and tenderness that tears welled in my eyes. *How could one so evil love a child,* I wondered.

And then I understood the darkness in his eyes. I felt his pain as he looked up into the face of his father with a yearning more anguished than any feelings I had yet known, a longing to understand how the man he most admired and loved could behave so cruelly. I understood in that moment that this son of the taskmaster was a slave himself, imprisoned on the wrong side. He belonged to my people as I belonged to him.

We met in secret and conceived a child. When my people saw my ripening belly, they taunted me and called me a whore. They said my child would be a bastard and should not be born.

I thought only of my beloved, the father of my child. Surely our love for one another could overcome all obstacles. But he could not stand to see me ridiculed.

He took up his father's whip to stop their jeers. And just then Moses the son of Pharaoh's daughter came upon us. In his self-righteous arrogance he turned the lash upon my champion and killed him.

Not long after that, I gave birth to my precious son, and I was shunned for disgracing my family. As my son grew to resemble his father, the taskmaster was constantly reminded of his loss, and in his anger he became even more cruel. Then I was blamed for causing even greater misery to my people. Distraught and lonely, I poured all my love into my son, trying to shield him from my pain.

We remained at the fringes of our slave society until the wondrous events of our people's deliverance unfolded. And then, suddenly we found ourselves in the wilderness. It was like we had been born anew—given a chance to redeem ourselves for past errors. I joined Miriam and the other women in their songs and celebration. We embraced and greeted one another with enthusiasm as if we were meeting for the first time.

But that feeling of togetherness passed. Some could not forget the taskmaster's blood in my son's veins. They tormented him and mocked me. Every innocent gesture was cause for ridicule. They teased me because of my name, Shelomith. If I greeted them with "shalom," they called me "Shalom-Shelomith," insinuating that I went around greeting people in an attempt to ingratiate myself with them. And they called me "Bat Dibri— the Chatty One," accusing me of flirting for simply having a conversation with a neighbor.

My son was not immune to the taunting, despite my efforts to protect him. We were isolated at the edge of the encampment, and he was ostracized and bullied. Where was the great Moses then? He'd been quick to murder my beloved for striking an Israelite in my defense but was nowhere to be found when my boy was being attacked. Did he ever speak up on our behalf or try to bring us within the camp? Did he insist that others accept us or that they cease abusing my innocent child? No! He showed no remorse for killing my beloved and no sympathy for our son's dilemma. You would think that since his own children were also half-Israelite he might have been more sympathetic to our situation. But perhaps that was his excuse; maybe Moses did not stand up for us because he was afraid the others would reject his sons as they had mine.

My beautiful Egyptian son . . . His dark eyes so like his father's were clouded by the same sadness that had broken my heart years before. Yet hope still burned in his soul as he sought a place for us within the tribal settlement. In vain he pleaded with Moses to judge in our favor, to allow us to dwell with my father's people among the tribe of Dan. But justice and mercy did not belong to the half-breed—just inflexible, uncompromising law. And the law said tribal identity could come only from the father, not the mother. My son's Egyptian birthright had been left behind at the Sea of Reeds.

His hope was shattered, his faith in justice denied. Of course he cursed the God of Moses, the God who had brought him to freedom only to enslave him by bigotry and hatred! And, like his father before him, he struck out in anger.

Once again, there was Moses, fortified by his laws, judging the son as he had judged his father and condemning him to death for the sin of his birth. No empathy or compassion for the tragedy of his lonely, dejected life. No thought for the mother, who dared to love, who saw her beloved murdered, who suffered ridicule and rejection, and who brought a dark-eyed son into the world despite it all.

So . . . let the Judge declare my boy guilty. Let the so-called blasphemer be put to stones. And the Judge shall be judged by the love of a mother named Shelomith.

CLASSICAL COMMENTARY AND MIDRASH:
The Biblical Tale of the Blasphemer

The "Blasphemer" story in the middle of Leviticus provides a disturbing view of ancient justice. In this brief and cryptic passage, we learn of a woman, Shelomith bat Dibri of the tribe of Dan, whose unnamed half-Egyptian son gets into a fight with an Israelite, blasphemes, is tried before Moses, and is put to death for that crime.

Among the most obvious questions arising from the text are the identities of the mother and father of this half-Israelite, half-Egyptian child. How did Shelomith come to have a half-Egyptian son? Who, and where, was the Egyptian father? Further, Shelomith of the tribe of Dan is the only woman named in the book of Leviticus; why, among all the women in the wilderness, was she given a name and pedigree? What provoked her son's fight with an Israelite, and what led him to commit blasphemy?

The Hebrew phrase *ben ish Mitzri*, *"son of an Egyptian man"* (Lev. 24:10) is as cryptic in the Hebrew as it is in English. Using the classic midrashic technique of analogy, Rashi and other commentators presume the phrase *"Egyptian man"* in this passage relates to the same *"Egyptian man"* whom Moses had killed after witnessing him beating an Israelite slave (Exod. 2:11–12).[1] If we accept this analogy and presume it is the same man, then other questions arise. What was the nature of the relationship between Shelomith, presumably an Israelite slave, and the Egyptian man? Did they have an illicit love affair, or did the Egyptian rape her? Was there a connection between the taskmaster's beating of the Israelite and his relationship with Shelomith?

Most commentators accept the traditional explanation that the Egyptian forced himself upon Shelomith. According to the most common version of this midrash, the Egyptian overseer lusted after Shelomith and ordered her Israelite husband away in the middle of the night. The Egyptian then entered her house and had relations with her, while Shelomith believed her husband was still in her bed.[2] Later the Egyptian sought to kill her husband, prompting Moses's intervention. According to this interpretation, Shelomith shared some of the blame for the situation because she willingly slept with him, even though she believed him to be her husband.[3] Exodus Rabbah weaves these themes together:

> The Rabbis said: The taskmasters were Egyptians but the officers were Israelites, one taskmaster being appointed over ten officers and one officer over ten Israelites. The taskmasters used go to the officers' homes early in the morning to drag them out to work at cock-crow. Once an Egyptian taskmaster went to a Jewish officer and set eyes upon his wife who was beautiful without blemish. He waited for cock-crow, when he dragged the officer out of his house and then returned to lie down with the woman who thought that it was her husband, with the result that she became pregnant from him. When her husband returned, he discovered the Egyptian emerging from his house. He then asked her: "Did he touch you?" She replied: "Yes,

for I thought it was you." When the taskmaster realised that he was caught, he made him go back to his hard labour, smiting him and trying to slay him. When Moses saw this, he knew by means of the Holy Spirit what had happened in the house and what the Egyptian was about to do in the field; so he said: "This man certainly deserves his death, as it is written: *And he that smiteth any man mortally shall surely be put to death* (Lev. 24:17). Moreover, since he cohabited with the wife of Dathan he deserves slaying, as it is said: *Both the adulterer and the adulteress shall surely be put to death*" (Lev. 20:10). Hence does it say: *And he looked this way and that way* (Ex. 2:12), namely, he saw what he did to him [Dathan] in the home and what he intended doing to him in the field.[4]

In a variant of this story, Shelomith smiled at the Egyptian taskmaster, encouraging him to stay behind after her husband left for the field.[5] In another version, when the Egyptian taskmaster entered their home to bring her husband to the fields, he was instantly smitten by Shelomith's beauty and compelled to claim her as his own.[6]

The midrashic assumption that the Egyptian father was the same Egyptian killed by Moses provides neat answers to questions that arise from this text, including the Egyptian's absence in the wilderness, where Shelomith and her son appear to be alone. It also explains why the man was beating the Israelite, who he was, and why Moses interceded. The death of the father by Moses' hand cleverly foreshadows the death of the son, also by Moses' decree. According to some sources, Moses killed the Egyptian with a curse, and so, too, his son was killed because of a curse.[7]

Who Were Shelomith and Her Husband?

In the passage cited previously, we glean that Shelomith was presumed to have been married to Dathan, an officer of the Israelites. Dathan is also thought to have been one of the two men Moses found fighting in the very next verse, along with his brother Abiram (Exod. 2:13). According to this midrash, Dathan and Abiram challenged Moses' authority to intercede and informed Pharaoh that Moses had killed the Egyptian, causing him to flee Egypt.[8] Dathan and Abiram are associated with numerous wicked deeds, like participating in Korah's notorious rebellion aimed at usurping Moses' leadership in the wilderness (Num. 16:1).[9] As punishment, God made the earth open up and swallow Korah, his followers, and their entire households (16:31–35). Although not mentioned specifically, if Shelomith was married to Dathan, we might wonder if she also would have been among the rebels who vanished that day.

The midrash provides several alternative identities for Shelomith's husband. In *Pirkei de-Rabbi Eliezer*, a midrashic collection from the eighth or ninth century, Shelomith is married to a man named Bedijah, a grandson of Dan, who was slain when the Egyptians raided the Israelites' homes to rape their wives and kill the men.[10] According to *Ḥizkuni*, a thirteenth-century commentary, her husband's name was Neriah.[11]

As for Shelomith herself, most commentaries and midrash take the fact that she uniquely is named among the women in the wilderness as a sign of shame, not honor.[12] The prevailing rabbinic presumption is that Shelomith alone was named because she was the only immoral woman of all those who left Egypt:

> R. Huna in the name of Bar Kappara said: Israel was redeemed from Egypt on account of four things . . . Whence do we know that they were not suspect of adultery? Because there was only one immoral woman and the Bible published her name, as it is said: *"And his mother's name was Shelomith, the daughter of Dibri."*[13]

Commentators also note the unusual placement of her name in the storyline—after her son commits blasphemy rather than in the introductory verse. Some see her not being named at the outset to her credit, suggesting that actually she was among those who brought her son to judgment. Others deduce that she was named only after he was brought to trial, because she defended him and in doing so her reputation was tarnished along with his.[14]

There is a rabbinic assumption that a person's nature is dictated by the circumstances of one's birth. Given this understanding, some sources blame the Egyptian father and others condemn Shelomith for their child's disgrace. Those who blame the father suggest that the evil act of the Egyptian taskmaster's rape of his mother established the child's character: "In every case the offspring follows the (nature of) the seed: if it be sweet, it will be due to the sweet (seed); if it be bitter, it will be due to the bitter (seed)."[15] Others explain that naming Shelomith was an indication that her genetic input predisposed her son to shame:

> By mentioning her name last, the Torah suggested that the original cause of such a terrible sin being committed was the mother of the sinner who had been guilty of a trespass. The baby grows out of the mother's blood, is nurtured for the length of the pregnancy by the mother's blood and even after the mother has given birth she nurses the child thus transmitting milk which originally was her blood. As a result of all this it is no more than reasonable that the child absorbs greater genetic input from his mother than from his father. This will eventually be reflected in his deeds which will reflect the mother's character more than that of the father.[16]

Any time a name is mentioned in the biblical text, the meaning of the name itself is the subject of midrashic interpretation. According to several commentaries, the specificity of Shelomith's lineage signifies that the shame caused by her son's blasphemy reflected not only on his mother and father, but also on his family and on the entire tribe of Dan.[17]

Numerous sources interpret the meaning of *Shelomith bat Dibri* in ways that reinforce the negative stereotype of a wanton woman. While the root of *Shelomith* is the same as for *shalom* (peace) and could be taken as a positive reference, when combined with *Dibri*, from the root *d-v-r*, meaning "to speak," Rashi and others portray her as a babbling, flirtatious woman with a loose tongue:

> *Shelomith* (connected with *shalom* "peace")—she was so called because she was always babbling: "Peace be with thee," "peace be with thee," "peace be with you"—she used to continually babble with

many words (she was a *bat dibri*)—she enquired after the health of everybody (Lev. R. 32:5). *Bat Dibri* (from the root *d-v-r* "to speak")—she was talkative—talking with any man, and in consequence of this she got into trouble.[18]

According to this interpretation, her name *Shelomith bat Dibri* does not mean "*Shelomith daughter of Dibri*," but rather "*Shelomith, the talkative* [or *chatty*] *one*"—implying that her loose character led to the events unfolding as they did and ultimately to her son's dishonor.

The Half-Israelite's Struggle

The only thing we know about the young man from the biblical text is that he was half-Israelite, half-Egyptian. Without additional information, it is logical to presume that the quarrel in which he was engaged had something to do with his lineage.

The ambiguity of the location might also provide a clue as to the nature of the argument. The text says that he "*came out*" among the Israelites, and yet the fight broke out "*in the camp*" (Lev. 24:10), leading to the question of whether he was outside or inside the camp. Since nothing in the biblical text is extraneous, commentators infer some relevance to the stated locations. Adding the reference to his mother's tribe of Dan, a picture begins to emerge in rabbinic texts:

But a wicked man, a rebel against the God of heaven, had come out of Egypt, the son of the Egyptian man who had killed the Israelite in Egypt, and had gone in unto his wife, who conceived and bore a son among the children of Israel. And while the Israelites were dwelling in the wilderness, he had sought to spread his tent in the midst of the tribe of the children of Dan; but they would not permit him, because in the arrangements of Israel every man dwelt with his family by the ensigns of the house of their fathers [not their mothers]. And they contended together in the camp.[19]

Being of mixed background, Shelomith and her son would have dwelled in the section of the camp reserved for the "mixed multitude." According to this depiction of events, her son *"went out"* from the mixed multitude encampment to the tribe of Dan in order to claim his mother's birthright. Once *"in the camp"* of Dan, the Israelites denied him a place to pitch his tent because the tribal designations were determined by the father's lineage, not the mother's.[20] Thus frustrated and dejected, Shelomith's son cursed God and was brought to Moses for judgment.

In a variation of this characterization of events, after being denied the right to pitch his tent with the tribe of Dan, Shelomith's son went to Moses to seek an exception to the rule. Rejected again, he *"went out"* from Moses's court and from there *"into the camp,"* whereupon the fight broke out. In this scenario, his anger was directed at both Moses and God, who could, but would not, make an accommodation for him and his mother. Ironically, the court to which he appealed for mercy was the same court that would soon condemn him to death.[21]

In yet another variant, during the argument, Shelomith's son learned that it was Moses who had killed his father, not by force, but through a curse. His own curse against Moses brings the story full circle.[22]

Employing the classical literary technique of playing on the juxtaposition of adjacent texts, some commentators connect the incident described in this passage with the section immediately preceding it, in which the Israelites receive laws regarding "showbread," the special loaves of bread to be prepared by the priests as an offering prior to the Sabbath. According to this interpretation, the half-Israelite ridiculed this practice, which led to an argument with others and his blasphemy.[23]

His presumed rejection of ritual practice illustrates a rabbinic disagreement as to whether the half-Israelite, half-Egyptian man was bound by the laws given at Sinai. If he was considered Egyptian, his rejection of the commandments given by the Israelites' God would not be surprising.[24] Still, the prohibition against blasphemy was one of the universal Noahide laws that would have applied to him regardless of his religious status.[25] That said, if he was considered a gentile, the punishment would have been by sword, whereas for an Israelite it was by stoning, as is the case in this story.[26] Ibn Ezra and others suggest that his Egyptian father had formally converted to Judaism, a clearly anachronistic reference, by interpreting the verse with a slightly different syntax than most translations. Instead of translating the text as, "*There came out among the Israelites a man whose mother was Israelite and whose father was Egyptian*," Ibn Ezra reads the verse more literally as "*There came out a son of an Israelite women, whose father was an Egyptian among the Israelites*."[27]

These rabbinic discussions help explain why the Israelites had to put the blasphemer in custody pending a determination of his punishment. Despite the clear evidence of his capital crime under Noahide laws, his religious status was unclear and therefore the proper punishment was also uncertain.

AUTHOR'S COMMENTARY: *A Mother's Anguish*

The story of the blasphemer is troubling on many levels. The ambiguity of his identity, the question of his status and place among the Israelites, and the dubious circumstances of his birth all contribute to the sad unfolding of events. At the center of all of that is Shelomith bat Dibri, a woman with a name but no voice.

The simple reading of this text tells us only that an Israelite woman named Shelomith bat Dibri had a son who was half-Egyptian. The fact that she is named at all, much less the only named woman in Leviticus, is cause for comment on her name. Since she is the mother of the notorious blasphemer, the rabbis are predisposed to seeing her as a negative character and take the various meanings of her name as evidence of her flirting and fawning persona. By contrast, in the sympathetic characterization in this modern midrash, the neighbors who have shunned Shelomith unfairly find fault with anything she does and use her name to make fun of her. It is ironic that Shelomith bat Dibri, who is accused of verbal transgressions and whose name itself refers to speaking, actually has no voice in the biblical text or later rabbinic interpretations. The retelling of events in "Testament of Shelomith" is an attempt to give her a voice of her own.

The fact that Shelomith is the only woman named in Leviticus is even more surprising when we consider that she actually has no role. Her unnamed son is the focus of the story, and the addition of his mother's name is a side comment with no obvious relevance to the story, except for the interpretations provided through midrash. For a change, it is the men in this story—her son and his father—who have no names. This comports with the general lack of interest in non-Israelite characters. In other modern midrash, the author has provided names for unnamed female characters; in this instance the male characters remain unnamed, keeping the focus on Shelomith and her point of view.

The classical midrash portrays a piteous version of her son's birth, presuming she was either raped or duped into sexual relations and guilty of licentious behavior regardless of the circumstances. According to ancient law, the mere fact of illicit relations between a man and a married woman constituted adultery for which both parties were guilty, irrespective of any extenuating circumstances. Sadly, even today, some countries retain such legal codes, and even rape victims have been found guilty of adultery. The rabbis also struggled with this concept, which was later abandoned, and those commentators who assigned moral blame to Shelomith imagined her to have been actively complicit in her liaison with the Egyptian father of her son.

Many commentaries assume that Shelomith was married to an Israelite man, yet nothing in the biblical text itself suggests that she was married. If we avoid the rabbis' leaps of midrashic fancy, we could just as easily interpret this text as a star-crossed love story. In this modern retelling of events, there has been no prior marriage and therefore no offense of adultery. Nor did the law prohibit having a relationship with a non-Israelite. Shelomith's "guilt" is only in violating cultural norms.

Imagining Shelomith's relationship with her son's father as a love affair leads to numerous questions, such as how she and the Egyptian met and fell in love, what happened when others found out about the affair, and why the Egyptian father is missing from the storyline. In "Testament of Shelomith," answers to many of these questions are revealed.

If we accept the linkage between this Egyptian father and the Egyptian killed by Moses, we would likely want to know those circumstances as well. Was the Egyptian overseer an evil brute beating a slave, as Moses presumed, or was he simply defending his beloved? Was Moses right to intercede, or did he jump to an erroneous conclusion that ultimately led to disastrous results for the protagonists? In the modern midrash, the foreshadowing of the son's death is more than a literary technique; it also depicts a cycle of violence that carries over from one generation to the next. The Egyptian taskmaster's son grows up witnessing his father's violence, and this learned behavior emerges as he violently strikes out to defend his lover. His bullied son also strikes out in anger, cursing and fighting out of his own frustration and rage. Moses too is locked in a violent cycle; having slain the father, he is the cause of the son's torment, and this eventually leads to his condemning the son to a gruesome death in punishment for his enraged response to the suffering Moses himself caused. The ripples of violence swirl around Shelomith, from the taskmaster, to her lover, to Moses, to her son, to the community that would stone him to death.

Although "Testament of Shelomith" does not accept the midrashic presumption of Shelomith's marriage to Dathan, an analogy can be made between these two characters. Dathan's character in both the biblical text and midrash is that of antagonist to the heroic Moses: he causes trouble, rejects Moses' counsel, denounces him to Pharaoh, and rebels against him in the wilderness. Likewise, Shelomith is an antagonist to Moses. She gives birth to a half-Egyptian child who is a constant unwanted reminder of the Israelites' past servitude, her son's demand for justice is a challenge to the newly ordained covenant, and her very presence will not allow Moses to forget his act of murder, for which he paid no price as dictated by that same law. Additionally, Shelomith and Moses seem to be locked in an epic battle, with love and mercy on one side and uncompromising devotion to God and law on the other. Her accusing, anguished rejection of Moses and his laws puts her right beside Dathan and the others who reject Moses' authoritarian leadership.

The classical sources depict Shelomith, the Egyptian, and their son as violators of social norms and law, who are punished accordingly. Conversely, in "Testament of Shelomith," these characters are reimagined as flawed human beings and victims—all casualties of an inflexible system of justice and discriminatory tribal norms overseen by its zealous guardian Moses. Yes, her son committed blasphemy, but given the extenuating circumstances, we might question the harshness of his punishment. We might ask whether the death penalty was the just sentence for a young man who committed an impulsive verbal crime in the context of being bullied, demoralized, and outraged by rules and social norms designed to prevent him from realizing his dreams.

Shelomith's actions are not depicted as either heroic or imprudent. She does not defy tradition to make a point—she simply fell in love. While others may have seen the Egyptian as the enemy or a forbidden relationship, she had no choice but to follow her heart. And her condemnation of Moses is neither an impulsive outburst like her son's nor a discourse on the legal system; it is the anguished reaction of a brokenhearted mother. At the end of "Testament of Shelomith," the blasphemer's sin is paralleled by Shelomith's own blasphemy in accusing Moses and God of lacking compassion and empathy. While Moses communes with God and executes the divine commands, Shelomith stands in judgment of them both, with all the audacity and bravado of a woman who has nothing left to lose. How we are to view her choices in the context of her life story and feelings is left to the reader.

Viewing this text critically and giving ourselves the latitude to question the traditional interpretations of this parable, we might find new lessons relevant to our own day and age. In fact, such reflective thinking is embedded within the evolution of Jewish law, as the rabbis themselves eventually eliminated the brutal punishments enumerated in the Bible and ameliorated some of the harsh provisions related to women. While our ancestors segregated insiders and outsiders in their encampment, we might instead seek a community of inclusion that embraces families of all types, including single parents, interfaith families, and individuals of different races and backgrounds. In imagining the struggles faced by Shelomith and her son, we might sympathize with those who feel ostracized or excluded and exhibit compassion for victims of bullying and discrimination. In the millennia since the story of the blasphemer was first told, our community has made progress on such matters, yet there is still much to do.

9

Miriam

Exiled by God, Dwelling Beyond the Camp

BIBLICAL TEXT: *Numbers 12:1–16*

Miriam and Aaron spoke against Moses because of the Cushite woman he had taken [into his household as his wife]: "He took a Cushite woman!"

They said, "Has God spoken only through Moses? Has [God] not spoken through us as well?" God heard it. Now Moses himself was very humble, more so than any other human being on earth. Suddenly God called to Moses, Aaron, and Miriam, "Come out, you three, to the Tent of Meeting." So the three of them went out. God came down in a pillar of cloud, stopped at the entrance of the Tent, and called out, "Aaron and Miriam!" The two of them came forward; and [God] said, "Hear these My words: When prophets of God arise among you, I make Myself known to them in a vision, I speak with them in a dream. Not so with My servant Moses; he is trusted throughout My household. With him I speak mouth to mouth, plainly and not in riddles, and he beholds the likeness of God. How then did you not shrink from speaking against My servant Moses!" Still incensed with them, God departed.

As the cloud withdrew from the Tent, there was Miriam stricken with snow-white scales! When Aaron turned toward Miriam, he saw that she was stricken with scales. And Aaron said to Moses, "O my lord, account not to us the sin which we committed in our folly. Let her not be like a stillbirth which emerges from its mother's womb with half its flesh eaten away!" So Moses cried out to God, saying, "O God, pray heal her!"

But God said to Moses, "If her father spat in her face, would she not bear her shame for seven days? Let her be shut out of camp for seven days, and then let her be readmitted." So Miriam was shut out of camp seven days; and the people did not march on until Miriam was readmitted. After that the people set out from Hazeroth and encamped in the wilderness of Paran.

MODERN MIDRASH: *Miriam's Fringes*

I shudder when I think back to that devastating moment when my brothers Aaron and Moses and I stood before God at the Tent of Meeting. Aaron and I were having a conversation with Moses, as we often did. He was considered a great leader to our people, but to me, he was still our baby brother and needed our guidance. My function was to advise him of the women's needs, and in this case I reminded him that as a role model for the Israelite men, it was important that he tend to the needs of his wife.

Suddenly, the Divine Voice called out in anger, and before I knew what was happening, I was blinded by pain coursing through my body. In a split second, my flesh became my enemy, no longer shielding my inner self, but attacking me from the outside in. And then we all saw it . . . the telltale crusty scabs and blisters that meant I was afflicted with the dreaded skin disease we all feared.

The next thing I knew, Aaron had dropped to his knees pleading with Moses to spare him from my fate. As if we had not just stood together before Moses saying the same thing! He was so self-absorbed and terrified it was pitiful. When he eventually spoke on my behalf, he couldn't even say the word—I was "stricken with scales," as if pronouncing L-E-P-R-O-S-Y made it more contagious.

Moses was no better. Looking back, I wonder if he would have done *anything* if Aaron hadn't begged him to intercede. Even then, the most my dear brother could muster was a mere five words on my behalf: "O God, pray heal her." After all I'd done for him—risking my life to save him as an infant, watching over him as he grew, helping him shepherd the women and children along the dangerous path through the waters, directing the women to refuse to give their jewelry to Aaron to build that abomination, standing by Moses whenever there was rebellion in the ranks—he could squeeze out only five little words for me?! Time and again throughout our journey he had beseeched God to deliver manna, water, and whatever else our band of ex-slaves needed in the wilderness; one would think he could have done more to spare me my ordeal. Was that really so much to ask?

In that moment, I felt deep, intense anger at my situation. In my agony, I needed to blame someone. First I blamed Aaron for his cowardly response and for abandoning me to suffer the consequences of our actions alone. Then I blamed Moses for his belated, stingy prayer. I was overwhelmed with pain and horror, and my own family was no help. My brothers let me down when I needed them most.

And I blamed God. If I was guilty of some offense, then certainly Aaron was also, yet only I was afflicted. And if defending Moses' wife was wrong—and I don't think it was!—it certainly did not warrant such a severe sentence. I was caught in a divinely set trap, cursed with illness and exiled outside the camp until a priest could declare me healthy again. But the only priests were my relatives Aaron and his sons, who were hence disqualified. No one could lift the decree . . . except the same God who had unjustly caused my anguish and who now declared that my exile would last seven days.

When I first left the camp, I was blind with anger. I cried. I screamed. I denounced God for being unfair and capricious. Despite my anger, I searched for some way to understand why God would do this to me. Was God using me as an example to others who would challenge authority? Was this experience part of some divine plan that only later would become clear?

If the lesson was about suffering, I learned it well. The physical pain of my rotting flesh crushed my spirit along with my body. I withdrew into the cold black hole of my own soul where rage, self-pity, and grief were my sole companions, shielding me from the world around. I felt as if I were at the bottom of a deep, dark well, alone, where no one could see me. Part of me longed for human contact, though the touch of another would have made the pain unbearable. Everything that had defined me—my body, spirit, faith, family, the sisterhood of women who'd danced and sung with me, my joy of living—were all gone.

After what seemed an eternity, I heard the faint sound of footsteps on the stones around me. I looked up and there was a woman, smiling, reaching out with a bowl of water. My throat was so parched from crying that I could not speak, but I took the bowl gratefully, and as I sipped, I slowly regained strength. The woman came back later with another bowl of water and a small plate of quail stew. She sat down next to me as I ate, watching me closely, curiously. "Why are you here?" she whispered. I struggled to put into words all that had happened, but in the end all I could say was, "I spoke against Moses, so God cursed me with this illness and exiled me for seven days." She nodded in understanding. "I know who you are, Miriam. I sang with you after we crossed the sea. You helped me find my voice." She choked back a tear as she rose and left me once more to my thoughts.

When she returned the next day, I was full of questions. *Who are you? How did you fall into this dark place?* She would not tell me her name, only that she was the mother of a murdered son and that she, too, had been cast out for speaking against Moses. "I understand your anger and your pain, Miriam," she said. "But look around you . . . you are not alone."

Eventually my eyes adjusted to the dark. Or, maybe, my focus changed, and this was the miracle after all. Indeed, I saw that I was not alone in this dark and terrible exile. With me were the other marginal people, the malcontents, the rejects, the forgotten, the holy.

At first, I merely observed the others, the ghostlike shadows that ringed the fringes, scarcely visible as they skirted in and out of the light. In my fascination with them, I forgot about my own pain. Here were people like me: damaged, wounded souls, broken bodies clinging to a life where each pain-filled breath was an act of courage. Their images remain imprinted on my spirit . . . A mother in mourning, offering her full breast to a stranger's child. A young man, skeletal, shaky, feeding another his daily meal. Children protecting each other from the daily horrors of life among the shadows. One woman gently preparing another for burial, her hands curled and racked with pain. An old man telling stories of the world beyond, teaching the children to sing.

Here were angels and heroes. Here was life. Life!

I later learned that the woman who had fed me was Shelomith, mother of the infamous blasphemer whom my brother had condemned to death by stoning. She and her half-Egyptian son had never been fully accepted into the community; she was tormented, and he was bullied. When he could take no more, he cursed God in anger and was stoned to death. In her anguish, Shelomith spoke out against Moses and the mercilessness of the new laws. Rejected by her clan and shunned by the community, she came here to dwell among the other outcasts. At the time, I had presumed God's judgment was just—but now I know better. Punishments do not always fit the crime. My heart broke for Shelomith. My ordeal would end after my week of exile, but she would forever mourn her son and the life that might have been. I was overwhelmed by the compassion she had shown me, the sister of the one who had caused her so much pain! If only the rest of us had been more forgiving and welcoming, perhaps their fates would have been different.

After my week of exile, I returned to the main camp, and then my people just got up and moved on, as if nothing had changed. No one asked what had happened during those seven days I dwelled at the edge of the camp. Had they asked, I could have taught them something about pain and death and something about life. I learned more about love, charity, and what is truly important in life in my exile than I had from all of God's or Moses' teachings. I lost some heroes, but others have replaced them. How ironic that my curse became a blessing. Living among the fringes, I discovered courage and hope; in adversity, I found faith.

I am no longer angry with Aaron or Moses, though I still feel some bitterness toward them. They were afraid that they, too, might be afflicted by that revolting disease. To immunize themselves, my brothers needed to believe there was a reason for my suffering, that it was not random and I must have done something to deserve it. Yes, they prayed for me to be healed, but they never acknowledged that what happened to me was unfair and unjust. I used to think my brothers looked so serene, so spiritual when they wrapped themselves for prayer while communing with the Almighty. But now I see that, despite their piety, their fringes separate them from the painful realities that surround us.

My anger against God has diminished too, for I now know that my illness was neither a punishment nor a test, but a difficult part of living. I don't even regret my suffering, for without it I would not have found this source of strength. Having faced this trauma, I still fear death, but it is no longer a lonely fear.

When I dance now, I gather my timbrels and dance around the edges of camp. When I sing of God's glory, these forgotten heroes are my chorus. When I am in need of healing, I drink from the well that gave us sustenance in our despair. And when I pray, these are the fringes with which I wrap myself for warmth and strength and courage.

CLASSICAL COMMENTARY AND MIDRASH:
Crime and Punishment

Why is it that when both Miriam and Aaron reproach Moses for something related to his Cushite wife, who may or may not be Zipporah, the Midianite woman whom Moses married during the Exodus narrative, only Miriam is punished, though both she and Aaron presumably committed the same offense? Why does God become directly involved in what seems to be a family quarrel? And why is Miriam's punishment so severe?

The rabbis explore all of these questions at length, although virtually none consider what actually happened to Miriam during her seven-day exile outside the camp.

What Concern Did Miriam and Aaron Raise?

The biblical text is vague about Miriam and Aaron's critique of Moses with regard to his Cushite wife. Because the issue involved his wife, most scholars suggest that Moses was neglectful in his marital duties. The rabbis acknowledge that siblings would not normally know about their brother's bedroom matters, so midrash suggests that Miriam found out about Moses's dereliction from his wife, Zipporah.

There are several depictions of this exchange. According to one account, Miriam discovered the neglect when she saw that Zipporah had stopped wearing jewelry because Moses was no longer attracted to her.[1] In another version, Miriam and Zipporah were standing together when Eldad and Medad began prophesizing (Num. 11:27), and Zipporah expressed concern for their wives, knowing that they too would be set aside when Eldad and Medad became prophets, as she had been.[2] In both scenarios, Miriam and Zipporah conferred in private, and then Miriam discussed the situation with Aaron before bringing their mutual concern to Moses. Hence, Miriam was the initial disseminator of information and the primary culprit, which was why she, and not Aaron, was punished.[3]

According to this interpretation, Miriam and Aaron criticized Moses for unnecessarily separating himself from his wife in order to remain pure for his interactions with God. They argued that they also enjoyed the gift of prophecy (Num. 12:2), as did the patriarchs, and yet they continued to fulfill their own marital obligations. Therefore, Moses was being unduly zealous by neglecting his duties to his wife.[4]

In Moses's defense, the rabbis respond that it was God who caused Moses to separate from his wife, since God might call upon Moses at any time and he therefore needed to remain chaste at all times.[5]

Some commentaries read the text more literally—"*because of the Cushite woman*" means that they criticized him for marrying a "*Cushite*," the biblical term for someone who is Black or from Ethiopia. Presumably this is a reference to Zipporah, despite the fact that she was Midianite; commentators explain that Zipporah was described as a Cushite woman as a way of remarking on her exceptional, dark-skinned beauty.[6] Rashi notes that 736, the numerical value of "*Cushite*" in Hebrew, is also the numerical equivalent of *yefat mareh*, "beautiful appearance."[7] Most of these sources suggest Miriam and Aaron were defending Zipporah because she was righteous and did not deserve to be neglected; however, others presume they disparaged her to Moses because her lineage was inferior to that of their own spouses.[8]

Another midrashic thread presumes that Moses' Cushite wife was not Zipporah, but rather a different woman altogether. According to variations of this midrash, when Moses fled Egypt, he went to the land of Cush (Ethiopia), became a great leader there for forty years, and was given the king's Cushite daughter as a bride as a reward for his military prowess.[9] This, not Zipporah, was the wife that he would later neglect.

Why Was Miriam's Punishment So Harsh?

Most commentaries consider Miriam and Aaron's offense to have been slander. According to this interpretation, when Miriam and Aaron spoke out against Moses, it was undeserved and a criticism not only of Moses, but also of God, who had directed Moses' actions. Although they spoke privately to Moses, nonetheless *"God heard it"* (Num. 12:2).[10]

Despite the fact that the siblings criticized their brother out of love and a desire to help correct aberrant behavior, Miriam's punishment was extremely harsh. According to midrash, this is one of ten examples when the Israelites "tested" God, but only slander merited such severe punishment:

With ten trials did our fathers try the Holy One, blessed be He, yet they were only punished because of their evil tongue, which was but one of them. . . . R. Simeon said: Upon those who utter slander does the plague of leprosy fall. We find it so with Aaron and Miriam who slandered Moses and were visited with punishment, as it is stated, *And Miriam and Aaron spoke against Moses.* [Nu. 12:1] Why does Scripture mention Miriam's name first before Aaron's? It teaches that Zipporah went and spoke of it to Miriam; Miriam went and spoke of it to Aaron, and both of them arose and spoke ill of that righteous man [Moses]. Because the two of them stood speaking ill of that righteous man, Divine punishment came upon them, as it is stated, *And the anger of the Lord was kindled against them, and departed.* [Nu. 12:9] What is the significance of the expression *and departed?* It suggests that [the leprosy] departed from Aaron and attached itself to Miriam, because Aaron did not enter into the details of the matter whereas Miriam did; therefore she was immediately punished with greater severity. Miriam said, "To me came the Word yet I did not separate myself from my husband." Aaron said, "To me came the Word yet I did not separate myself from my wife. The Word also came to our fathers of old and they did not separate themselves from their wives. But [Moses], in his arrogance, has separated from his wife!" They did not criticize him to his face but only behind his back, and their criticism was not stated as a fact but only as a surmise; since it was a matter of doubt whether he had acted so from arrogance or not. Now is there not here an inference from the less to the greater? If Miriam, who spoke only against her brother, spoke only in secret and spoke only behind Moses' back, was punished, how much greater will be the punishment of an ordinary man who speaks ill to the face of his fellow and puts him to shame![11]

Immediately following this story is the tale of the spies who return with a negative report from the Promised Land. The rabbis use the juxtaposition of these two stories to explain that the spies knew the severity of punishment for slander based on what had happened to Miriam and therefore had no excuse for committing the same crime:

> *And Miriam and Aaron spoke against Moses* (ib. XII, 1) and after that, *Send thou men*. This bears on what Scripture says: *They know not, neither do they understand; for their eyes are bedaubed, that they cannot see* (Isa. XLIV, 18). What reason had Scripture for saying, after the incident of Miriam, *Send thou men*? The fact is that the Holy One, blessed be He, foresaw that the spies would utter a slander about the Land. Said the Holy One, blessed be He: "They shall not say, 'We did not know the penalty for slander.'" The Holy One, blessed be He, therefore placed this section next to the other—for Miriam had spoken against her brother and had been smitten with leprosy—in order that all might know the penalty for slander, and that if people were tempted to speak slander they might reflect [on] what had happened to Miriam.[12]

Criticism of Moses was an implied criticism of God, since certainly the all-knowing God would be aware of Moses' actions and did not require

Aaron and Miriam to intercede. Sforno imagines God being furious that Miriam and Aaron could believe either that God knew of Moses' misdeeds and permitted them or that God did not know as much as they did.[13] This understanding helps explain the degree of God's wrath and direct involvement in the situation. After the rebuke, the biblical text reminds us that *"Moses was very humble"* (Num. 12:3), and then *"suddenly"* (Num. 12:4) God commands the three siblings to gather at the Tent of Meeting. It seems that Moses is so humble that he is incapable of standing up for himself, and so God steps in to defend him. Rabbeinu Bahya explains the unusual use of the biblical term *"suddenly"*: by calling Miriam and Aaron *"suddenly,"* God found them unfit to stand before the Divine, proving that Moses had been right to remain separate from his wife in anticipation of being called at any time. Furthermore, the suddenness prevented them from repenting due to the severity of their offense:

> *"Suddenly."* Rashi explains that G'd surprised them in [a] state of ritual impurity occasioned due to their having had marital relations with their respective spouses. They then exclaimed: "water, water," implying the need to purify themselves as well as recognition that Moses had been correct in separating from his wife so as not to be ritually impure when G'd would choose to address him. Seeing that there were no fixed periods of time when G'd would appear, Moses had to be in constant readiness for such a communication.
>
> Some commentators understand the word [*"suddenly"*] as meaning that the suddenness of G'd's reaction was designed to prevent Miriam and Aaron from repenting on what they had said at that time. Their sin included desecration of the name of the Lord, a sin which is so severe that people guilty of it are not presented with opportunities to repent. Miriam and Aaron had to know that speaking out against G'd's prophets was considered as on a level with speaking out against the Shechinah.[14]

The idea that Miriam and Aaron had committed an offense against God is made clear in God's response to Moses' plea on Miriam's behalf: *"But God* said to Moses, 'If her father spat in her face, would she not bear her shame for seven days?'" (Num. 12:14). The comparison is to a daughter who shames her father and in response he spits in her face, either metaphorically or literally, and then she is barred from his presence for seven days. The rabbis comment that if one who disgraces a human father is ostracized for seven days, one who commits an affront to God should suffer even longer. This is an example of the midrashic technique of *kal vaḥomer*, drawing an inference from a lesser matter to a major matter. Others do the math differently; her offense against Moses is worth seven days and minimally another seven days for God, so her sentence should have been at least fourteen days. However, since Moses seems to have forgiven his sister, the sentence is reduced to just seven days.[15] In effect, while the sentence would seem harsh for a sibling spat, the rabbis consider the punishment rather light for the offense of slander against God's prophet and the implicit disparagement of God.

Why Was Only Miriam Punished?

Although both Aaron and Miriam shared their concerns with Moses, only Miriam is stricken and temporarily exiled from the community. The rabbis offer several explanations for this. As noted previously, according to midrash, Miriam learned of Moses' misconduct from Zipporah and shared the information with Aaron; thus, she was considered the initiator and primary offender. Other commentaries note that in Num. 12:1 the feminine singular verb is used for "*And Miriam spoke*" (*vatidabeir*), where one would have expected the plural verb for both "*Miriam and Aaron spoke*" (*vayedabeiru*). Given the singular verb usage, the nuance of this phrase could be read as "*And Miriam spoke, and Aaron, against Moses,*" with Miriam being the key speaker and Aaron following along silently.[16]

Some commentaries use this text to view Miriam as a negative model for all women. According to *Da'at Zekenim*, a twelfth- to thirteenth-century compendium of commentaries, "Seeing that it is a fact that women indulge more in loose talk, Miriam is mentioned here first, seeing that she was a woman."[17] Similarly, Deuteronomy Rabbah cites Miriam's actions as an example of negative female traits:

R. Levi said, Women possess the four following characteristics: they are greedy, inquisitive, envious, and indolent. . . . The rabbis add two more characteristics; they are querulous and gossips. . . . And whence do we know that they are gossips? For it is written, *"And Miriam spoke."* R. Joshua of Siknin said: When God was about to create Eve from Adam, He was considering whence to create her. . . . God said: . . . "I will not create her from the mouth that she may not be talkative," yet of Miriam the pious, it is written, *"And Miriam spoke."* And see what befell her, *Remember what the Lord thy God did unto Miriam.*[18]

Further in the biblical text, we read that God was angry with *them*, not just Miriam (Num. 12:9). Some take this to mean that both Miriam and Aaron were in fact stricken with leprosy. That leads to the corollary question of why Aaron's affliction is not spelled out in the text just like Miriam's. According to these sources, Aaron's punishment was not publicly pronounced out of respect for him; or, alternately, he was healed immediately due to his merit and thus did not require quarantine outside the camp.[19]

Aaron and Moses' Reactions

The rabbis discuss the merit of both brothers' responses to their sister's crisis. The fact that Aaron sought Moses' intercession begs the question of why Moses did not intercede on his sister's behalf without being prompted. According to the eighteenth-century commentary *Or ha-Ḥayim*, Aaron believed Moses was offended by their actions and needed to forgive them in order for Miriam to be healed. The text, however, states that Moses was a *"humble man"* (Num. 12:3) to indicate that he was not insulted by their rebuke. That said, it was not his prerogative to forgive the affront committed against God by virtue of their criticism of God's servant. Consequently, his own forgiveness or plea on Miriam's behalf would not have helped her, so it did not occur to Moses to intervene.[20]

An alternative description of Aaron's plea to Moses suggests that he appealed to Moses' vanity by reminding him that the Israelites would hear that the sister of Moses and Aaron was leprous, and it would reflect negatively upon them.[21] Others suggest that Aaron explained Miriam's dilemma to Moses: only an unrelated priest could perform the inspections to allow someone's return to the community, yet Aaron and his sons, the sole priests, were all related to Miriam and unable to execute that function on her behalf; thus, only God had the authority to determine her state of fitness and the duration of her quarantine.[22]

The rabbis also point to a redundancy in Moses' plea to God once he was motivated to pray for his sister's relief: *"Moses cried out to God, saying, 'O God, pray heal her!'"* (Num. 12:13). The redundancy of *"crying out"* and *"saying"* indicates the depth of his anguish and intention and also offers a message about the efficacy of prayer:

> *"Moses cried out to the Lord:"* he expressed his pain over Miriam's fate and prayed for her. The reason the Torah continues with the word *"leimor"* ("saying"), was to tell us that this prayer by Moses was not merely in his heart but that he verbalized it. This is the meaning of Berachot 31 *"if someone prays he must move his lips and enunciate the words of his prayer."* The reason is that by moving one's lips the letters one says assume a certain shape (in the atmosphere) through the use of voice, breath, and verbalising them. When such a prayer has assumed a certain shape it ascends to the celestial regions and arrives in the presence of the Lord.[23]

The rabbis also use the brevity of the five-word prayer offered by Moses to teach that prayers should be kept short.[24] It is also deemed to be a credit to Moses that he did not elongate his prayer so as not to show favoritism to his sister.[25] Since the Hebrew word *na*, a term of supplication, is repeated twice in the prayer, several commentaries suggest that the first use was an entreaty to God, whereas the second was a more demanding appeal for immediate action.[26] According to Rashi, this is a model for the correct form of prayer: a few precatory words of supplication followed by the request being made.[27] *Targum Jonathan* embellishes on the five-word prayer to offer a more effusive depiction of Moses' words: "And Mosheh did pray, and seek mercy before the Lord, saying: I pray through the compassions of the merciful God, O Eloha, who hast power over the life of all flesh, heal her, I beseech thee."[28]

Miriam's Exile Outside the Camp

Little has been written about Miriam's experiences during the seven days she was exiled outside the camp. One depiction, in Deuteronomy Rabbah, explains that she was sent to the mines with other malcontents:

> Remember [*what your God did to Miriam on the journey after you left Egypt*. Deut. 24:9]. The Rabbis say: This can be compared to a king who returned [in triumph] from war, and a noble lady sang his praises, and the king decreed that she should be called the Mother of the Senate. [A title of honour.] Later, she began to cause disorder in the royal provisions [royal headquarters]. Said the king thereupon: 'Is that what she does? Let her be sent away to the mines.' [Where malefactors were sent.] So, when God waged war at the Red Sea, Miriam chanted a song, and she was named prophetess, as it is said, *And Miriam the prophetess . . . took* (Ex. XV, 20). When, however, she slandered her brother, God commanded that she should be sent to the mines, as it is said, *And Miriam was shut up* (Num. XII, 15).[29]

It was a great credit to Miriam that the Israelites remained encamped for the duration of her quarantine, awaiting her return. Numerous commentaries suggest that this was her reward for having watched over Moses as he floated down the Nile; just as she waited for Moses for one hour, the Israelites would wait for her for the full seven days.[30] Also acknowledged is Miriam's well, the magical well said to have been the sole source of the Israelites' water in the wilderness, following them along the way and only ceasing upon Miriam's death—another reward for Miriam's protection of Moses from the waters.[31] The waters of Miriam's well were known to have healing powers, even to cure leprosy.[32] Ensuring the continuing presence of Miriam's well was additional motivation for the Israelites to remain in place until Miriam was able to travel with them once again.

As a prophetess and a wise leader of the women during the Exodus and wilderness experiences, Miriam is one of the most celebrated women in biblical history. A great deal of commentary is devoted to her character, the various episodes of her life journey, and what grievous sin she must have committed to have been afflicted with leprosy and exiled from the community for seven days. A glaring exception to this exposition is her personal experience during her seven days of exile outside the camp. Filling in that gap is the subject of the modern midrash "Miriam's Fringes."

A core component is Miriam's evolving feelings toward her brothers Moses and Aaron. Sibling relationships can be complicated, and these three had certainly been through a lot together! Miriam's watchful eye and rescue of Moses as an infant suggest a loving protectiveness of her younger brother, which continued later in life—both she and Aaron play significant supportive roles in bolstering Moses throughout the wilderness journey—and yet, Moses' prayer on her behalf comes only after Aaron's insistence, and even then, it is extremely brief. Given this history, it seems natural that Miriam would be angry at Moses for not doing more for her at her moment of need, as she had for him throughout his life.

As for Aaron, it seems likely that Miriam would have felt abandoned by him. While both of them had a common mission to see their brother succeed and both approach Moses together, only she suffers the consequences for their shared actions. Whether Aaron's efforts to intercede with Moses were the most or the least he could do is unclear. In that moment of trauma, Miriam would likely not have been inclined to give him the benefit of the doubt.

That Miriam is considered "*as one dead*" (Num. 12:12) during this period of time leads to the consideration of the five stages of grief and loss famously documented by Elizabeth Kübler-Ross: denial, anger, bargaining, depression, and acceptance. In the midrash, we see Miriam go through several of these stages, including anger, depression, and eventually acceptance. Anyone who has experienced a significant ordeal or loss like Miriam's will probably recognize many of these emotions. At such fraught moments, family relationships can become strained, and old resentments can percolate.

A traumatized person might misdirect disappointment and anger at close family and friends, thwarting their efforts to provide support during the crisis. This midrash leaves open the question of whether her brothers' responses to her ordeal were appropriate; regardless, Miriam was likely to direct some of her pain, grief, and rage toward them. It is noteworthy that the five-word prayer, which is often used in healing services today, is counted as a credit to Moses by the rabbis, yet Miriam perceives it as deficient. Perhaps this explains why *Targum Jonathan* creatively embellished the words of his prayer.

"Miriam's Fringes" reintroduces the biblical character Shelomith bat Dibri, another outcast who suffers on account of Moses (Lev. 24:10–14) and who gets to tell her own story in this volume (see "Testament of Shelomith" in chapter 8). While neither the biblical text nor classical midrash provide an ending to Shelomith's tale of woe—we know nothing of what happens to her after her son is stoned to death—this modern midrash provides a conclusion, imagining her as sojourning with the outsiders and malcontents just beyond the Israelites' camp, along with the rest of "Miriam's fringes." Including the character of Shelomith in this story personalizes the powerful images Miriam witnessed—these were not just illusions, but real people with real stories to share. In connecting with Shelomith and listening to her story, Miriam's curiosity is transformed into empathy; she is no longer a temporary resident but becomes part of the community at the fringes of the camp. Shelomith almost acts as a spirit guide, helping Miriam to see beyond her own pain to find the beauty and holiness around her.

After her sojourn with the outcasts, Miriam cannot simply return to her prior station in life and move on so easily, as the rest of the camp does. From her newly opened eyes, the fact that these heroic, virtuous individuals have been cast out of the camp is an indictment of Moses' and Aaron's leadership. A caring community would not have left these vulnerable individuals to fend for themselves. Although Moses and Aaron valiantly uphold the ritual and legal doctrines required by God, they neglect the many commandments to care for the poor and vulnerable. She can no longer ignore these people's plight, and she loses some respect for her brothers, who do.

The book of Deuteronomy commands us to remember what happened to Miriam: "*Remember what God did to Miriam on the journey after you left Egypt*" (Deut. 24:9). Several verses later, there is a similar command to remember the Israelites' nemesis, Amalek: "*Remember what Amalek did to you on your journey after you left Egypt*" (Deut. 25:17). And what did Amalek do? He attacked the Israelites from the rear, cutting off the stragglers, those who were most weary. For that sin of attacking the most vulnerable, the memory of Amalek was to be blotted out entirely (Deut. 25:18–19). In this modern midrash, Miriam's ordeal reminds us who those vulnerable people were: they were her fringes—the human souls who were left defenseless at the edge of the camp. Perhaps there is a lesson in juxtaposing Miriam's exile outside the camp with Amalek's sin: rather than leaving the stragglers behind, the most vulnerable should have been protected and embraced by the camp.

In this midrash, Miriam experiences many of the stages of death and dying and emerges with greater wisdom, awareness, and empathy for others who are outsiders. Inspired by Miriam, readers might also give thought to individuals on the fringes of our own communities—people who suffer from illness and addiction, or struggle to survive poverty, or live as social outcasts, or are elderly, vulnerable, and alone. These and other dejected people are worthy of attention and care rather than apathy. Miriam is no longer able to disregard the people who reside just outside the camp; they have become her people—what if they could become ours?

10

Noah

Daughter of Zelophehad

BIBLICAL TEXT: *Numbers 27:1–8, 36:1–12*

The daughters of Zelophehad, of Manassite family—son of Hepher son of Gilead son of Machir son of Manasseh son of Joseph—came forward. The names of the daughters were Mahlah, Noah, Hoglah, Milcah, and Tirzah. They stood before Moses, Eleazar the priest, the chieftains, and the whole assembly, at the entrance of the Tent of Meeting, and they said, "Our father died in the wilderness. He was not one of the faction, Korah's faction, which banded together against God, but died for his own sin; and he has left no sons. Let not our father's name be lost to his clan just because he had no son! Give us a holding among our father's kinsmen!"

Moses brought their case before God.

And God said to Moses, "The plea of Zelophehad's daughters is just: you should give them a hereditary holding among their father's kinsmen; transfer their father's share to them.

"Further, speak to the Israelite people as follows: 'If a householder dies without leaving a son, you shall transfer his property to his daughter.'" . . .

The family heads in the clan of the descendants of Gilead son of Machir son of Manasseh, one of the Josephite clans, came forward and appealed to Moses and the chieftains, family heads of the Israelites. They said, "God commanded my lord to assign the land to the Israelites as shares by lot, and my lord was further commanded by God to assign the share of our kinsman Zelophehad to his daughters. Now, if they become the wives of persons from another Israelite tribe, their share will be cut off from our ancestral portion and be added to the portion of the tribe into which they become [wives]; thus our allotted portion will be diminished. And even when the Israelites observe the jubilee, their share will be added to that of the tribe into which they become [wives], and their share will be cut off from the ancestral portion of our tribe."

So Moses, at God's bidding, instructed the Israelites, saying: "The plea of the Josephite tribe is just. This is what God has commanded concerning the daughters of Zelophehad: They may become the wives of anyone they wish, provided they become wives within a clan of their father's tribe. No inheritance of the Israelites may pass over from one tribe to another, but the Israelite [heirs]—each of them—must remain bound to the ancestral portion of their tribe. Every daughter among the Israelite tribes who inherits a share must become the wife of someone from a clan of her father's tribe, in order that every Israelite [heir] may keep an ancestral share. Thus no inheritance shall pass over from one tribe to another, but the Israelite tribes shall remain bound each to its portion."

The daughters of Zelophehad did as God had commanded Moses: Mahlah, Tirzah, Hoglah, Milcah, and Noah, Zelophehad's daughters, became the wives of their uncles' sons, becoming wives within clans of descendants of Manasseh son of Joseph; and so their share remained in the tribe of their father's clan.

MODERN MIDRASH: *Noah and Elishama—A Love Story*

All my life people told me I was brave. I never felt brave. Mahlah, my older sister—*she* was brave. She always seemed so sure of herself and spoke her mind, even to men. Father loved her best; she was his first-born and the sparkle in his eyes. My sisters and I knew that, but it was okay. I think we all loved Mahlah most. She was funny and forthright and smart. One of the first to be born in the wilderness after the journey through the Reed Sea, she became a symbol of the new life we would forge one day in the Promised Land. Even the other men of our tribe indulged her, permitting her to join them at tribal council meetings to study the new rules and laws handed down by Moses.

When I got older, Father sometimes let me tag along with Mahlah to sit by his side. I was in awe of Mahlah; she spoke her mind and even the men respected her opinion. I was more reserved, though not really shy. I could speak up when I had something to say, though I rarely had anything to say that Mahlah had not already said before me.

Our clan of Manasseh, among the most honorable descendants of Joseph, grew quickly. Father and Mother did their part, as my sisters and I came one right after the other—Mahlah, me (Noah), Hoglah, Milcah, and Tirzah. The annual clan gatherings were joyous and lively affairs. Sometimes we joined with our cousins from the tribe of Ephraim, also descendants of Joseph. The women cooked together and danced with timbrels, just as the elders had done with Miriam when they began their sojourn in the wilderness. The men gathered around the fires to tell stories of heroism and bravery, rejoicing in their newfound freedom even as they remembered the torment of slavery. Some of the men had even seen Moses, our great leader, at the Tent of Meeting. They told wondrous tales of pillars of clouds rising from the desert floor to lead us at day and columns of flames to guide us at night.

During these gatherings, while Mahlah was with Father and the men at the campfire and my younger sisters were at my mother's skirts, I was free to play with the older children of the two tribes of Joseph; we were like one, big happy family. My best friend and playmate then was Elishama, from the tribe of Ephraim, who like me, was curious and loved to explore. We would go from one campfire to the next, listening to heroic tales of battles at one and then joining the women and children dancing, and then on to another circle of men debating the new laws, and then back to games with the other children. There was so much to see and hear—we never grew tired of being together. Though Eli and I saw each other only during those clan reunions with both Manasseh and Ephraim, it felt like the two of us grew up together in the wilderness.

As time went on, we spent less time playing games and more time sharing our thoughts and dreams. He was learning to be a warrior, preparing to enter and fight for our Promised Land as our journey was, hopefully, nearing its end. And I was learning the proper ways to be a wife and care for a household of my own one day.

When I reached the age of womanhood, propriety dictated that Eli and I could no longer be alone together. I hid my face behind a veil just like the other women whenever I left the family tent, but, I could tell, my Eli always knew me. He knew my eyes and the way I walked. And I could pick out his voice from any size crowd at the gathering. When our eyes locked across the clan fires, it was as if no one else existed. Our childhood friendship had blossomed into love, and we knew we were intended for one another.

Over the years, my heart swelled with pride as I watched him grow from a boy into a man, a brave warrior, and a leader of Ephraim.

Meanwhile, Mahlah and I were growing into young women, and soon it would be our time to wed. I anxiously awaited Mahlah's marriage, because I knew mine would come soon after. Everyone assumed Eli and I would wed—our love for each other was no secret. Marriages between our tribes were common; many couples found one another during those tribal gatherings.

When Mother's monthly cycles stopped, Father grew despondent. He watched the other clansmen and their sons longingly. As the father of only daughters, he worried about who would follow in his footsteps and carry on the family name and what kind of future his daughters would have without the protection of a male heir to secure the family rights. Mother worried that the family would not have enough for our dowries to ensure good marriages for all five of us. So Father had to work even harder to prepare for our future marriages, and without sons to help with the herds, he was constantly worried and exhausted.

Father left one day but did not return. We were not concerned, for he often spent days on end with the herds. But then Gamaliel, head of our tribe, showed up unannounced at our tent. Immediately we knew something was drastically wrong.

Father, Gamaliel, explained to us, had been caught gathering on the Sabbath day, violating the new laws proclaimed by Moses. As a result, he had been brought to the Tent of Meeting to await a ruling about the punishment for this crime.

Before Gamaliel could say another word, we hastily gathered ourselves and set out with Gamaliel to witness the proceedings at the Tent of Meeting. When we arrived, we saw that men from all the tribes had gathered there to learn what would happen when someone violated the new laws about the Sabbath.

Mahlah did not wait to hear the final decree—she spoke up as soon as we arrived, much to the surprise of everyone except our family. She begged and pleaded with Moses to spare Father. "His crime was one of love," she cried. "Love for our mother, love for his five daughters. With no sons, he has to work extra hard all by himself to provide for us. Surely a just God would know Father's heart! And a kind and generous God would understand that these rules are new for our people and would forgive a first-time infraction. A merciful God would not leave a wife and five daughters alone in this world of men, without means of support and sustenance and without dowries!"

While Mahlah addressed the community and tribal leaders (she was so brave!), I searched for Eli. Perhaps he could help us and speak on Father's behalf. Our eyes met, as they always did, and with a slight nod of silent communication we stole away for a private rendezvous.

I fell into his arms, weeping and begging him to help us. Eli comforted me, cooing softly until my sobs subsided. "My love," he gently whispered, "I'm so sorry for you and your family. I know your father is a good man. But we must trust in our wise leader, Moses, and have faith that the ruling will be just. God is our Judge. Even if the worst happens, do not fear for yourself. I will marry you and care for you. And I will care for your mother and sisters too, if they do not wed."

Despite my despair over my father's plight, I could not stop my heart from dancing. My hopes and dreams might finally come true—I would be wed to Elishama, son of Ammihud, my beloved and my best friend, who would one day be chieftain of Ephraim. I proclaimed my devotion and gave Eli my pledge to become his wife.

Despite Mahlah's pleading, the worst did happen, as Eli had warned me. Moses said he had no choice; the decree came directly from God. The punishment would be death by stoning. They would make an example of Father, lest anyone doubt the seriousness of these new laws. There would be no flexibility and no recourse.

The days that followed were a blur. We had just witnessed the horror of the execution of our father, and then immediately after the period of mourning, our uncles came to Mother to devise a plan for our future. Since Mother was too old to bear a son, they released her of the obligation to marry under the levirate law. Mahlah would be wed immediately to our cousin Aniam, son of Shemida, and the rest of us would follow in due course. I hoped that soon the despair would lift from our household and I would find myself once more in the arms of my beloved.

But Mahlah was not satisfied. She would wed Aniam, but she insisted that we not relinquish our share of the land that was Father's birthright to receive at the end of our journey through the wilderness. Having paid attention during those days when she accompanied Father to the clan meetings, she knew about the plans to apportion land to the tribes according to each male descendant. As the first-born of the first-born, she insisted that daughters in our situation should receive their own shares, just like sons. Since Moses and the tribal leaders had taken Father from us and stoned him to death, it would not be fair for them to also take our inheritance.

For the first time, I pushed back. I was not interested in another fight with the tribal leaders. I wanted her to marry Aniam and make way for Eli and me finally to be together. His inheritance would be enough for me, and I did not want Mahlah's greed and arrogance to stand in our way. "We will soon enter the Promised Land, and there will be enough for us all," I argued. "The laws are difficult—we know that better than anyone—but our family has followed Moses this far, and now it's our turn to have faith and follow the laws of the God of Israel. Please, Mahlah, be satisfied with what you will have with Aniam, and allow us to move on."

But it was no use; Mahlah was determined. Tirzah and Mother agreed with her, and Hoglah and Milcah went along. While I knew Eli would take care of me—and the rest of them if necessary—they wanted assurance that we would not be left destitute or at the mercy of our uncles without our own property.

So first Mahlah went to our tribal elders to demand our share of Father's inheritance. They said it was not their decision to make and deferred to the next level of authority. When those judges also rejected her claim, she went to even higher authorities, appealing one ruling after another until finally reaching the highest court: the Tent of Meeting, the very site of our Father's demise. She stood before Moses, Eleazar the priest, the chieftains, and all the other men and said, *"Our father died in the wilderness. He was not one of the faction, Korah's faction, which banded together against God, but died for his own sin; and he has left no sons. Let not our father's name be lost to his clan just because he had no son! Give us a holding among our father's kinsmen!"*

Just as he had done before, Moses heard Mahlah's arguments and then retreated into the Tent to consult with the Holy One. When he emerged, he reported on the Divine ruling: *"The plea of Zelophehad's daughters is just: you should give them a hereditary holding among their father's kinsmen; transfer their father's share to them."*

Mahlah got her way, and she married Aniam too. Finally it was my turn to wed.

Aniam's father, pleased with the additional property from Father's inheritance that his family would receive, wanted to betroth me to his other son, Likhi.

But I refused. "I made a pledge to wed Elishama son of Ammihud," I proclaimed to the Manasseh Tribal Council elders. "With no father or husband to annul it, my vow to Elishama is binding." Mahlah was not the only sister who had paid attention! I insisted on following the new laws to the letter—which included my promise to wed Eli. My pledge had to be fulfilled.

The men of the council took my plea under advisement but then moved on to more pressing matters. As our tribes neared the Land of Israel, the tribes of Reuben and Gad had decided they did not want to travel across the River Jordan. They would establish settlements east of the river, though first they would send their armies with the rest of the tribes to assure a successful victory over the Canaanite clans to the west. Our tribal council discussed whether to cross the river or remain with Reuben and Gad in the east, but they could not come to a consensus, so they decided to let each family choose which way to go. My uncles sided with those who would remain east of the Jordan.

I was devastated! That meant I would be separated from Mother and my sisters. Since my future was with Eli and his tribe of Ephraim, once we married I would travel across the Jordan with him, while Mother and my sisters remained behind.

Just when I thought everything had been decided, my uncle Shemida and the other men of Manasseh appealed Moses' ruling regarding our inheritance. They were not going to give up Father's share of the lands, even if these were on the east side of the river. They demanded that my shares of the family's inheritance remain with them and not be allotted to Ephraim, Eli's tribe.

So once more Mahlah, my sisters, and I found ourselves standing before Moses at the Tent of Meeting—though this time Eli and I stood against Mahlah and her husband as he and the other men of Manasseh argued, *"God commanded my lord to assign the land to the Israelites as shares by lot, and my lord was further commanded by God to assign the share of our kinsman Zelophehad to his daughters. Now, if they become the wives of persons from another Israelite tribe, their share will be cut off from our ancestral portion and be added to the portion of the tribe into which they become wives; thus our allotted portion will be diminished. And even when the Israelites observe the jubilee, their share will be added to that of the tribe into which they become wives, and their share will be cut off from the ancestral portion of our tribe."*

Immediately Moses issued a ruling that he explained came from God's bidding: *"The plea of the Josephite tribe is just. This is what God has commanded concerning the daughters of Zelophehad: They may become the wives of anyone they wish, provided they become wives within a clan of their father's tribe. No inheritance of the Israelites may pass over from one tribe to another, but the Israelite heirs—each of them—must remain bound to the ancestral portion of their tribe. Every daughter among the Israelite tribes who inherits a share must become the wife of someone from a clan of her father's tribe, in order that every Israelite heir may keep an ancestral share. Thus no inheritance shall pass over from one tribe to another, but the Israelite tribes shall remain bound each to its portion."*

It took me a moment to process what I had heard. First Moses had said I could marry anyone I wanted, but now he was saying I had to marry someone from my own tribe. It didn't matter that Eli and I were both descendants of Joseph. It didn't matter that we loved each other and had pledged ourselves to one another. If I wed, it had to be a man of Manasseh. I would not be able to marry my beloved Eli! And even if neither of us married, we still would be separated, our tribal lands on opposite sides of the Jordan. Eli would lead Ephraim in battle to the west, while I was obliged to settle with Father's people in the east. No matter what we did, Eli and I would be lost to one another!

Once more, I found myself in Eli's arms, this time both of us crying at the cruelty of our fate. As a young tribal leader, Eli could never abandon his people. Like the rest of us, he was sworn to uphold the new rules. He would not defy Moses or disobey the law, which came directly from God Almighty. And so, my betrothed, my Eli, released me from my vow, and I released him.

Heartbroken, angry, and bitter, I determined never to marry. If I could not be with my Eli, I would remain alone. So I bestowed upon Tirzah my rightful place as second sister, and she wed shortly thereafter. Hoglah and Milcah also took their turns under the canopy with men of Manasseh.

And so, I remained with the tribe of Manasseh along with Mother and my sisters, while Elishama departed to lead the tribe of Ephraim to fight for our birthright. We hadn't even been able to say goodbye to one another because my uncles feared we might defy their authority and run off together.

Though my love story ended when Elishama crossed the Jordan without me, my life story continued. After Mother died, Mahlah and Aniam brought me to their camp. Tirzah, Hoglah, and Milcah, and their husbands, too, made sure I was cared for. They knew that the happiness they had found came at my expense, and though they did not regret their own happiness, they nonetheless took pity on me. Over the years I heard tales of Eli's conquests and his valor, but our eyes never met again.

With the passage of time, I grew restive, and longed for a tent of my own. The passion of youth eventually gave way to the wisdom of age. And so, when Likhi was widowed and his bed grew cold, I joined him. It took many years, but I did, eventually, do as I was told.

The daughters of Zelophehad did as God had commanded Moses: Mahlah, Tirzah, Hoglah, Milcah, and Noah, Zelophehad's daughters, became the wives of their uncles' sons, becoming wives within clans of descendants of Manasseh son of Joseph; and so their share remained in the tribe of their father's clan.

CLASSICAL COMMENTARY AND MIDRASH:
Five Righteous Women

The story of Zelophehad's daughters is rather unique in ancient tradition. The five sisters are not only named, but their names are repeatedly included in genealogical lists throughout the Bible. The women speak with their own voice to make a case for inheritance rights, arguing directly before Moses and the other leaders empowered to issue rulings under the new law code created in the wilderness. The resulting decision establishes the right of women to inherit in cases where there are no male heirs, thus ensuring that property will be passed down to their father's descendants. Also, initially these five women are granted the right to marry as they please. However, after male members of their extended clan object, a subsequent ruling amends women's right to inherit to stipulate that here and henceforth, daughters who will inherit their fathers' property must marry within their tribe in order to preserve the prescribed contours of tribal lands. Though these ancient rulings conferred some ownership rights to women, it did so with significant limitations. Their right to own property meant giving up their right to marry freely.

Who Was Zelophehad and How Did He Die?

According to biblical genealogical lists, Zelophehad was a descendant of Joseph through his son Manasseh, his great-great-grandfather.[1] Zelophehad is presumed to have been a first-born son and, as such, entitled to a double portion of his father's estate, which would make his daughters' property claim that much more significant. The biblical text indicates that he died with no male heirs but does not say how or when he died. His daughters allude to his death in their argument before the court: *"Our father died in the wilderness. He was not one of the faction, Korah's faction, which banded together against God, but died for his own sin; and he has left no sons"* (Num. 27:3). This curious admission prompts numerous questions. Why did the daughters feel the need to reference his death? What was the sin for which he died? What is the connection between his death and the fact that he had no sons, which is linked within the verse?

According to the commentators Sforno and Ibn Ezra, the daughters must have presumed that descendants of Korah's followers would not have been entitled to inherit.[2] Consequently, they raised and addressed that concern up front—a common legal maneuver. Since the Korah rebellion took place in the biblical passages preceding this story and many men died at that time in the wilderness, the judges might have viewed Zelophehad's death, and therefore his daughters' plea, less favorably had insurrection been the cause. But once that cause of death had been discounted, nothing more would have had to be said about his death to make their inheritance claim. It is peculiar, then, that the daughters assertively raise the subject of his death at all, which is obvious based on their case. It is even more surprising that they unnecessarily acknowledge that some unnamed sin was involved.

The commentaries consider and disagree as to what that sin might have been. Several presume that Zelophehad had committed a capital offense and was put to death. In that case, his punishment of death would have had the effect of atonement for his crime. The Talmud contains an interesting debate about this. Citing Rabbi Akiva, an analogy is made between Zelophehad, who died *"in the wilderness"* (*ba-midbar*) (Num. 27:3), and an earlier story of an unnamed man gathering wood on Shabbat *"in the wilderness"* (*ba-midbar*) (Num. 15:32), who is taken before Moses and stoned to death by divine decree. Akiva asserts that the use of the same term *"in the wilderness"* in both passages signifies that it was one and the same man, and therefore, the crime of gathering wood on Shabbat was the crime for which Zelophehad was tried and put to death.

However, other rabbis in that same talmudic passage dispute this assumption, presuming his sin was that of the entire generation who had left Egypt, all of whom were doomed to die in the wilderness after the incident with the spies and the Israelites' incessant complaining (Num. 14).[3] The verse immediately prior to the story of Zelophehad's daughters reiterates the decree that all those who came out of Egypt, except Caleb and Joshua, would die before reaching the Promised Land. Numerous commentaries and midrash pick up on the juxtaposition of these passages as well as the language of that text, which states specifically that not one "man" (*ish*) would be left (Num. 16:65). This becomes one of several examples of how the women, compared to the men, are considered more righteous and praiseworthy in their actions throughout the journey. The placement of that text immediately before this story is evidence that the plea of Zelophehad's daughters is an example of the women's valor:

> *Then drew near the daughters of Zelophehad* (Num. XXVII:1). In that generation the women built up the fences [in the moral sense] which the men broke down. Thus you find that Aaron told them: *Break off the golden rings, which are in the ears of your wives* (Ex. XXXII, 2), but the women refused and checked their husbands; as is proved by the fact that it says, *And all the people broke off the golden rings which were in their ears* (ib. 3), the women not participating with them in making the Calf. It was the same in the case of the spies, who uttered an evil report: *And the men . . . when they returned, made all the congregation to murmur against him* (Num. XIV, 36), and against this congregation the decree [not to enter the Land] was issued, because they had said: *We are not able to go up* (ib XIII, 31). The women, however, were not with them in their counsel, as may be inferred from the fact that it is written in an earlier passage of our section, *For the Lord had said of them: They shall surely die in the wilderness. And there was not left* a man *of them, save Caleb the son of Jephunneh* (ib. XXVI, 65). Thus the text speaks of "*a man*" but not of "*a woman.*" This was because the men had been unwilling to enter the Land. The women, however, drew near to ask for

an inheritance in the Land. Consequently the present section was written down next to that dealing with the death of the generation of the wilderness, for it was there that the men broke down the fences and the women built them up.[4]

Several commentaries cite Rabbi Judah Halevi, who proposed that the phrases "*[he] died for his own sin*" and "*he has left no sons*" should be understood as linked; in other words, Zelophehad had no sons and he died, both because of his sin.[5] The Talmud conveys a similar message that suggests that God is angered if a man dies without a male heir. This notion is derived through a play on words. In the passage, "*you shall transfer [veha'avartem] his property to his daughter*" is linked with the day of wrath, "*That day shall be a day of wrath [evra]*" (Zephaniah 1:15).[6]

Whatever Zelophehad's sin may have been, the biblical text is clear that it did not bar his daughters from seeking their inheritance. In legal terms, their opening statements clarify that there is no cause to dismiss their case, and the judges are able to proceed to consider the merits of their claim.

The Righteous Daughters

Throughout the biblical text and the commentaries, the daughters of Zelophehad are deemed to be admirable women. The fact that they are named in the text along with their honorable pedigree dating back to Joseph indicates that they and their ancestors were all righteous.[7] Rashi adds that their link with Joseph is also exemplified by their love for, and desire to inherit, property in the Promised Land, just as Joseph sought to be buried there.[8] Despite the fact that the sisters boldly step forward to speak directly to Moses, it is presumed that they are actually timid and respectful and gain the required self-confidence only after consulting with their tribal elders.[9]

More than that, Zelophehad's daughters are considered to be wise interpreters of Jewish law.[10] They understand how the new laws pronounced at Sinai are to be implemented once the Israelites traverse the wilderness into the Promised Land. The depiction of the sisters' plea for justice provided by Ginzberg in *Legends of the Jews* is particularly powerful:

When Zelophehad's daughters, that had lived piously and wisely like their father and their ancestors, heard that the land was being divided among the male members of the tribe, but not among the female, they took counsel together, discussing what they could do, so that they might not find themselves come out empty-handed. They said: "God's love is not like the love of a mortal father; the latter prefers his sons to his daughters, but He that created the world extends His love to women as well as to men, 'His tender mercies are over all His works.'" They now hoped that God would take pity on them and give them their share of the promised land, which they loved with as great devotion as their grandsire Joseph, who had upon his death-bed exhorted his children to transfer his body to the Holy Land.[11]

According to midrash, the daughters wisely outlined the legal conundrum. If their situation is comparable to a man who dies childless and has no heirs, then the levirate laws would apply, and their mother should be married to the nearest male relative to produce the required male heir. However, if a man with daughters is not considered childless for levirate purposes, then he must have heirs, and therefore, logically, the daughters should be treated as if they were sons for inheritance purposes.[12]

The commentators do not agree as to why Moses turned to God to issue the ruling. Some assert that Zelophehad's daughters had bested Moses; they were wiser and more insightful even than Moses, who did not know the answer and needed God to confirm that the women had been accurate in their interpretation of the law. Others, however, assume Moses actually knew the correct answer. However, since the women had first approached the lower court for a ruling, that court consulted with a higher court, that court consulted with an ever-higher court, and so on, successively moving their claim up the chain until it reached Moses, he chose to consult the next and highest level of judicial authority as well, out of modesty and respect for custom. In this scenario, God's declaration that the women were correct is not seen as a critique of Moses, but rather as a credit to the women:

Now it is written, *and Moses brought their cause* (27, 5). Some hold that the law was hidden from Moses. There are cases where righteous men have boasted of some matter connected with a precept and the Holy One, blessed be He, weakened their power. . . . It is the same here. Moses had said: "*The cause that is too hard for you ye shall bring unto me.*" When the daughters of Zelophehad, however, came, He concealed the law from him, *and Moses brought their cause before the Lord. The daughters of Zelophehad speak right* (27, 7). This, He meant, is the law! The Holy One, blessed be He, said to him: "Did you not say, '*The cause that is too hard for you ye shall bring unto me*'? The law with which you are unacquainted is decided by the women!"

Another exposition of the text, *and Moses brought their cause*, etc. Resh Lakish says: Moses our Teacher knew this law, but the women came in the first instance before the chiefs of ten who said: "This is a case concerning inheritance and is not within our scope. It belongs to our superiors." The women came to the chiefs of fifty. Seeing that the chiefs of ten had shown them honour, the chiefs of fifty said: "In our case also there are superiors to us." The same reply was given by the chiefs of hundreds, by the chiefs of thousands, and by the princes. They all answered them in the same strain, for they were unwilling to begin considering it before their superior. So they went to Eleazar and he told them: "Behold, there is Moses our Teacher!" All parties came before Moses. When Moses saw that each one had shown respect to his superior, he thought: If I tell them the law I shall be appropriating all the greatness. So he said to them: "I too have a Superior! Therefore, Moses brought their cause before the Lord. The Holy One, blessed be He, answered him: The daughters of Zelophehad speak right." This indicates that the Holy One, blessed be He, acknowledged the justice of their words.[13]

The fact that the women brought their case not only to Moses, but also to Eleazar the priest, the chieftains, and the entire community is note-worthy. According to *Or ha-Ḥayim*, this was to ensure that everyone heard this important ruling, which was on the sensitive topic of women's inheritance rights.[14]

The presence of Eleazar the priest also begged an obvious question: where was Aaron? The rabbis answer that question by explaining that Aaron had already died by this time, which, according to the biblical text, was in the fortieth year of the wilderness journey (Num. 33:38).[15] Based on this timeline, the daughters of Zelophehad also brought their claim in the fortieth year, leading the rabbis to ask why the five daughters waited until the fortieth year to bring this claim, noting that they would have been well past marriageable age by then. This becomes additional evidence of the sisters' merit and superiority over Moses. While Moses had remained apart from his wife for forty years in the wilderness so as to remain pure when he stood before God (see chapter 9), these women were not commanded to remain chaste for those forty years, yet they chose to do so until the ruling would be made and proper husbands found. They were rewarded for their piety by the miracle of children, even though they were all over forty years old when they wed.[16]

In Num. 36:10–12, after the second ruling restricting their marriages to men of their own clan, the sisters are listed in a different order than the genealogical listings in 26:33 and 27:1 and later in Josh. 17:3. In most instances, Noah is listed second and Tirzah is listed last, but in the passage related to their marriage, these two names are reversed. Speculating on this variation in the name sequence, some rabbis suggest that the genealogical references provide the sisters' chronological birth order and Num. 36:11 the order in which they were wed.[17] Others suggest that their chronological order and marriage order would have been the same, since the custom, known from the Leah-Rachel narrative, was for older sisters to wed first. Therefore, some other criteria must have been used to list Noah second and Tirzah last in the other verses. The Talmud agrees with this view, explaining that the listing in Num. 36:11 is both their chronological birth and marriage order, whereas elsewhere they are listed according to their degree of intelligence, just as scholars are seated in order based on their wisdom.[18] Rashi, the father of three beloved daughters, considers the names interchangeable, because the sisters were all equal in intelligence and wisdom.[19]

The rabbinic sources wrestle with the inconsistency between the two statements in Num. 36:6, which states that the daughters could marry whomever they wanted but also that they had to marry within the tribe. According to the Talmud, the second clause restricting their husbands to men of the clan was only a recommendation, and to their credit, the sisters followed the recommended course.[20] Sforno takes note of the women's personal sacrifice; although they complied with the restriction voluntarily, their husbands were not the ones they would have chosen had the restriction not been in place.[21] In a variation of this perspective, some interpret the ruling as granting dispensation to marry freely only to the daughters of Zelophehad, while all other women inheriting land had to marry within their clan. Other commentaries suggest that the restriction did, in fact, apply to Zelophehad's daughters as well as all other women who were inheriting land; however, it only applied to the first generation of those who entered the Promised Land. By way of explanation, these rabbis clarify that only in that first generation were the lands apportioned according to the males numbered in the census.[22] The Talmud refers to a special holiday on the fifteenth of the month of Av (Tu b'Av, also known as the "Jewish Valentine's Day"), which marked the celebration that took place when the restriction was lifted and intermarriage among the different tribes was permitted once again.[23]

AUTHOR'S COMMENTARY: *Rights Given and Taken Away*

The story of Zelophehad's daughters is celebrated for establishing an ancient precedent for women's rights. The five sisters are given the right to inherit, or, more accurately, the right to have their inheritance pass through them to their male heirs. They are also granted the right to choose their own husbands at a time when that was not the norm, although that right was subsequently restricted.

While these laws are impressive when considering the era in which they were established, they are limited and certainly not equal to the privileges enjoyed by their male counterparts. Men could inherit and marry whomever they wished; however, women with no male siblings were required to marry within their immediate clan. And despite the laudatory precedent related to women's rights, the women did not actually inherit the property themselves—it was merely preserved for their sons or husbands to inherit. Although there would have been an economic benefit to ensuring that their male heirs were protected, the women themselves were not entitled to own property. In effect, this precedent restricted women's marital rights without conferring any real property rights.

The real-life implication of these rulings on women's lives in ancient days can only be imagined, but it is not difficult to see that the effect may not have been entirely beneficial to the women themselves. The modern midrash "Noah and Elishama—A Love Story" explores the dilemma faced by one of the sisters as the two-sided nature of the ruling becomes evident. Her male uncles and cousins are able to retain her share of her father's land grant, while she is prevented from marrying the man she loves.

It is notable that Mahlah, Noah, Hoglah, Milcah, and Tirzah are repeatedly named and the biblical narrative records their own words, unlike so many unnamed biblical women who have no voice. That said, the biblical text and commentaries provide little information about the women themselves—who they were as individuals, their family life, how they related to each other, or what it meant for them to go before the tribunal of men. From the text we only know that they sought and received a ruling in their favor related to their clan's rights. From the classical midrash, we learn that the sisters were wise, righteous, and married late in life.

"Noah and Elishama—A Love Story" weaves together the midrash related to Zelophehad, the legal issues of their case, and biblical genealogy while incorporating elements from nearby biblical passages related to inheritance laws, the Korah rebellion, the allotment of tribal lands, and the tribe of Manasseh's decision to remain in the Diaspora. In the biblical narrative, the laws regarding the vows of women also come at this point in the storyline (Numbers 30), between Zelophehad's daughters' successful plea for their inheritance and the tribe of Manasseh's demand that lands remain within the tribe. As depicted in this modern midrash, a woman's vow could be annulled by her father or, after she was wed, her husband; if her father or husband did not disavow it, her pledge would stand.

The selection of the featured sister was influenced by the unusual shift in name sequence. Why was Noah, the second sister named in genealogical lists, suddenly relegated to the last position in chapter 36? The rabbinic speculation that the change was related to the order of the sisters' marriages added an interesting element to explore in Noah's story. Envisioning her love interest as a man from a different tribe illustrates the impact of the imposed marriage ban; even if she and her prospective husband were willing to renounce her property claim, by law she was not permitted to marry outside the tribe. The separation of families that would have resulted from the decision of the tribe of Manasseh to remain on the east side of the Jordan River added yet another tragic dimension to her story.

Elishama's and other names were chosen from genealogical lists. Elishama ben Ammihud was a warrior and tribal leader representing the tribe of Ephraim at the Tent of Meeting.[24] Aniam and Likhi, sons of Shemida, are listed in the genealogical lists for the tribe of Manasseh.[25] The tribes of Manasseh and Ephraim were related through their common ancestor, Joseph, so Noah and Elishama would have been distant cousins. Hence, the origin of their love story at imagined clan gatherings became a logical story element.

The star-crossed lovers' separation at the Jordan River when the tribe of Manasseh remained behind is not directly related to the story of Zelophehad's daughters. That said, these events would have taken place at around the same time, just prior to entering the Promised Land, according to biblical chronology. The request of the tribes of Gad, Reuben, and half of Manasseh to remain east of the Jordan occurs in between the two rulings related to Zelophehad's daughters (Numbers 32). That tribal decision, like the inheritance ruling, would have led to tragic separations among families.

The connection between Zelophehad's daughters' story and the holiday of Tu b'Av, commemorating the moment when tribes could once again intermarry, offers a happy ending of sorts. Although Noah and other similarly situated women of her generation were not permitted to marry beyond their clan, eventually the ban was lifted. Once the apportionment of tribal lands under Joshua was completed and the land grant matters resolved, women in the five sisters' predicament could marry beyond the confines of their own tribe. Although Noah and Elishama's love story ended unhappily, her descendants would once again know the possibility of inter-tribal love and marriage.

APPENDIX

Overview of Midrash

From the moment the biblical text was codified, scholars have sought to understand every nuance of every word of the Bible in order to learn its deepest, most salient lessons. Biblical exegesis, the art of interpreting and expounding upon the biblical text, developed over the centuries to create a fulsome body of Jewish literature, from legal codes, to commentaries, to collections of midrash. That creative process continues to this day, as students of Scripture continue to apply our ancient wisdom to today's realities. The brilliance of our tradition is found in that ongoing process of engagement with the text; no matter how many times we read and reread our sacred texts, there are always new lessons to be learned and new ways to find meaning within, and between, the words on the page.

Through the midrashic process, we are able to interpret not only the letters of the text, but also the white space in between. Midrash allows us to "mine the gaps" in the text, finding meaning and relevance not only in what is written, but also through what is missing, allowing our imagination and creativity to fill in the blanks. If the lessons of our ancient texts are unclear or if they fail to address the current circumstances affecting our communities, the tools of midrash allow us to uncover hidden meanings and discover new insights.

The word *midrash* is derived from the Hebrew root *d-r-sh*, meaning "to seek." As noted in the introduction, historically midrash developed as the rabbis plumbed the text for knowledge about its deeper meaning and for direction in how to guide their own communities in their own days. Over time, the literature that developed was organized into two primary types of midrash: *midrash halakhah* (halakhic/legal midrash), which clarifies the rules and regulations governing the Jewish community; and *midrash aggadah* (aggadic/narrative midrash), which explores biblical tales and legends to derive ethical and theological lessens from the experiences of our ancestors. Occasionally, these elements overlap; a collection of halakhic midrash may include aggadic material and vice versa.

There are also different literary forms of midrash. *Exegetical midrash*, explaining a particular verse or word, is generally short and to the point. In many of the traditional commentaries, this type of midrash can be quite cryptic. *Homiletical midrash* tends to be lengthier; like a modern sermon, biblical texts are woven together creatively to build a case for a particular message.

HERMENEUTICAL RULES

As rabbis and scholars sought to explain the biblical text, they developed specific concepts and rules for biblical interpretation, or exegesis. *Hermeneutics* is the application of these generally accepted interpretive methods to biblical study. These rules of construction helped bring order to the midrashic process, even as they enabled creativity in the reading and understanding of the text.

The earliest compilation of these hermeneutical rules are seven principles (*middot*) ascribed to Hillel in the first century BCE. In the subsequent generation, these rules were later amplified in a set of thirteen rules ascribed to Rabbi Yishmael, and found at the beginning of the Sifra, a compilation of midrash from the third century. In the second century CE Rabbi Eliezer ben Yose ha-Galili expanded the thirteen rules to thirty-two rules.

The hermeneutical rules are largely based in principles of logic. For example, *kal vaḥomer* is an inference from a minor (*kal*) matter to a major (*ḥomer*) matter, as well as the reverse. This can be understood by the English phrase "If X is true, then *all the more so*, Y must be true." Similarly, *kelal uferat* is an argument from a general (*kelal*) principle to a specific (*perat*) subject and the reverse. Other commonly applied rules include "analogy," which involves deducing the meaning of a word based on its usage elsewhere in the biblical text, and "juxtaposition," which links matters together based on their adjacent placement in the text.

Expansion and *limitation* are other common techniques. If each word has significance, then the presence of certain particles such as the Hebrew equivalents of "and," "but," or "with" permits the extension or restriction of a principle outlined in the text. A linguistic repetition, redundancy, or superfluous word in the text is an invitation to expound upon the meaning of a verse. Similarly, unusual words, letters, or diacritical marks give rise to midrashic explanations. *Gematria*, applying a numerical value to letters and words, can also be used to uncover deeper meanings within the text.

The rabbis even used puns and wordplays to provide new and creative understandings of the text. A particularly creative principle is *ein mukdam ume'uḥar ba-Torah*, "nothing is early or late in the Torah," meaning that chronological logic need not apply to the Torah. For example, this concept allows the midrash to envision Moses seated in a classroom taught by Rabbi Akiva (BT *Menaḥot* 29b).

One of the keys to understanding classical midrash is determining what questions the rabbis themselves were asking as they endeavored to discover the proper meaning of a text for their day. Similarly, a helpful rule of thumb for studying midrash is to refer to the full verse being referenced by the rabbis; the inclusion of a biblical citation to either raise or answer a particular question may not be understandable from the few words offered as shorthand in the midrash itself.

A HISTORY OF MIDRASH

Midrash as a type of interpretive literature can be found embedded throughout Jewish sources. Although the biblical stories date from as early as 1200 BCE, it was not until around the latter part of the first millennium BCE that it began to take final shape and become codified. At that point, it took on canonical status and could no longer be changed, and yet the need to interpret and understand it continued. Eventually the sages organized these interpretations and explanations. Rabbi Yehudah ha-Nasi synthesized and codified what became the Mishnah around 200 CE. At around the same time, another compendium with the same structure, the Tosefta (meaning "Addition"), also was codified with additional material. Subsequent commentary on the Mishnah, the Gemara, developed over the next several hundred years through the two major centers of Jewish scholarship, one in the Land of Israel and the other in Babylonia, modern-day Iraq. The Mishnah and the Gemara combined became the Talmud. The Jerusalem, or Palestinian, Talmud (Talmud Yerushalmi) was finalized around the fourth to fifth century CE, while the Babylonian Talmud (Talmud Bavli) was finalized about a hundred years later. While both contain much of the same material, there are variations as each responded to the different circumstances facing their communities. Midrash can be found sprinkled throughout each of these texts.

At around the same time the Mishnah and Talmud were developing, the Hebrew Bible was translated into Aramaic, the common spoken language of the Jewish community by the end of the biblical era. These translations (*Targumim*) often contain elements of midrash that were commonly known at the time but not part of the biblical text itself. Translation is a form of interpretation, and the word choices and amplification of the text found in these translations can provide insights into how early scholars understood the nuances of the text. *Targum Onkelos*, the most commonly utilized Aramaic translation, likely dates to the second to first century BCE. *Targum Jonathan*, more properly referred to as *Targum Yerushalmi* or *Targum Pseudo-Jonathan*, is a later Aramaic translation, and its dating—ranging from the fourth century to the fourteenth century—remains a subject of debate. In addition to the Aramaic translations, the Hebrew Bible was translated into Greek (the Septuagint) and eventually Latin (the Vulgate); each of these translations embed interpretive choices that also impact the nuance of a verse.

Hellenistic Literature

Elements of biblical stories that did not make it into the final canon none-theless found their way into other ancient sources. The Apocrypha, a collection of books that were not canonized in the Hebrew Bible but were recognized as authoritative in some Jewish communities as early as the second century BCE, includes two books of the Maccabees, additions to several biblical books, and wisdom literature. Another collection of works, the Pseudepigrapha, is falsely ascribed to biblical personages; the book of *Jubilees* and the *Testaments of the Twelve Patriarchs* are two examples. Preserved through the Greek and Latin translations of the Bible, these Hellenistic works are part of the Christian canon but contain many early rabbinic interpretations.

Antiquities of the Jews, written by Josephus Flavius, a first- to second-century Jewish general who later became a Roman historian, offers a retelling of biblical history that also preserves elements of biblical stories that were known at the time but not incorporated into the Hebrew Scripture we read today. Similarly, texts found among the Dead Sea Scrolls in Qumran contain works that were contemporaneous with the Bible but did not make it into the canon. Technically these Hellenistic works are not considered midrash, but they contain material that supplements the biblical text and sheds light on how early sages expounded upon the biblical stories, just as midrash does.

Early Midrashic Anthologies

At around the same time as the Talmud was developing, compilations of midrash primarily organized around the books of the Bible began to emerge. The early collections became known as the tannaitic midrashim because they are attributed to the *tannaim*, the rabbinic sages named in the Mishnah, although it is more likely that the following generation of scholars compiled them. Classified as *midrash halakhah*, though they contain aggadic material as well, these include the *Mekhilta de-Rabbi Yishmael* on Exodus, the *Sifra* on Leviticus, the *Sifrei Bamidbar* on Numbers, and the *Sifrei Devarim* on Deuteronomy.[1] These collections probably reached their final form in the third or fourth century. *Seder Olam Rabbah*, a collection of midrash tracking the chronological history of Israel from Creation to Alexander the Great, also includes early midrashic material from the second century but likely did not reach its final form until the twelfth century.[2]

The extensive collection of midrash known as Midrash Rabbah is often mistakenly referred to as "the Midrash," which developed over several hundred years. Like earlier compilations, Midrash Rabbah is organized according to the books of the Bible. The earliest section, Genesis Rabbah, attributed to sages from the third- and fourth-century post-Mishnah amoraic period, likely reached its final form around the early fifth century. The later Rabbah collections, such as Numbers Rabbah, were finalized much later. These midrashim look to the history of the Jewish people as told in Genesis to glean lessons for the world as it had been and would become in the future. According to scholar Jacob Neusner:

> Their [the sages'] conviction is that what Abraham, Isaac, and Jacob did in the past shaped the future history of Israel. If, therefore, we want to know the meaning of present events and those in the future, we look back to find out. But the interest is not merely in history as a source of lessons; it is history as the treasury of truths about the here and now and especially about tomorrow. . . . And that is why they looked to a reliable account of the past and searched out the meanings of their own day. Bringing to the stories of Genesis the conviction that it told not only the story of yesterday but also the tale of tomorrow, the sages whose words are before us in this anthology transformed a picture of the past into a prophecy for a near tomorrow.[3]

Other midrashic collections from around the same period that Genesis Rabbah was developed include Leviticus Rabbah, Lamentations Rabbah, and *Pesikta de-Rav Kahana*. Later sections of the Midrash Rabbah collection for Exodus, Numbers, Deuteronomy, and other biblical books were compiled later, reaching their final forms at various times between the eighth and eleventh centuries. Midrashic collections that developed during this later period include *Pesikta Rabbati*, *Pirkei de-Rabbi Eliezer*, *Tanna de-Vei Eliyyahu*, and *Midrash Tanḥuma*. Still later sources include *Yalkut Shimoni*, likely from the eleventh to twelfth century, and *Sefer ha-Yashar* from as late as the fourteenth to fifteenth century.[4]

Medieval Commentators

While the desire to unravel the mysteries of the biblical text was endemic to Jewish life from its earliest days, biblical commentary emerged in the Middle Ages as a significant addition to the corpus of Jewish literature. Eminent scholars culled through hundreds of years of Jewish sources and applied many of the classic midrashic techniques to continue the process of interpreting the Bible and comprehending the Talmud to keep them relevant and understandable to their medieval Jewish communities.

The influence of Islamic scholarship in Spain and the Ottoman Empire during this period greatly influenced many of these rabbis. They sought to distill the text to its simplest form, to clarify the *peshat* (simple meaning) of the words found in Scripture as these might have been understood when originally written. Other scholars expounded upon the text in order to develop the *derash* (interpretation), curating lessons to be learned with a more homiletical approach. Over centuries, these commentators learned from each successive generation of scholars and added their own insights and knowledge to develop an extensive body of rabbinic literature.

Eventually, the writings of the most distinguished scholars were incorporated within printed texts of the Bible and Talmud. Among the most prominent of these commentators were Rabbi Shlomo ben Yitzhak (Rashi, 1040–1105, France), Rabbi Shmuel ben Meir (Rashbam, 1085–1174, France, Rashi's grandson), Rabbi Abraham ben Meir Ibn Ezra (1089–1164, Spain), Rabbi David Kimhi (Radak, 1160–1235, Provence), Rabbi Moshe ben Nahman (Nahmanides or Ramban, 1194–1270, Spain), and Rabbi Levi ben Gershon (Gersonides or Ralbag, 1288–1344, France).[5] These brilliant scholars and others like them laid the foundation for later biblical scholars and modern biblical studies. Their commentaries continue to be studied today in order to grasp the many nuances of our sacred Scripture.

As classical texts are being translated and educational resources and tools are increasingly available online, more individuals are being exposed to the richness of midrash as a way to make Scripture relevant to today. And thus, midrash continues as a thriving, living art form today, just as it has throughout the ages.

GLOSSARY OF CLASSICAL SOURCES

Antiquities of the Jews: A retelling of biblical history, including elements of biblical stories that were known at the time but not incorporated into Hebrew Scripture, written by Josephus Flavius, the first- to second-century Jewish general who later became a Roman historian.

Apocrypha: A collection of books that were not canonized in the Hebrew Bible but were recognized as authoritative in some Jewish communities as early as the second century BCE. These writings, as well as the Pseudepigrapha, were preserved through the Greek and Latin translations of the Bible.

Avot de-Rabbi Natan: A minor tractate included in most editions of the Talmud, homiletically linked to Pirkei Avot (Sayings of the Fathers), a collection of ethical teachings dating perhaps as late as the seventh to tenth century.

Bible: This author's use of the term "Bible" refers to Hebrew Scripture. Most scholars agree that the text was largely finalized by the first or second century BCE. The translation used throughout this publication is *The Contemporary Torah: A Gender-Sensitive Adaptation of the JPS Translation*.

Da'at Zekenim: A collection of commentaries by the later Franco-German tosafists of the twelfth to thirteenth century, generally included in editions of the Bible with commentaries.

Ein Yaakov (Well of Jacob): A compilation of aggadic midrash and stories drawn from the Talmud compiled by Rabbi Yaakov ibn Habib following his expulsion from Spain and completed by his son Rabbi Levi ibn Habib in the sixteenth century. The Glick edition of *Ein Yaakov* is an English translation produced by Rabbi Shmuel Tzvi-Hirsch Glick in Chicago in 1921.

Gemara: When combined with the Mishnah, the Gemara completes the Oral Law of the Talmud. Once the Mishnah was codified, generations of sages continued to study, debate, and amplify its rulings, and these additions became known as the Gemara (from the Hebrew root *g-m-r*, meaning "to finish" or "to complete").

Ḥizkuni: A thirteenth-century commentary on the Bible by Rabbi Hezekiah ben Manoah (likely France, ca. 1250–1310), who based his work on earlier midrashic commentaries and widely cited Rashi's commentary

Ibn Ezra: Abraham ben Meir Ibn Ezra (Spain, ca. 1089–1164), an itinerant scholar who traveled throughout Europe; wrote his commentaries in Spain, Italy, France, and England; and took a philological (linguistic) approach to the study of the biblical text in order to determine the simple meaning of the text (*peshat*), setting the stage for modern biblical criticism.

Joseph and Asenath: A book in the Pseudepigrapha containing stories and intrigues around Joseph's marriage to Asenath, presumed to be a Jewish source from the Hellenistic era.

Jubilees: A book in the Pseudepigrapha containing a retelling of biblical stories, probably written originally in Hebrew and dating from as early as 150 BCE.

Kitzur Baal ha-Turim: An abridged version of the *Tur ha-Arokh*, a Torah commentary by Rabbi Jacob ben Asher (Spain, ca. 1269–1343), also known as Rabbeinu Asher.

Kli Yakar: A homiletical commentary written in the sixteenth century by Rabbi Shlomo Ephraim ben Aaron Luntschitz (Prague, 1550–1619).

Luzzatto: Samuel David Luzzatto (Italy, 1800–1865), known as Shadal, a scholar, philosopher, and poet whose commentary applied a modern critical approach to the biblical text.

Maimonides/Rambam: Rabbi Moses ben Maimon (Spain, 1138–1204), also known as Rambam, a legal expert, philosopher, and physician learned in science and Islamic culture, who incorporated midrash and other Jewish texts within his expansive writings. Maimonides' *Mishneh Torah*, a code of Jewish law, provided the basis for later law codes and is still considered authoritative today.

Malbim: Commentary by Rabbi Meir Leibush ben Yehiel Michel Wisser (Ukraine, 1809–79), which is characterized by the author's presumption that there are no superfluous words in the biblical text and all laws can be gleaned from either the *peshat* (simple meaning) or the *derash* (exegesis) of the words in the Torah.

Mekhilta de-Rabbi Yishmael, or the *Mekhilta:* A halakhic (legal) midrash on the book of Exodus, which also incorporates aggadic (narrative) material, ascribed to the school of Rabbi Yishmael ben Elisha ha-Kohen and likely composed around the third or fourth century.

Midrash Rabbah (the Great Midrash): An extensive collection of midrashim organized according to the books of the Bible and developed over several hundred years, roughly from the fifth through the eleventh century. Genesis Rabbah, the earliest section, is largely attributed to sages from the fifth to early sixth century; Leviticus Rabbah and Lamentations Rabbah were likely from this same time period. The sections for Exodus, Numbers, Deuteronomy, and other biblical books were compiled later, reaching their final forms at various times between the eighth and eleventh centuries.

Midrash Sekhel Tov: An early twelfth-century compilation of aggadic and halakhic midrash and philological (linguistic) commentary by Rabbi Menahem ben Shlomo, likely from Italy. While the complete text is no longer extant, Solomon Buber printed portions of it in 1900.

Midrash Tanḥuma: A midrashic collection ascribed to Rabbi Tanhuma from the amoraic period (200–500 CE), but it is more likely to have been compiled in the sixth to ninth century. Solomon Buber published a version of *Midrash Tanḥuma* in 1885 based on an early manuscript, incorrectly asserting the date to be much earlier.

Mishnah: A codification of Jewish biblical legal texts by Rabbi Yehudah ha-Nasi, ca. 200 CE. After the biblical text was canonized, the sages distilled and organized its legal rulings and applied them to real-life situations in their day. Rabbi Yehudah's subsequent codification laid the foundation for what became known as the Oral Law, as distinguished from the Written Law of the Bible.

Or ha-Ḥayim: An eighteenth-century Torah commentary by Rabbi Hayyim ben Moshe ibn Attar (Morocco, ca. 1696–1743), who is sometimes referred to as the Or ha-Hayim, after his commentary.

Pesikta de-Rav Kahana: A compilation containing homiletical midrash dating possibly from the fifth to early sixth century but likely not reaching its final form until the early eighth century. Who Rabbi Kahana was or which Rabbi Kahana inspired this collection, remains unclear.

Pesikta Rabbati: A homiletical midrash for festivals and special Sabbaths dated to the eighth or ninth century.

Pirkei de-Rabbi Eliezer: A collection of aggadic (narrative) midrash on the biblical text from Genesis to the Israelites' journey in the wilderness, ascribed to Rabbi Eliezer ben Hyrcanus from the tannaitic period (first to second century), but likely composed in the eighth or ninth century.

Pseudepigrapha: Generally combined with the Apocrypha, the Pseudepigrapha is a noncanonical collection of books purported to have been written by Jewish and biblical personages. This publication makes reference to the Pseudepigrapha's *Jubilees* and *Testaments of the Twelve Patriarchs*, likely from the second to first century BCE. Fragments of both books were found among the scrolls discovered at Qumran.

Rabbeinu Bahya: Rabbi Bahya ben Asher (Spain, 1255–1340), who infused his biblical commentary with midrash as well as Kabbalah, often citing prior generations of commentators, particularly Ramban (Nahmanides).

Radak: Rabbi David Kimhi (Provence, 1160–1235), who approached the biblical text from a linguistic and grammatical perspective, though he also shared philosophical and ethical interpretations of the text.

Ramban: Rabbi Moses ben Nahman (Spain, 1194–1270), also known as Nahmanides, who wrote an extensive commentary on the Bible, often citing earlier scholars such as Rashi and Ibn Ezra, though not always agreeing with his predecessors. His commentary includes simple explanations of the text and often is infused with philosophy and mysticism.

Rashbam: Rabbi Shmuel ben Meir (France, ca. 1085–1174), a grandson of Rashi whose commentaries on the Bible and Talmud focus on the simple explanations of the text, though without the midrashic embellishments offered by Rashi.

Rashi: Rabbi Shlomo ben Yitzhak (France, 1040–1105), the most prominent of the medieval commentators, who provided simple, logical explanations of the texts while also incorporating a rich trove of midrashic elements. His commentaries on the Bible and Talmud have a central place in printed editions of these texts and provide the basis for many subsequent commentaries.

Seder Olam Rabbah (**The Great Order of the World**): A compilation of early aggadic (narrative) midrash likely dating to the second century, though probably not reaching its final form until the twelfth century. It follows the chronological history of Israel from Creation to Alexander the Great, filling in gaps in the biblical narrative.

Sefer ha-Yashar: A medieval narrative midrash covering biblical history from Creation until the period of the Judges, likely composed in Italy and dating from the tenth to the sixteenth century. *Sefer ha-Yashar* is also known as the *Toledot Adam*, *Divrei ha-Yamim he-Arukh*, and in English, the *Book of Jasher*, which supposedly is based on a biblical allusion to it, in Joshua 10:13.

Sforno: Ovadiah ben Yaakov Sforno (Italy, ca. 1475–1550) a scholar and physician, who approached the biblical text from an exegetical, philological perspective, seeking out the original meaning of the text and rejecting mystical interpretations.

Sifra: A halakhic (legal) midrash on the book of Leviticus, likely compiled by the school of Rabbi Yishmael in the third to fourth century. The *Sifra* (Book) begins with a listing of the thirteen hermeneutical principles articulated by Rabbi Yishmael.

Sifrei Bamidbar: A halakhic (legal) midrash on the book of Numbers, likely compiled by the school of Rabbi Yishmael ben Elisha ha-Kohen around the third to fourth century.

Sifrei Devarim: A halakhic (legal) midrash on the book of Deuteronomy, likely compiled by the school of Rabbi Akiva around the third to fourth century.

Siftei Ḥakhamim: A "supercommentary" on Rashi's Bible commentary by Shabbetai ben Joseph Bass (Poland, 1641–1718). This overlay of Rashi's work often appears in editions of the Bible with commentary.

Talmud: The combination of the Mishnah and the Gemara, which completed the Oral Law. Once the Mishnah was codified, generations of sages continued to study, debate, and amplify its rulings, and these additions became known as the Gemara (from the Hebrew root *g-m-r*, meaning "to finish" or "to complete"). The scholars from academies in the Land of Israel finalized the Jerusalem Talmud (Talmud Yerushalmi) around 400 CE, while the academies from Babylonia codified their Talmud (Talmud Bavli) around 500 CE. References to the Babylonian Talmud and Jerusalem Talmud in this volume are abbreviated as BT and JT respectively.

Targum (plural: *Targumim*): Literally "translation," in the context of biblical studies, the term used for a translation of Hebrew Scripture into Aramaic, the common spoken language of the Jewish community by the end of the biblical era. These translations often contain midrashic elements that were commonly known at the time but not part of the biblical text itself.

Targum Jonathan: A later Aramaic translation of the Bible, dating from as early as the fourth century, also known as *Targum Yerushalmi* or *Targum Pseudo-Jonathan*.

Targum Onkelos: The most commonly utilized Aramaic translation of the Bible, likely dating to the second to first century BCE.

Testaments of the Twelve Patriarchs: A book of the Pseudepigrapha containing the purported deathbed testimonials of the twelve sons of Jacob sharing their confessions and advice to their descendants, likely originally written in Greek, from the second century BCE.

Tosafot (Additions): Explanatory notes on the Talmud by French and German scholars from the twelfth through the fourteenth century. The earliest of the tosafists were Rashi's disciples, including his sons-in-law and grandsons.

Tosefta: A compilation of Oral Law that is comparable to, and contemporaneous with, the second-century Mishnah. The word *tosefta* means "addition" or "supplement." While it is organized with the same structure as the Mishnah, the Tosefta contains some variations and additional material.

Tractate *Kallah Rabbati* (Great bride): A minor tractate written in Aramaic included in most printed editions of the Talmud, likely composed after the talmudic period, in the eighth or ninth century.

***Tur ha-Arokh* or *Perush ha-Tur ha-Arokh al ha-Torah*:** A Torah commentary by Rabbi Jacob ben Asher (Spain, ca. 1269–1343), also known as Rabbeinu Asher and as the Ba'al ha-Turim, from his major halakhic work, *Arba'ah Turim* (the *Tur*). His Torah commentary is generally included in editions of the Bible with commentary. The *Kitzur Baal ha-Turim* is an abridged version of this Torah commentary.

***Yalkut Shimoni*:** A late compilation of aggadic (narrative) midrash that follows the biblical storyline, likely assembled in the eleventh to twelfth centuries.

NOTES

INTRODUCTION

1. Holtz, *Back to the Sources*, 213–14.
2. See Holtz, *Back to the Sources*, 255, for a listing of these significant commentators.
3. Holtz, *Back to the Sources*, 179–80.

1. KETURAH

1. According to Gen. R. 67:9, all of the matriarchs, including Rebekah, were prophets.
2. Rashi on Gen. 25:6.
3. Rashi on Gen. 25:1, citing Gen. R. 61.
4. The various Aramaic translations of the biblical text are known as *Targumim* (meaning "translations").
5. Ibn Ezra and Rashbam on Gen. 25:1; Rashbam on Gen. 25:6.
6. Gen. R. 61:4.
7. Rashi on Gen. 25:1, citing Gen. R. 61:4, as translated in Rosenbaum and Silbermann, *Pentateuch with Targum Onkelos, Haphtaroth and Rashi's Commentary*, 111.
8. *Tur ha-Arokh* on Gen. 25:1, as translated in Munk, *Tur on the Torah by Rabbi Yaakov ben Rabbeinu Asher*.
9. *Kli Yakar* on Gen. 25:1, as translated in Davis, *Sifsei Chachamim Chumash*.
10. BT *Bava Kamma* 92b.
11. *Midrash Tanḥuma*, Ḥayyei Sarah 9:1, as translated in Townsend, *Midrash Tanhuma*.
12. OTP, *Jubilees* 19:13.
13. BT *Bava Kamma* 92b.

14. See, for example, Deut. 7:3.

15. Rabbeinu Bahya on Gen. 25:6, as translated in Munk, *Torah Commentary by Rabbi Bachya ben Asher*.

16. Radak on Gen. 25:1, as translated in Munk, *Mikraot Gedolot*. See also *Tur ha-Arokh* on Gen. 25:6.

17. *Tur ha-Arokh* on Gen. 25:6, as translated in Munk, *Tur on the Torah by Rabbi Yaakov ben Rabbeinu Asher*.

18. Radak on Gen. 25:1, as translated in Munk, *Mikraot Gedolot*. See also Rabbeinu Bahya on Gen. 25:6.

19. *Siftei Ḥakhamim* on Gen. 25:6, as translated in Davis, *Sifsei Chachamim Chumash*.

20. Gen. R. 38:10.

21. Gen. R. 61:5, as translated in Freedman, *Midrash Rabbah*, 2:544.

22. Sforno on Gen. 25:6.

23. *Ḥizkuni* on Gen. 25:6.

24. Rashi on Gen. 25:6.

25. See, for example, BT *Sotah* 13a; BT *Sanhedrin* 91a.

26. BT *Sanhedrin* 59b. See also Maimonides, *Mishneh Torah*, Kings and War, 10:8.

27. Gen. R. 68:11. See also Lev. R. 36:5; Num. R. 2:13.

28. BT *Sanhedrin* 91a.

29. Gen. R. 61:5.

30. Radak on Gen. 25:3.

2. LEAH AND RACHEL

1. *"I am my beloved's, and my beloved is mine"* (Song of Songs 6:3) is often used in wedding ceremonies.

2. In the time between the births of Joseph and Benjamin, Jacob had returned to Canaan with his family, wrestled with an angel, and reunited with and then separated from his older brother, Esau.

3. Believing Joseph to be dead, Jacob cherished Rachel's second son, Benjamin, above the others. See Judah's depiction of Jacob and Benjamin's relationship in Gen. 44:20 and 44:30.

4. This depiction is a reference to the well-known image of Rachel crying for her children: *"A cry is heard in Ramah—Wailing, bitter weeping—Rachel weeping for her children. She refuses to be comforted for her children, who are gone"* (Jer. 31:15).

5. See *Seder Olam Rabbah* 2; *Sefer ha-Yashar*, Toledot 6.

6. See, for example, BT *Bava Batra* 123a.

7. BT *Bava Batra* 123a; Gen. R. 70:16, 71:2; Rashi, Ibn Ezra, Radak, and *Tur ha-Arokh* on Gen. 29:17; *Midrash Tanḥuma Buber*, Va-yetse' 12:1.

8. See, for example, *Targum Jonathan* on Gen. 29:9; *Pirkei de-Rabbi Eliezer* 36:5; *Or ha-Ḥayim* on Gen. 29:6.

9. See, for example, *Tur ha-Arokh* on Gen. 29:9; *Or ha-Ḥayim* on Gen. 29:6.

10. See, for example, Ramban, *Ḥizkuni*, and *Tur ha-Arokh* on Gen. 29:9; Rabbeinu Bahya on Gen. 29:11 and 29:15.

11. See, for example, Gen R. 70:12; Ramban on Gen. 29:9; Rabbeinu Bahya on Gen. 29:11; Ruth Rabbah 2:21; Sforno on Gen. 29:18.

12. See, for example, Ibn Ezra, *Ḥizkuni*, and *Or ha-Ḥayim* on Gen. 29:12.

13. See, for example, Rashi, *Tur ha-Arokh*, and *Siftei Ḥakhamim* on Gen. 29:12.

14. *Tur ha-Arokh* on Gen. 29:10, as translated in Munk, *Tur on the Torah*. In a variation of this commentary, Rashi, citing Gen. R. 70:13, suggests that Jacob's description implied that if Laban proved deceitful, he would be his "brother" (match) in deception; however, if he proved honest, then Jacob similarly would be pious like the son of Laban's sister Rebekah. See also *Targum Jonathan* on Gen. 29:12; *Ein Yaakov, Megillah* 1:25.

15. Gen. 29:18, author's translation.

16. Rashi on Gen. 29:18, citing Gen. R. 70:17, as translated in Rosenbaum and Silbermann, *Pentateuch with Targum Onkelos, Haphtaroth and Rashi's Commentary*, 137. See also Rabbeinu Bahya on Gen. 29:15.

17. See, for example, BT *Bava Batra* 123a; BT *Megillah* 13b; Rashi and Radak on Gen. 29:25; *Ein Yaakov, Megillah* 1:25. Other sources suggest that Rachel gave Jacob a particular token or that Rachel whispered to Jacob from outside the bridal chamber so he would not discover Leah's true identity. See, for example, Tractate *Kallah Rabbati* 3:18.

18. See, for example, *Seder Olam Rabbah* 2; *Sefer ha-Yashar*, Toledot 6.

19. See, for example, *Targum Jonathan* and *Da'at Zekenim* on Gen. 29:22.

20. *Or ha-Ḥayim* on Gen. 29:26, as translated in Munk, *Or HaChayim*.

21. *Or ha-Ḥayim* on Gen. 29:23.

22. Ramban on Gen. 29:31.

23. See, for example, Gen. R. 70:19; *Midrash Tanḥuma Buber*, Va-yetse' 11:1.

24. See, for example, Radak, Rabbeinu Bahya, and *Tur ha-Arokh* on Gen. 29:30–31.

25. Gen. R. 71:2, as translated in Freedman, *Midrash Rabbah*, 2:653.

26. See, for example, Gen. R. 72:6; *Ḥizkuni* on Gen. 30:1; Rabbeinu Bahya on Gen. 29:21; *Tur ha-Arokh* on Gen. 30:9. Rashi suggests, alternatively, that Rachel was envious of her sister's good deeds, presuming that Leah was privileged to bear children due to her righteousness. See Gen. R. 71:6; Rashi on Gen. 30:1.

27. Radak on Gen. 30:1 and 30:15 suggests that Jacob slept with Rachel more often than Leah because she had no children. According to *Or ha-Ḥayim* on Gen. 30:15, Jacob had no obligation to spend his nights equitably among his wives

and merely had to perform his minimal marital obligations with Leah. See also Radak, Ramban, *Ḥizkuni*, Rabbeinu Bahya, *Tur ha-Arokh*, Sforno, and *Or ha-Ḥayim* on Gen. 29:30, which all comment that Jacob loved Rachel more than Leah, even though Leah was his first wife.

28. See, for example, Gen. R. 98:4.
29. See, for example, Radak and *Or ha-Ḥayim* on Gen. 30:1. According to *Targum Jonathan* on Gen. 30:16, the braying of an ass alerted Leah to Jacob's arrival, while other sources suggest that Jacob's ass led him to Leah's tent through God's intervention (see *Siftei Ḥakhamim* on Gen. 30:16). This is a play on Gen. 49:14, "*Issachar is a strong-boned ass.*" Issachar was the son born after that encounter, and the verse could also be translated as "*Issachar: the ass was the cause.*" Referencing the idiom "Like mother like daughter," some commentaries see Leah's brazenness as immoral, noting that the same phrase used to describe Leah's "going out" to meet Jacob is used for her daughter Dinah's "going out" to see the daughters of the land (Gen. 34:1), which led to her assault and her brothers' subsequent brutal retaliation against the town. See, for example, Gen. R. 80:1; *Midrash Tanḥuma*, Va-yeshev 6:2 and Va-yishlaḥ 7:1; Rashi on Gen. 34:1.
30. Rabbeinu Bahya on Gen. 29:21, citing Gen. R. 72:3, as translated in Munk, *Torah Commentary by Rabbi Bachya ben Asher*. See also Rashi on Gen. 30:15.
31. *Targum Jonathan* on Gen. 30:21, as translated in Etheridge, *The Targums of Onkelos and Jonathan Ben Uzziel on the Pentateuch*. According to Gen. R. 72:6, Rachel is the one who prayed, and through her merit the gender of the fetus changed. See also BT *Berakhot* 60a; *Midrash Tanḥuma*, Va-yetse' 8:3; Radak, Rabbeinu Bahya, and *Tur ha-Arokh* on Gen. 30:21.
32. See, for example, *Da'at Zekeinim* and *Ḥizkuni* on Gen. 30:8; *Midrash Tanḥuma Buber*, Va-yetse' 19:1.
33. Gen. R. 70:15, as translated in Freedman, *Midrash Rabbah*, 2:647.

3. BAT SHUA

1. *Midrash Tanḥuma*, Ki Tissa' 22:1, as translated in Townsend, *Midrash Tanhuma*. See also Rashi on Gen. 39:1; *Midrash Tanḥuma Buber*, Va-yeshev 8:2 and 12:1.
2. Gen. R. 85:3, as translated in Freedman, *Midrash Rabbah*, 2:790. See also BT *Sotah* 13b; *Midrash Tanḥuma Buber*, Va-yeshev 13:11.
3. See, for example, Gen. R. 85:1; *Midrash Tanḥuma Buber*, Va-yeshev 9; Bialik and Ravnitsky, *Book of Legends/Sefer Ha-Aggadah*, 51:92.
4. OTP *Jubilees* 41:7.
5. OTP *Testament of Judah* 8:1–3 in *Testaments of the Twelve Patriarchs*.
6. OTP *Testament of Judah* 13:3, in *Testaments of the Twelve Patriarchs*.

7. *Sefer ha-Yashar*, Va-yeshev 22. A variation of this name, Alet, is indicated in Ginzberg, *Legends of the Jews*, 2:37.

8. *Targum Onkelos* on Gen. 38:2; BT *Pesaḥim* 50a. See also Rashi, Rashbam, Radak, Ramban, Rabbeinu Bahya, *Tur ha-Arokh*, and *Or ha-Ḥayim* on Gen. 38:2.

9. See, for example, Ibn Ezra on Gen. 38:2.

10. *Targum Jonathan* on Gen. 38:2.

11. *Or ha-Ḥayim* on Gen. 38:2, as translated in Munk, *Or HaChayim*.

12. Gen. R. 85:4. See also OTP *Testament of Judah* 13:3.

13. *Testament of Judah* 11:1, 13:4–8, 17:1–2, in *Testaments of the Twelve Patriarchs*, as translated in Charlesworth, *The Old Testament Pseudepigrapha*, 1:798–99.

14. See, for example, *Targum Jonathan* on Gen. 38:3; Gen. R. 85:4. See also Ginzberg, *Legends of the Jews*, 2:32, citing *Targum Yerushalmi* and *Midrash ha-Gadol* 1:570.

15. See, for example, Gen. R. 85:4; *Targum Jonathan* and Ramban on Gen. 38:3.

16. See, for example, Gen. R. 85:4; *Targum Jonathan* on Gen. 38:3, 38:4, and 38:5; Rashi, Ramban, *Da'at Zekenim, Ḥizkuni*, and Sforno on Gen. 38:5. *Tur ha-Arokh* on Gen. 38:2 provides a particularly comprehensive overview of the various meanings offered for the sons' names.

17. See, for example, Radak, Ramban, *Tur ha-Arokh*, and others on Gen. 38:5.

18. Gen. R. 85:5. The commentaries wrestle with the seemingly contradictory precepts of the levirate law and laws against incest and offer a variety of explanations. See, for example, Ramban, *Tur ha-Arokh*, and *Siftei Ḥakhamim* on Gen. 38:8.

19. See Sforno on Gen. 38:9.

20. See, for example, BT *Yevamot* 34b; *Targum Jonathan*, Rashi, Rashbam, Radak, *Ḥizkuni*, and others on Gen. 38:7; *Sefer ha-Yashar*, Va-yeshev 22.

21. See Tractate *Kallah Rabbati* 2:7; Rabbeinu Bahya on Gen. 38:10.

22. BT *Yevamot* 34b; Rashi, Rashbam, and Radak on Gen. 38:7.

23. OTP *Jubilees* 41:2–4.

24. See, for example, *Midrash Tanḥuma Buber*, Va-yiggash 10:3.

25. Ramban on Gen. 38:7, as translated in Chavel, *Ramban (Nachmanides) Commentary on the Torah*, 468. See also *Tur ha-Arokh* on Gen. 38:7.

26. See, for example, Gen. R. 85:5; Rashi, Radak, and Rabbeinu Bahya on Gen. 38:11.

27. *Ḥizkuni* on Gen. 38:11.

28. OTP *Testament of Judah* 11:1–5. See also Ginzberg, *Legends of the Jews*, 2:33.

29. *Tur ha-Arokh* on Gen. 38:11, as translated in Munk, *Tur on the Torah*. See also Ramban, Rabbeinu Bahya, and Sforno on Gen. 38:11.

30. Sforno and Malbim on Gen. 38:12.

4. BILHAH

1. See Radak on Gen. 35:27.
2. OTP *Testament of Naphtali* 1:9–12. References to Bilhah's lineage are found in Qumran scrolls as well. See *Testaments of the Twelve Patriarchs*, in Charlesworth, *The Old Testament Pseudepigrapha*, 1:776.
3. See, for example, *Targum Jonathan* on Gen. 29:29; *Pirkei de-Rabbi Eliezer* 36:10.
4. Rashi on Gen. 31:50. See also Gen. R. 74:13.
5. Rashi on Gen. 30:10, citing Gen. R. 71:9, as translated in Rosenbaum and Silbermann, *Pentateuch with Targum Onkelos, Haphtaroth and Rashi's Commentary*, 140. See also Ginzberg, *Legends of the Jews*, 1:365.
6. *Targum Jonathan* and *Ḥizkuni* on Gen. 30:4; Radak on Gen. 35:22; *Or ha-Ḥayim* on Gen. 30:3.
7. Gen. R. 87:6. The *Tur ha-Arokh* on Gen. 35:22 provides a complete overview of all these interpretations. See also *Or ha-Ḥayim* on Gen. 35:23.
8. *Mishnah Megillah* 4:10; BT *Megillah* 25a.
9. Rabbeinu Bahya on Gen. 35:22.
10. *Tur ha-Arokh* on Gen. 35:22.
11. Ramban on Gen. 35:22 and 49:4; *Tur ha-Arokh* on Gen. 35:22.
12. See, for example, *Ḥizkuni*, Rabbeinu Bahya, and *Tur ha-Arokh* on Gen. 35:22.
13. BT *Shabbat* 55b, Rashi, *Targum Jonathan*, and *Siftei Ḥakhamim* on Gen. 35:22.
14. Sforno on Gen. 35:22.
15. BT *Sotah* 7b; BT *Makkot* 11b; *Midrash Tanḥuma Buber*, Va-yeshev 17:7.
16. Radak on Gen. 35:22.
17. *Targum Jonathan*, Rashi (citing Gen. R. 84:19), and *Da'at Zekenim* on Gen. 37:29; *Pesikta de-Rav Kahana* 24:9; *Pesikta Rabbati*, piska 50:4.
18. OTP *Jubilees* 33:2ff. See also OTP *Testament of Reuven* 3:11, in *Testaments of the Twelve Patriarchs*. In the latter version, Bilhah gets drunk, passes out naked on her bed, and isn't aware that she is defiled.
19. *Midrash Tanḥuma*, Va-yeshev, siman 7; Rashi, Rashbam, Radak, and Ramban on Gen 37:2.
20. *Tur ha-Arokh* on Gen. 37:2, as translated in Munk, *Tur on the Torah by Rabbi Yaakov ben Rabbeinu Asher*.
21. Gen. R. 84:11; *Targum Jonathan* and Ramban on Gen. 37:2:2; Ibn Ezra on Gen. 37:10. See also OTP *Testament of Benjamin* 1:3, in *Testaments of the Twelve Patriarchs*.
22. Gen. R. 84:11.
23. OTP *Jubilees* 34:15–17.
24. *Pesikta Rabbati*, piska 3.4.

25. Rashi on Gen. 50:16.

26. *Tanḥuma*, Tsav 7:1 as translated in Townsend, *Midrash Tanhuma*. See also *Targum Jonathan* on Gen. 50:16; *Midrash Tanḥuma Buber*, Shemot 2:1.

5. POTIPHAR'S UNNAMED WIFE

1. Noting the ambiguity of the term *sar hatabaḥim*, the NJPS translation indicates (a type of) Egyptian official, whereas the earlier (OJPS) translation of the text was "chief steward." A similar phrase, *rav tabaḥim*, is found in Jer. 39:13, translated as "chief of the guards."

2. Josephus, *Antiquities of the Jews*, book 2, 4:1; OTP *Jubilees* 34:12 and 39:2; *Targum Jonathan* on Gen. 39:1; BT *Sotah* 13b; *Sefer ha-Yashar*, Va-yeshev 13.

3. Rabbeinu Bahya on Gen. 39:1:1–2, as translated in Munk, *Torah Commentary by Rabbi Bachya ben Asher*. Also *Midrash Tanḥuma Buber*, Va-yeshev 14:1.

4. Gen. R. 85:2, as translated in Freedman and Simon, *Midrash Rabbah*, 2:788.

5. Rashi on Gen. 39:1.

6. Gen. R. 86:3, as translated in Freedman and Simon, *Midrash Rabbah*, 2:802. See also BT *Sotah* 13b.

7. See Gen. R. 86:2.

8. *Or ha-Ḥayim* on Gen. 39:2:1, as translated in Munk, *Or HaChayim*.

9. Gen. R. 86:3. See also *Targum Jonathan* and Rabbeinu Bahya on Gen. 39:6:1.

10. Rashi on Gen. 39:6:2.

11. Radak on Gen. 39:6:2. See also *Tur ha-Arokh*, citing Nahmanides, on Gen. 39:6:2.

12. Rashi on Gen. 39:6, as translated in Rosenbaum and Silbermann, *Pentateuch with Targum Onkelos, Haphtaroth and Rashi's Commentary*, 191. *Siftei Ḥakhamim*, a seventeenth-century "supercommentary" on Rashi, explains why Rashi called her a bear: "And he calls her a bear because a bear has no rest; it is always moving. So too was Potiphar's wife—she had no rest because of her pursuit of Yoseif to have relations with him" (*Siftei Ḥakhamim* on Gen. 39:6, as translated in Davis, *Sifsei Chachamim Chumash*).

13. Sforno on Gen. 39:6 as translated in Munk, *Mikraot Gedolot*.

14. *Midrash Tanḥuma*, Va-yeshev 5:2 as translated in Berman, *Midrash Tanhuma-Yelammedenu*. See also a variant of this tale in *Sefer ha-Yashar*, Vayeshev 15.

15. See also Ginzberg, *Legends of the Jews*, 2:38–39.44ff. In addition to the Qur'an, Potiphar's wife has this name in Islamic literature and an epic Persian love poem, "Yusuf and Zuleikha."

16. *Sefer ha-Yashar*, Va-yeshev 16, as translated in Browne, *Sefer ha-Yashar*.

17. Ginzberg, *Legends of the Jews*, notes on Genesis, 5:339, n. 111, citing the Zohar 3:213b.

18. *Da'at Zekenim* on Gen. 39:12:1, as translated in Munk, *Daat Zekenim*. See also *Sefer ha-Yashar*, Va-yeshev 15.

19. BT *Sotah* 3b.

20. Ibn Ezra on Gen. 39:10; Rashi on Gen. 39:10, citing Gen. R. 87:6. See also *Tur ha-Arokh* on Gen. 39:10:1.

21. See, for example, Radak on Gen. 39:9; Rabbeinu Bahya on Gen. 39:10:1–3.

22. *Midrash Tanḥuma*, Va-yeshev 8:6.

23. *Tur ha-Arokh*, Gen. 39:9:1, as translated in Munk, *Tur on the Torah*.

24. OTP *Testament of Joseph* 3:8 in *Testament of the Twelve Patriarchs*.

25. OTP *Testament of Joseph* 11"1–16:5 in *Testament of the Twelve Patriarchs*.

26. OTP *Testament of Joseph* 4:4, 5:1–4, 7:1–8 in *Testament of the Twelve Patriarchs*.

27. Gen. R. 87:7.

28. BT *Sotah* 36b.

29. *Midrash Tanḥuma*, Va-yeshev 9:1.

30. BT *Sotah* 36b.

31. *Ḥizkuni* on Gen. 39:11:1, as translated in Munk, *Chizkuni*.

32. See, for example, *Tur ha-Arokh* on Gen. 39:17:1; *Or ha-Ḥayim* on Gen. 39:17:2.

33. *Sefer ha-Yashar*, Va-yeshev 18.

34. See, for example, *Targum Jonathan* on Gen. 41:45 and 46:20; *Pirkei de-Rabbi Eliezer* 38:2; Rabbeinu Bahya on Gen. 41:45:2–3.

35. *Pirkei de-Rabbi Eliezer* 38–39. See also Rabbeinu Bahya on Gen. 41:45:2–3 and *Ḥizkuni* on Gen. 41:45:2. Ginzberg tells this story at great length in *Legends of the Jews*, 2:38–39 and the related notes 5:336–337.

36. *Ḥizkuni* on Gen. 41:45:2, as translated in Munk, *Chizkuni*.

37. *Joseph and Asenath* 1:5, as translated in Charlesworth, *The Old Testament Pseudepigrapha*, 2:203.

6. THE SACRED SISTERHOOD

1. *Targum Onkelos* (Exod. 1:15) and Rashbam's commentary on Exod. 1:15 are among those that assert the midwives were Hebrew women. Josephus, *Antiquities of the Jews*, book 2, 9:2, and Sforno's commentary on this verse declare them to be Egyptian women. Samuel David Luzzatto's nineteenth-century commentary on the verse provides a detailed review of the various arguments and concludes that the logic of the text requires understanding them to be Egyptian, and not Hebrew, women.

2. Sarna, *Exploring Exodus*, 25.

3. BT *Sotah* 11b, as translated in Epstein, *The Babylonian Talmud*, 57. See also *Targum Jonathan* on Exod. 1:15 and Exod. R. 1:13 for alternative explanations of the meanings of Shiphrah and Puah. Various interpretations of the meanings of

their names are offered to connect them to their midwifery roles or to events in the lives of Jochebed and Miriam.

4. BT *Sotah* 12a; Exod. R. 1:13.
5. Ibn Ezra on Exod. 1:15. See also *Or ha-Ḥayim* on Exod. 1:15.
6. Sforno on Exod. 1:15:1.
7. *Midrash Tanḥuma*, Pekudei 9:1.
8. *Or ha-Ḥayim* on Exod. 1:15.
9. BT *Sotah* 12a.
10. *Tur ha-Arokh* on Exod. 1:10, as translated in Munk, *Tur on the Torah*.
11. *Sefer ha-Yashar*, Shemot 18; *Ḥizkuni* on Exod. 1:16.
12. *Or ha-Ḥayim* on Exod. 1:16.
13. Exod. R. 1:18.
14. *Or ha-Ḥayim* on Exod. 1:16.
15. BT *Sotah* 11b. See also Exod. R. 1:14; *Ḥizkuni* on Exod. 1:16.
16. Exod. R. 1:18; *Midrash Tanḥuma*, Va-yak'hel 5:1.
17. Exod. R. 1:18.
18. See, for example, Josephus, *Antiquities of the Jews*, book 2, 9:2; *Targum Jonathan* on Exod. 1:15; Exod. R. 1:18; Rashi on Exod. 1:16; *Tur ha-Arokh* on Exod. 1:10. See also Sarna, *Exploring Exodus*, 29–30; Gaster, *Myth, Legend, and Custom in the Old Testament*, 224–30.
19. *Siftei Ḥakhamim* on Exod. 1:10.
20. Luzzatto on Exod. 1:15.
21. According to *Sefer ha-Yashar*, Shemot 18, Pharaoh threatened to burn the midwives and their households to death if they defied him.
22. BT *Sotah* 11b:17–18; also Exod. R. 1:15; Rashi, *Siftei Ḥakhamim*, and *Or ha-Ḥayim* on Exod. 1:17; Sforno on Exod. 1:18.
23. Exod. R. 1:15, as translated in Freedman, *Midrash Rabbah*, 3:20.
24. *Ḥizkuni* on Exod. 1:20.
25. See, for example, Exod. R. 1:12; *Or ha-Ḥayim* on Exod. 1:19.
26. *Or ha-Ḥayim* on Exod. 1:20.
27. *Tur ha-Arokh* on Exod. 1:21.
28. Exod. R. 1:16.
29. BT *Sotah* 11b; Exod. R. 1:17; *Midrash Tanḥuma*, Va-yak'hel 4:10; Rashi on Exod. 1:21.
30. *Tur ha-Arokh* on Exod. 1:21 as translated in Munk, *Tur on the Torah*.
31. *Da'at Zekenim* and *Ḥizkuni* on Exod. 1:21.
32. The significant amount of traditional midrash on the suffering of the Hebrew slaves has not been incorporated into this chapter because it does not directly

relate to the midwives' own experiences, except to the extent that they sympathized with the Israelites' plight.

33. See, for example, *Targum Jonathan* on Gen. 41:45 and 46:20; *Pirkei de-Rabbi Eliezer* 38–39; *Ḥizkuni* and Rabbeinu Bahya on Gen. 41:45. Ginzberg tells this story at great length in *Legends of the Jews*, 2:38–39 and the related notes 5:336–337.

7. THE PRINCESS AND THE SLAVE GIRL

1. BT *Sotah* 12a; Exod. R. 1:13.
2. Exod. R. 1:20.
3. BT *Sotah* 12a; Exod. R. 1:20; *Sefer ha-Yashar*, Shemot 23.
4. BT *Sotah* 12a; Exod. R. 1:13, 20.
5. BT *Sotah* 12a; *Targum Jonathan, Da'at Zekenim*, and *Ḥizkuni* on Exod. 2:2:1.
6. BT *Sotah* 12b; Exod. R. 1:24. This depiction of Moses is also found in *Pseudo-Philo* 9:15, a first-century text in the Pseudepigrapha.
7. BT *Sotah* 12a; Exod. R. 1:20; *Pirkei de-Rabbi Eliezer* 48:8; *Ḥizkuni* 2:2:1.
8. See, for example, Sarna, *Exploring Exodus*, 29–30; Gaster, *Myth, Legend, and Custom in the Old Testament*, 224–30.
9. Josephus, *Antiquities of the Jews*, book 2, 9:5 and 9:7; *Jubilees* 47:5.
10. See, for example, Josephus, *Antiquities of the Jews*, book 2, 9:5 and 9:7.
11. BT *Megillah* 13a; Lev. R. 1:3; *Sefer ha-Yashar*, Shemot 24.
12. BT *Sotah* 12b; BT *Megillah* 13a; Exod. R. 1:23; *Midrash Tanḥuma*, Shemot 7:3; *Ḥizkuni* on Exod. 2:5.
13. *Midrash Mishlei* 31:5; *Pirkei de-Rabbi Eliezer* 48:8.
14. *Targum Jonathan* on Exod. 2:5. According to this text, all of Egypt was plagued with a skin ailment, and when the handmaids discovered and picked up the child, they immediately were cured. See also Exod. R. 1:23; *Pirkei de-Rabbi Eliezer* 48:8; *Tanḥuma*, Shemot 7:3.
15. *Sefer ha-Yashar*, Shemot 24.
16. Sforno on Exod. 2:5.
17. BT *Sotah* 12b, as translated in Epstein, *The Babylonian Talmud, Sotah* 12b, 62. See also *Ḥizkuni* and *Siftei Ḥakhamim* on Exod. 2:5.
18. *Ḥizkuni* and *Siftei Ḥakhamim* on Exod. 2:5.
19. *Or ha-Ḥayim* on Exod. 2:5.
20. Rashbam on Exod. 2:3.
21. Rashi on Exod. 2:5. See also BT *Sotah* 1:42; *Da'at Zekenim* and *Ḥizkuni* on Exod. 2:5; *Ein Yaakov, Sotah* 1:42.
22. Sforno on Exod. 2:5.
23. *Or ha-Ḥayim* on Exod. 2:5.

24. BT *Sotah* 12b; Exod. R. 1:24; Rashi and *Or ha-Ḥayim* on Exod. 2:6.

25. BT *Sotah* 12b; Exod. R. 1:24; Rashi on Exod. 2:6.

26. *Ḥizkuni* and *Kitzur Baal ha-Turim* on Exod. 2:6.

27. See, for example, Josephus, *Antiquities of the Jews*, book 2, 9:2; Exod. R. 1:18; *Targum Jonathan* on Exod. 1:15; *Midrash Tanḥuma*, Va-yak'hel 5:1; Rashi on Exod. 1:16; *Tur ha-Arokh* on Exod. 1:10.

28. BT *Sotah* 12b; Exod. R. 1:21, 24.

29. BT *Sotah* 12b; Exod. R. 1:25; Rashi and Sforno on Exod. 2:7; *Or ha-Ḥayim* on Exod. 2:6.

30. BT *Sotah* 12b; Exod. R. 1:25; Rashi on Exod. 2:9.

31. See, for example, BT *Sotah* 11b; Exod. R. 1:2 and 1:15; Rashi on Exod. 1:17; Sforno on Exod. 1:18. Regarding their punishment, see *Da'at Zekenim, Ḥizkuni*, and *Tur ha-Arokh* on Exod. 1:21.

8. SHELOMITH BAT DIBRI

1. See, for example, Lev. R. 32:4; *Midrash Tanḥuma*, Emor 24; Rashi on Lev. 24:10.

2. Exod. R. 1:28; *Targum Jonathan* on Lev. 24:10; *Pirkei de-Rabbi Eliezer* 48:15.

3. Rabbeinu Bahya on Va-yikra' 24:11.

4. Exod. R. 1:28, as translated in Freedman, *Midrash Rabbah*, 3:36.

5. Lev. R. 32:4.

6. *Midrash Tanḥuma*, Shemot 9:2. See also *Midrash Sekhel Tov*, Exod. 2:11.

7. *Da'at Zekenim*, Rabbeinu Bahya, and *Siftei Ḥakhamim* on Lev. 24:10.

8. Exod. R. 1:30–31.

9. Exod. R. 1:29–31. See also BT *Sanhedrin* 109b; BT *Nedarim* 64b; Rashi on Exod. 5:20 and 18:4.

10. *Pirkei de-Rabbi Eliezer* 48:15.

11. *Ḥizkuni* on Lev. 24:11.

12. See, for example, Exod. R. 1:28; Lev. R. 32:5; Rashi on Lev. 24:11.

13. Exod. R. 1:28, as translated in Freedman, *Midrash Rabbah*, 3:35. See also Rashi on Lev. 24:11.

14. *Or ha-Ḥayim* on Lev. 24:11.

15. *Pirkei de-Rabbi Eliezer* 48:15, as translated in Friedlander, *Pirke de Rabbi Eliezer*.

16. Rabbeinu Bahya on Lev. 24:11, as translated in Munk, *Torah Commentary by Rabbi Bachya ben Asher*.

17. *Midrash Tanḥuma*, Va-yak'hel 4:5; *Midrash Tanḥuma Buber*, Va-yak'hel 3:1; Rashi on Lev. 24:11.

18. Rashi on Lev. 24:11, as translated in Rosenbaum and Silbermann, *Pentateuch with Targum Onkelos, Haphtaroth and Rashi's Commentary*, 112. See also Lev. R. 32:5.

19. *Targum Jonathan* on Lev. 24:10, as translated in Etheridge, *The Targums of Onkelos and Jonathan Ben Uzziel on the Pentateuch.*

20. See, for example, Lev. R. 32:3; Rashi on Lev. 24:10.

21. See, for example, *Sifra,* Emor 14:1; Rashi on Lev. 24:10.

22. *Da'at Zekenim,* Rabbeinu Bahya, and *Siftei Ḥakhamim* on Lev. 24:10.

23. Rashi and *Tur ha-Arokh* on Lev. 24:10.

24. *Da'at Zekenim* and Sforno on Lev 24:10.

25. BT *Sanhedrin* 56a; *Ḥizkuni* on Lev. 24:10.

26. *Da'at Zekenim* on Lev. 24:12.

27. Ibn Ezra on Lev. 24:10. Also Rashi, Rabbeinu Bahya, and *Or ha-Ḥayim* on Lev. 24:10 and *Sifra,* Emor 14:1.

9. MIRIAM

1. *Sifrei Bamidbar* 99:1; *Ḥizkuni* on Num. 12:1.

2. *Midrash Tanḥuma,* Tsav 13:1; Rashi on Num. 12:1.

3. *Sifrei Bamidbar* 100:1; *Avot de-Rabbi Natan* 9:2.

4. See, for example, *Avot de-Rabbi Natan* 9:2; *Sifrei Bamidbar, Targum Jonathan,* Ibn Ezra, and *Or ha-Ḥayim* on Num. 12:2.

5. BT *Shabbat* 87a; *Midrash Tanḥuma,* Tsav 13; Rashi and Rabbeinu Bahya on Num. 12:4; Rashi, *Da'at Zekenim,* and *Siftei Ḥakhamim* on Num. 12:8.

6. See, for example, BT *Mo'ed Katan* 16b; *Sifrei Bamidbar* 99:1; *Pirkei de-Rabbi Eliezer* 53:5; *Midrash Tanḥuma,* Tsav 13:1; *Targum Onkelos,* Rashi, Ibn Ezra, Rabbeinu Bahya, *Tur ha-Arokh,* and *Siftei Ḥakhamim* on Num. 12:1.

7. Rashi on Num. 12:1.

8. *Tur ha-Arokh* on Num. 12:1.

9. Josephus, *Antiquities of the Jews,* book 2, 10:2; *Targum Jonathan,* Rashbam, Ibn Ezra (citing *Yalkut Shimoni,* Shemot 168), *Da'at Zekenim,* and *Ḥizkuni* on Num 12:1.

10. Ibn Ezra and *Or ha-Ḥayim* on Num. 12:2.

11. *Avot de-Rabbi Natan* 9:2, as translated in Cohen, *The Minor Tractates of the Talmud.* See also *Sifrei Bamidbar* 99:1; *Midrash Tanḥuma,* Metsora' 2:1.

12. Num. R. 16:6, as translated in Freedman and Simon, *Midrash Rabbah,* 6:677. See also *Midrash Tanḥuma,* Shelaḥ-Lekha 5:1.

13. Sforno on Num. 12:8. See also *Or ha-Ḥayim* on Num. 12:11.

14. Rabbeinu Bahya on Num. 12:4, citing Rashi on Num. 12:4, as translated in Munk, *Torah Commentary by Rabbi Bachya ben Asher.*

15. BT *Zevaḥim* 69b and *Bava Batra* 111a; *Avot de-Rabbi Natan* 9:2; *Targum Jonathan,* Rashi, *Da'at Zekenim,* and *Ḥizkuni* on Num. 12:14.

16. *Sifrei Bamidbar* 99:1; Ibn Ezra and Rabbeinu Bahya on Num 12:1.

17. *Da'at Zekenim* on Num. 12:1, as translated in Munk, *Daat Zkenim*.
18. Deut. R. 6:11, as translated in Freedman and Simon, *Midrash Rabbah*, 7:128.
19. BT *Shabbat* 97a; *Sifrei Bamidbar* 105:1; *Midrash Tanḥuma*, Metsora' 2:1; *Midrash Tanḥuma Buber*, Metsora' 6:1; Rabbeinu Bahya on Num. 12:1; *Ḥizkuni* and *Or ha-Ḥayim* on Num. 12:9–10.
20. *Or ha-Ḥayim* on Num. 12:11,13.
21. *Midrash Tanḥuma*, Tsav 13:1; *Pirkei de-Rabbi Eliezer* 54:1.
22. BT *Zevaḥim* 101b–102a; *Sifrei Bamidbar* 105:1; Lev. R. 15:8; *Midrash Tanḥuma*, Tsav 13:1.
23. Rabbeinu Bahya on Num. 12:13, as translated in Munk, *Torah Commentary by Rabbi Bachya ben Asher*.
24. See, for example, *Mekhilta de-Rabbi Yishmael*, Be-shallaḥ 4:7 and Vayassa' 1:99.
25. See, for example, *Sifrei Bamidbar* 105:1; *Mekhilta de-Rabbi Yishmael* 14:15 and 15:25; *Midrash Tanḥuma*, Tsav 13:1; *Avot de-Rabbi Natan* 9:2; Rashi on Num. 12:13; *Ein Yaakov, Berakhot* 5:13.
26. *Da'at Zekenim*, *Ḥizkuni*, Sforno, and *Or ha-Ḥayim* on Num. 12:13.
27. Rashi on Num. 12:13, citing *Sifrei Bamidbar* 105; also *Midrash Tanḥuma*, Tsav 13:1.
28. *Targum Jonathan* on Num. 12:13, as translated in Etheridge, *The Targums of Onkelos and Jonathan Ben Uzziel on the Pentateuch*.
29. Deut. R. 6:12, as translated in Freedman and Simon, *Midrash Rabbah*, 7:129.
30. *Mishnah Sotah* 1:9; BT *Sotah* 9b; *Mekhilta de-Rabbi Yishmael* 13:19; *Sifrei Bamidbar* 106:1; *Midrash Tanḥuma*, Tsav 13:1 and Be-shallaḥ 2:4; Rashi on Num. 12:15; *Ein Yaakov, Sotah* 1:32; Rabbeinu Bahya on Num. 12:15.
31. BT *Shabbat* 35a and *Ta'anit* 9a; *Targum Jonathan*, Rabbeinu Bahya, and *Siftei Ḥakhamim* on Num. 20:2.
32. Tosefta, *Sukkah* 3; Lev. R. 22:4; Num. R. 18:22; *Midrash Tanḥuma*, Ḥukkat 1:1; Shulḥan Arukh, *Oraḥ Ḥayyim* 299:10. See also Ginzberg, *Legends of the Jews*, 3:54.

10. NOAH

1. See, for example, the genealogical listing of the tribes just prior to this section in Num. 26:33, where Zelophehad's lineage is described as Joseph-Manasseh-Mechir-Gilead-Hepher-Zelophehad.
2. Sforno and Ibn Ezra on Num. 27:3.
3. BT *Shabbat* 96b. See also *Sifrei Bamidbar* 133:3; Rashi and *Siftei Ḥakhamim* on Num. 27:3.
4. Num. R. 21:10, as translated in Freedman and Simon, *Midrash Rabbah*, 6:836. See also *Sifrei Bamidbar* 133:1; *Tanḥuma*, Pinḥas 7:1.

5. See, for example, Ibn Ezra, Ramban, Rabbeinu Bahya, and *Tur ha-Arokh* on Num. 27:3.
6. BT *Bava Batra* 141a. See also Rashi on Num. 27:7; *Ein Yaakov, Bava Batra* 8:4 and 9:2.
7. See, for example, Rashi, Rabbeinu Bahya, and *Or ha-Ḥayim* on Num. 27:1.
8. Rashi on Num. 27:1.
9. *Or ha-Ḥayim* on Num. 27:1.
10. See for example BT *Bava Batra* 119b; Num. R. 21:11–12; *Tanhuma*, Pinhas 8:1.
11. Ginzberg, *Legends of the Jews*, 3:391–392.
12. See, for example, BT *Bava Batra* 119b; Num. R. 21:11; Rashi and *Or ha-Ḥayim* on Num. 27:4; *Or ha-Ḥayim* on Num. 27:7; *Ein Yaakov, Bava Batra* 8:11.
13. Num. R. 21:12, as translated in Freedman and Simon, *Midrash Rabbah*, 6:837ff. See also *Sifrei Devarim* 17:7; *Tanḥuma*, Pinḥas 8:1; Rashi on Num. 27:7.
14. *Or ha-Ḥayim* on Num. 27:2 and 27:6.
15. *Sifrei Bamidbar* 133:3; Rashi on Num. 27:2.
16. BT *Bava Batra* 119b; Num. R. 21:11; *Or ha-Ḥayim* on Numbers 27:1; *Ein Yaakov, Bava Batra* 8:11; Ginzberg, *Legends of the Jews*, 3:394–95.
17. Ibn Ezra and Rabbeinu Bahya on Num. 36:11; *Or ha-Ḥayim* on Num. 27:1.
18. BT *Bava Batra* 120a.
19. Rashi on Num. 27:1 and 36:11. See also BT *Bava Batra* 120a.
20. BT *Bava Batra* 120a.
21. Sforno on Num. 26:10.
22. BT *Bava Batra* 120a, 121a, and *Ta'anit* 30b; *Targum Jonathan* and *Or ha-Ḥayim* on Num. 36:6.
23. BT *Ta'anit* 30b and *Bava Batra* 121a; *Ein Yaakov, Ta'anit* 4:11 and *Bava Batra* 8:13.
24. See, for example, Num. 1:10, 2:18, 7:48, 7:53, 10:22; 1 Chron. 7:26.
25. See lineage at Num. 26:32 and 1 Chron. 7:19.

APPENDIX

1. Neusner, *The Midrash*, 31ff., provides a detailed overview of the composition and literary form of each of these compilations.
2. Strack, *Introduction to the Talmud and Midrash*, 225.
3. Neusner, *The Midrash*, 142.
4. Holtz, *Back to the Sources*, 188–89.
5. Holtz, *Back to the Sources*, 255.

BIBLIOGRAPHY

Berman, Samuel S., ed. *Midrash Tanhuma-Yelammedenu.* New York: KTAV, 1996.

Bialik, Hayim Nahman, and Yehoshua Hana Ravnitsky, eds. *The Book of Legends / Sefer Ha-Aggadah: Legends from the Talmud and Midrash.* New York: Schocken, 1992.

Braude, William G., trans. *Pesikta Rabbati.* New Haven: Yale University Press, 1968.

Braude, William G., and Israel J. Kapstein, trans. *Tanna Debe Eliyyahu: The Lore of the School of Elijah.* Philadelphia: Jewish Publication Society of America, 1981.

———, trans. *Pesikta de-Rab Kahana.* Philadelphia: Jewish Publication Society, 1975.

Browne, Edward B. M., trans. *Sefer ha-Yashar.* New York: n.p., 1876.

Charlesworth, James H., ed. *The Old Testament Pseudepigrapha.* New York: Doubleday, 1985.

Chavel, Charles B., trans. and annotator. *Ramban (Nachmanides): Commentary on the Torah.* New York: Shilo, 1971.

Cohen, Abraham. *The Minor Tractates of the Talmud: Massektoth Ketannoth.* London: Soncino, 1965.

Davis, Avraham. *Sifsei Chachamim Chumash.* Metsudah, 2009.

Epstein, Isidore, ed. *The Babylonian Talmud.* London: Soncino, 1936.

Etheridge, J. W., trans. *The Targums of Onkelos and Jonathan Ben Uzziel on the Pentateuch.* London: Longman, Green, and Roberts, 1862.

Freedman, H., and Maurice Simon, eds. *Midrash Rabbah.* London: Soncino, 1983.

Friedlander, Rabbi Gerald, trans. *Pirke de Rabbi Eliezer.* London: Kegan Paul Trench, Trubner, 1916.

Gaster, Theodor H. *Myth, Legend, and Custom in the Old Testament.* Gloucester MA: Peter Smith, 1981.

Ginzberg, Louis. *The Legends of the Jews.* Philadelphia: Jewish Publication Society, 1967.

Glick, Shmuel Tzvi-Hirsch., ed. and trans. *En Jacob: Agada of the Babylonian Talmud.* Chicago: Glick, 1921.

Holtz, Barry W., ed. *Back to the Sources: Reading the Classic Jewish Texts.* New York: Summit, 1984.

Lauterback, Jacob Z., trans. *Mekilta de-Rabbi Ishmael.* Philadelphia: Jewish Publication Society, 1976.

Munk, Eliyahu, trans. and annotator. *Chizkuni.* New York: KTAV, 2013.

———, trans. *Daat Zekenim.* urimpublications.com, accessed at sefaria.org.

———, trans. and annotator. *Mikraot Gedolot: Multi-Commentary on the Torah— HaChut Hameshulash, Commentaries on the Torah by Rabbeinu Chananel, Rash'bam, R'dak, and Seforno.* New York: KTAV, 2003.

———, trans. and annotator. *Or HaChayim: Commentary on the Torah.* New York: KTAV, 1998.

———, trans. and annotator. *Torah Commentary by Rabbi Bachya ben Asher.* New York: KTAV, 1998.

———, trans. and annotator. *Tur on the Torah by Rabbi Yaakov ben Rabbeinu Asher (R'osh).* New York: KTAV, 2005.

Neusner, Jacob. *The Midrash: An Introduction.* Northvale NJ: Jason Aronson, 1994.

Newman, J. *Halachic Sources.* Leiden: E. J. Brill, 1969.

Rosenbaum, M., and A. M. Silbermann. *Pentateuch with Targum Onkelos, Haphtaroth and Rashi's Commentary.* Jerusalem: Silbermann Family, 1932.

Sarna, Nahum M. *Exploring Exodus: The Heritage of Biblical Israel.* New York: Schocken, 1986.

———. *Understanding Genesis: The Heritage of Biblical Israel.* New York: Schocken, 1978.

Stein, David E. S., ed. *The Contemporary Torah: A Gender-Sensitive Adaptation of the JPS Translation.* Philadelphia: Jewish Publication Society, 2006.

Strack, Hermann L. *Introduction to the Talmud and Midrash.* New York: Atheneum, 1978.

Townsend, John T. S., trans. *Midrash Tanhuma: S. Buber Recension.* New York: KTAV, 1989.

Whiston, William, trans. *The Works of Flavius Josephus.* Nashville TN: Broadman, 1974.